American Progressivism

American Progressivism

A Reader

Edited and Introduced by
Ronald J. Pestritto and William J. Atto

LEXINGTON BOOKS

A division of
ROWMAN & LITTLEFIELD PUBLISHERS, INC.
Lanham • Boulder • New York • Toronto • Plymouth, UK

LEXINGTON BOOKS

A division of Rowman & Littlefield Publishers, Inc.
A wholly owned subsidary of The Rowman & Littlefield Publishing Group, Inc.
4501 Forbes Boulevard, Suite 200
Lanham, MD 20706

Estover Road
Plymouth PL6 7PY
United Kingdom

British Library Cataloguing in Publication Information Available

Library of Congress Cataloging-in-Publication Data

American progressivism : a reader / edited and introduced by Ronald J. Pestritto and
    William J. Atto.
    p. cm.
    Includes index.
    ISBN-13: 978-0-7391-2303-4 (cloth : alk. paper)
    ISBN-10: 0-7391-2303-3 (cloth : alk. paper)
    ISBN-13: 978-0-7391-2304-1 (pbk. : alk. paper)
    ISBN-10: 0-7391-2304-1 (pbk. : alk. paper)
    1. Progressivism (United States politics)—History—Sources. 2. United States—
Politics and government—1865–1933—Sources. 3. United States—Social policy—
Sources. 4. Political science—United States—History—Sources. 5. Political
leadership—United States—History—Sources. 6. Democracy—United States—
History—Sources. I. Pestritto, Ronald J. II. Atto, William J., 1967–
E661.A54325 2008
324.2732'7—dc22   2008001519

Printed in the United States of America

⊗™ The paper used in this publication meets the minimum requirements of American
National Standard for Information Sciences—Permanence of Paper for Printed Library
Materials, ANSI/NISO Z39.48-1992.

Contents

Part III: Social Justice, Social Gospel, and Education

Part IV: Leadership and the American Presidency

Part V: National Administration

Preface and Acknowledgments

The goal of this collection is to provide a resource for professors and students studying the Progressive Era—either in its own right or as part of courses in American political thought, American political development, or American history, among other possibilities. Because of the richness and variety of Progressive-Era material and because our goal here is to provide an affordable, single-volume book, we have had to make difficult choices in selecting some pieces for inclusion and leaving others. No doubt there may be grounds to quarrel with some of these choices, but that is an inevitability in an enterprise such as this, where it is simply impossible to include every worthy or important piece. We have been guided in our selection of texts by a desire to focus largely on the national progressives whose writings and speeches have had an influence in shaping the politics of our own time. It is hoped that by bringing these selections together in a single volume, the need for extensive assembling of photocopied course reading packets can be lessened, and that these important and influential writings will gain a wider dissemination.

ORGANIZATION, SOURCES, AND TEXTS

The selections in this book are not presented in chronological fashion. Instead, they are organized around the key tenets of progressive thought. We begin with the more thematic pieces, focusing first on defining progressivism and then looking at its conception of the ends and scope of government. The progressives' account of history gets special attention because history is a loaded term in progressive thought and the progressives' idea of government cannot be understood separately from their idea of history. Progressivism was also caught up in the important religious, social, and educational reform movements of the day, and selections are offered which give a representation of progressive writing in each of those areas. We then turn to the arguments made by progressives for reforming American political institutions, and focus particularly on the presidency, national administration, the party system, and the direct-democracy movement. Selections pertaining to the 1912 presidential election are also provided, given the significance of that contest to the movement. Finally, the principles of progressive internationalism are addressed, as is the relationship of progressive ideas to America's role in the world.

We offer guidance to the reader in two ways. First, in our introduction we focus on the ideas and arguments of progressivism, laying out the key themes of progressive thought and explaining certain premises that underlie our argument and our selection of texts. Second, because the selections are not presented in chronological fashion, brief headnotes are provided with each piece, in an effort to give the reader some historical context for the piece and to offer a very concise summary of the author's main point. Beyond this, we intentionally leave the reader to his own investigation of these important works. For this reason, and because we strived to present the authors' original texts as accurately as possible, we have intervened editorially only in cases of extreme need. Where we have done so we have used brackets. In order to avoid frequent interruptions of the text, we have not employed the notation "sic," even when the original text seemed to cry out for it. For the sake of brevity, we have usually omitted authors' footnotes; readers should consult our note at the beginning of each piece for more on this.

If provided a limitless number of pages, we would have strongly preferred to present each selection in its entirety. Many are so presented. Given the limitations of a single-volume collection and the desire to keep the collection modestly priced, however, some of the selections are excerpts. Where this has been done, it is so noted at the beginning of the selection, and excerpted parts are indicated by an ellipsis. Where the word "excerpt" does not appear in the editorial note, the particular speech, essay, or chapter is presented in its entirety.

Every one of the selections presented was drawn from works in the public domain. With all but one selection the version of the text we present is the version from the place of original publication or from the standard source. The exception is the excerpt from Woodrow Wilson's "Leaders of Men," a speech which was given several times in 1889 and 1890 and which existed for many years only in handwritten form. It first appeared in print in T. H. Vail Motter's 1952 edited volume, *Leaders of Men*, and the copyright on that volume has since been allowed to expire.

ACKNOWLEDGMENTS

The editors would like to thank their home institutions, Hillsdale College and the University of Dallas, for their much-appreciated support. In addition, we would like to acknowledge the Ashbrook Center for Public Affairs at Ashland University for the opportunity to team-teach a course on the progressives in its master's program for the past several summers. That course has enabled us to think about and refine our argument on the progressives, and the reading list for it served as the foundation for the selections in this book. We would like to thank, in particular, the Center's executive director, Peter Schramm, and its deputy director, Roger Beckett.

Ronald J. Pestritto would like to acknowledge the Earhart Foundation, which provided a fellowship research grant to support his work on this volume, and to thank the Foundation's Ingrid A. Gregg and Montgomery B. Brown for their support and encouragement. He would also like to thank the Shipley Foundation, whose endowment of his chair at Hillsdale College makes possible so much of his scholarly work, and the indefatigable Larry Arnn, president of Hillsdale College, for his confidence and support. Ronald Pestritto also acknowledges the Claremont Institute and its president, Brian T. Kennedy, whose support in recent years has been particularly important to his work on Wilson and the progressives. Finally, Marcy Rader at Hillsdale College was very helpful in the preparation of some of these manuscripts, and her work is much appreciated.

William J. Atto wishes to acknowledge gratefully the assistance of Ms. Alice Puro in the Interlibrary Loan Department at the University of Dallas. Also, special thanks are due Mr. Sola Babatunde of the Government Information Resources Department of Fondren Library at Southern Methodist University and Ms. Nancy Mulhern of the Wisconsin State Historical Society for their valuable assistance in locating a number of documents for this collection.

1

Introduction to American Progressivism

Ronald J. Pestritto and William J. Atto

It has become fashionable today for those who once called themselves "liberals" to refer to themselves, instead, as "progressives."[1] This phenomenon is partly due, even now, to the influence of the national political debate in the 1980s, where "liberal" became a dirty word. But for those who study American politics and history, the phenomenon is felicitous for several reasons, among which is the effect of helping to clear up any confusion that might exist between modern liberals—those who favor an expansive and active central government of the kind we have seen in America since the early part of the twentieth century—and those whom we might call classical liberals, who see the fundamental purpose of government as the protection of individual rights and thus view with suspicion any extension of governmental power into spheres beyond this limited purpose. More important, by increasingly identifying themselves as progressives, modern liberals have come home. The progressive movement in America was the launching point for modern liberalism, and thus for the shape of American politics even to this day.

As students of American politics and history, if we are to understand the principles of our polity today, and how it came to be this way, there may be no more important era to study than that of the progressives. Regardless of whether we think it a good development or bad, there is no question that the purpose and scope of American government today is a far cry from what was envisioned in the constitutional thinking of the American founders. The welfare-state politics of the twentieth and now twenty-first century are built upon a direct and conscious rejection of the original principles of the American Constitution. While it is the case that, in practical terms, this revolution in American politics was implemented by Franklin Roosevelt's New Deal, subsequently extended by Lyndon Johnson's Great Society, and since been maintained by the programmatic liberalism of presidents of both major political parties, it is also the case that the intellectual roots of the New Deal and its progeny took hold in the Progressive Era. This is a fact acknowledged by no less an authority than Franklin Roosevelt himself, who openly grounded his 1932 presidential campaign on the ideas of Theodore Roosevelt and, especially, Woodrow Wilson.[2]

In offering a collection of "progressive" writings, and especially in offering an essay which speaks of "progressivism" as a single, coherent, identifiable idea or principle, we will no doubt run the risk of criticism from those who would point to important differences among the prominent progressives on the major issues of the day. Most obviously, the two most prominent national progressives featured in this collection—Roosevelt and Wilson—not only were from different political parties but opposed one another in a hard fought presidential election. Perhaps even more importantly, there was a split among national progressives about the viability of the two-party system itself, to mention just one of the differences on the issues that characterized Progressive-Era debates. Nonetheless, we do contend, emphatically, that progressivism can be understood as a coherent set of principles with a common purpose. The differences among progressives over issues such as reforming the party system were, in the end, differences over particular means, not over fundamental ideas of what government is or ought to be, and certainly not over the need with which all progressives identified to revolutionize both the theory and practice of American government.

It is because of the coherent set of principles that characterizes this movement that leads us to think of it as an "-ism" as much as we think of it as an "era." The meaning of progressivism, and its profound relevance for American politics today, transcends any boundaries that might be placed upon it by a particular set of dates or figures. Progressivism and the ideas that constitute it are alive and well today, as is evidenced by the reclaiming of that title by today's liberals. Understanding progressivism thus requires both an historical and theoretical perspective. One cannot comprehend progressivism without paying careful attention to the particular events and figures of the Progressive Era and thinking about how these shaped the character of the movement; nor can one comprehend the progressives without perceiving the core ideas that gave them their identity and thinking about the relevance of these ideas in their own right.

What, then, is progressivism? The bulk of this essay will be spent laying out its basic characteristics, but in short we can think of it as an argument to progress, or to move beyond, the political principles of the American founding. It is an argument to enlarge vastly the scope of national government for the purpose of responding to a set of economic and social conditions which, progressives contend, could not have been envisioned at the founding and for which the founders' limited, constitutional government was inadequate. Whereas the founders had posited what they held to be a permanent understanding of just government, based upon a permanent account of human nature, the progressives countered that the ends and scope of government were to be defined anew in each historical epoch. They coupled this perspective of historical contingency with a deep faith in historical progress, suggesting that, due to historical evolution, government was becoming less of a danger to the governed and more capable of solving the great array of problems besetting the human race. Historically, these ideas formed a common thread among the most important American thinkers from the 1880s into the 1920s and beyond, and this collection shows how they manifested themselves in the writings and speeches of Theodore Roosevelt, Woodrow Wilson, Herbert Croly, John Dewey, Robert La Follette, and several others. The most relevant biographical particulars of these figures will be laid out in the brief headnotes that accompany each selection of the book; the essay here aims to speak to the fundamental characteristics in the thought of these figures that gave them common cause as progressives.

THE PRINCIPLES OF PROGRESSIVISM

The Progressive Era was the first major period in American political development to feature, as a primary characteristic, the open and direct criticism of the Constitution. While criticism of the Constitution could be found during any period of American history, the Progressive Era was unique in that such criticism formed the backbone of the entire movement. Progressive-Era criticism of the Constitution came not from a few fringe figures, but from the most prominent thinkers and politicians of that time. Readers are reminded, in almost any progressive text they pick up, that the Constitution is old, and that it was written to deal with circumstances that had long ago been replaced by a whole new set of pressing social and economic ills. The progressives understood the intention and structure of the Constitution very well; they knew that it established a framework for limited government, and that these limits were to be upheld by a variety of institutional restraints and checks. They also knew that the limits placed on the national government by the Constitution represented major obstacles to implementing the progressive policy agenda. Progressives had in mind a variety of legislative programs aimed at regulating significant portions of the American economy and society and at redistributing private property in the name of social justice. The Constitution, if interpreted and applied faithfully, stood in the way of this agenda.

The Constitution, however, was only a means to an end. It was crafted and adopted for the sake of achieving the natural-rights principles of the Declaration of Independence. The progressives understood this very clearly, which is why many of the more theoretical works written by progressives feature sharp attacks on social compact theory and on the notion that the fundamental purpose of government is to secure the individual natural rights of citizens. While most of the founders and nearly all ordinary Americans did not subscribe to the radical epistemology of the social compact theorists, they did believe, in Lockean fashion, that men as individuals possessed rights by nature—rights that any just government was bound to uphold and which stood as inherent limits to the authority of government over individual liberty and property. The regulatory and redistributive aims of the progressive policy agenda, therefore, were on a collision course with the political theory of the founding. This basic fact makes understandable Woodrow Wilson's admonition—in an address ostensibly honoring Thomas Jefferson—that "if you want to understand the real Declaration of Independence, do not repeat the preface."[3] Do not, in other words, repeat that part of the Declaration that enshrines natural rights as the focal point of American government.

Taking Wilson's advice here would turn our attention away from the timelessness of the Declaration's conception of government, and would focus us instead on the litany of grievances made against George III; it would show, in other words, the Declaration as a merely practical document, to be understood as a specific, time-bound response to a set of specific historical circumstances. Once the circumstances change so too must our conception of government. It is with this in mind that Wilson urged that "we are not bound to adhere to the doctrines held by the signers of the Declaration of Independence," and that every Fourth of July, instead of a celebration of the timeless principles of the Declaration, should instead "be a time for examining our standards, our purposes, for determining afresh what principles, what forms of power we think most likely to effect our safety and happiness."[4] Like Wilson, Frank Goodnow acknowledged that the founders' system of government "was permeated by the theories of social compact and natural right," and he complained that such theories were "worse than useless," since they "retard development"[5]—that is, that the protections for individual liberty and property inhibit the expansion of government. In contrast to the principle of natural rights that undergirded the American system, Goodnow praised political systems in Europe where, he explained, "the rights which [an individual] possesses are, it is believed, conferred upon him, not by his Creator, but rather by the society to which he belongs. What they are is to be determined by the legislative authority in view of the needs of that society. Social expediency, rather than natural right, is thus to determine the sphere of individual freedom of action."[6]

Goodnow, Wilson, and other progressives championed historical contingency against the Declaration's talk of the permanent principles of just government. The natural-rights understanding of government may have been appropriate, they conceded, as a response to the prevailing tyranny of that day, but, they argued, all government has to be understood as a product of its particular historical context. The great sin committed by the founding generation was not, then, its adherence to the doctrine of natural rights, but rather its notion that that doctrine was meant to transcend the particular circumstances of that day. It was this very facet of the founders' thinking that Abraham Lincoln recognized, and praised, in 1859 when he wrote of the Declaration and its primary author: "All honor to Jefferson—to the man who, in the concrete pressure of a struggle for national independence by a single people, had the coolness, forecast, and capacity to introduce into a merely revolutionary document, an abstract truth, applicable to all men and all times."[7] Recognizing the very same characteristic of the founders' thought, John Dewey complained, by contrast, that the founding generation "lacked historic sense and interest," and that it had a "disregard of history." As if speaking directly to Lincoln's praise of the founding, Dewey endorsed, instead, the doctrine of historical contingency. Natural-rights theory, Dewey argued, "blinded the eyes of liberals to the fact that their own special interpretations of liberty, individuality and intelligence were themselves historically conditioned, and were relevant only to their own time. They put forward their ideas as immutable truths good at all times and places; they had no idea of historic relativity."[8] The idea of liberty was not frozen in time, Dewey argued, but had instead a history of evolving meaning. The history of liberalism, about which Dewey wrote in *Liberalism and Social Action*, was progressive—it told a story of the move from more primitive to more mature conceptions of liberty. Modern liberalism, therefore, represented a vast improvement over classical (or what Dewey called "early") liberalism.

This coupling of historical contingency with the doctrine of progress—shared by all progressives to one degree or another—reveals how the progressive movement became the means by which German historicism was imported into the American political tradition. The influence of German political philosophy is evident not only from looking at the ideas espoused by progressives, but also from the historical pedigree of the most influential progressive thinkers. Almost all of them were either educated in Germany in the nineteenth century or had as teachers those who were. This reflects the sea change that had occurred in American higher education in the second half of the nineteenth century, a time when most Americans who wanted an advanced degree went to Europe to get one. By 1900, the faculties of American colleges and universities had become populated with European Ph.D.s, and the historical thinking that dominated Europe (especially Germany) in the nineteenth century came to permeate American higher education. Johns Hopkins University, founded in 1876, was established for the express reason of bringing the German educational model to the United States and produced several prominent progressives, including Wilson, Dewey, and Frederick Jackson Turner.

Among other things, American progressives took from the Germans—and especially from the German philosopher G. W. F. Hegel and his disciples—their critique of individual rights and social compact theory and their organic or "living" notion of the national state. Wilson, in reflecting on what it meant to be a progressive, wrote of government as a "living thing," which was to be understood according to "the theory of organic life." This "living" notion of a constitution, Wilson contended, was far superior to the founders' model, which had considered government a kind of "machine" that could be constantly limited through checks and balances.[9] As a living entity, the progressives reasoned, government had to evolve and adapt in response to changing circumstances. While early American conceptions of national government had carefully circumscribed its power due to the perceived threat to individual liberties, progressives argued that history had brought about an improvement in the human condition, such that the will of the people was no longer in danger of becoming factious. Combined with a whole new host of economic and social ills that called out for a governmental remedy, progressives took this doctrine of progress and translated it into a call for a sharp increase in the scope of governmental power.

There may be no greater example of this phenomenon than Theodore Roosevelt's speech on the New Nationalism in 1910, which became the foundation for his 1912 campaign to regain the presidency. The speech reflects Roosevelt's turn, after his presidency, to a more radical brand of progressivism and reflects the extent to which other progressives like Herbert Croly had come to influence his thinking. Roosevelt called in the New Nationalism for the state to take an active role in effecting economic equality by way of superintending the use of private property. Private property rights, which had been serving as a brake on the more aggressive progressive policy proposals, were to be respected, Roosevelt argued, only insofar as the government approved of the property's social utility:

> We grudge no man a fortune in civil life if it is honorably obtained and well used. It is not even enough that it should have been gained without doing damage to the community. We should permit it to be gained only so long as the gaining represents benefit to the community. This, I know, implies a policy of a far more active governmental interference with social and economic conditions in this country than we have yet had, but I think we have got to face the fact that such an increase in governmental control is now necessary.[10]

New circumstances, Roosevelt argued, necessitated a new conception of government, and natural rights were no longer to serve as a principled boundary that the state was prohibited from crossing. Wilson had outlined a similar view of the extent of state power in a concise but revealing essay on the relationship between socialism and democracy. Wilson's essay starts out by defining socialism, suggesting that it stands for unfettered state power, which trumps any notion of individual rights. It "proposes that all idea of a limitation of public authority by individual rights be put out of view" and "that no line can be drawn between private and public affairs which the State may not cross at will." After laying out this definition of socialism, Wilson explained that he found nothing wrong with it in principle, since it was merely the logical extension of genuine democratic theory. It gives all power to the people, in their collective capacity, to carry out their will through the exercise of governmental power, unlimited by any undemocratic idea like individual rights. He elaborated:

> In fundamental theory socialism and democracy are almost if not quite one and the same. They both rest at bottom upon the absolute right of the community to determine its own destiny *and that of its members*. Limits of wisdom and convenience to the public control there may be: limits of principle there are, upon strict analysis, none.[11]

In this view, rights-based theories of self-government, such as the republicanism to which the American founders subscribed and of which Wilson was sharply critical, are far less democratic than socialism. As Wilson and his fellow progressives believed, rights-based theories of government limit the state's sphere of action, thus limiting the ability of the people to implement their collective will and thus representing something less than a real democracy.

PROGRESSIVE INTERPRETATIONS OF HISTORY

Given their reliance on the doctrine of progress, historical interpretation was of critical importance to a significant number of leading national progressives. Both Roosevelt and Wilson had a keen sense of history and were historians in their own right, each producing a number of scholarly historical works. And both were dramatically influenced by the changes that accompanied the professionalization of historical study in the academy in the late nineteenth century. By the time Roosevelt became president in 1901, a quarter-century of change had swept the field of its attachment to purely literary narrative and Romantic expression; the prose of Francis Parkman and the celebratory works of George Bancroft (though Bancroft often praised the values progressives

cherished, such as popular democracy and individual autonomy) yielded to
the "new learning." To assert their legitimate place in the university, historians maintained, they must adopt new methodologies and incorporate the multitudes of information and the insights provided by the new fields of sociology, psychology, and statistics.

Among the earliest of the new approaches to historical methodology was
the "Teutonic-germ theory" of Herbert Baxter Adams at Johns Hopkins University. Adams's assertion that democratic institutions in America owed their
existence to Germanic developments centuries earlier held sway briefly
among historians in the 1880s. Among Adams's closest students were Wilson
and Turner, and Turner's early writings clearly suggest the influence of
Adams and the Germanic model. As late as 1891, Turner published an article
entitled "The Significance of History" that quoted Adams extensively and
demonstrated his support for Adams's ideas. Turner wrote:

> The story of the peopling of America has not yet been written. We do not un-
> derstand ourselves. . . . One of the most fruitful fields of study in our country
> has been the process of growth of our own institutions, local and national. The
> town and the country, the germs of our political institutions, have been traced
> back to old Teutonic roots.[12]

Nonetheless, Turner ultimately rejected the germ theory as an inadequate ex-
planatory model and replaced it in 1893 with one far more influential. He
posited the "frontier thesis" as the means to understand American development, and the thesis, with its emphasis on democratic individualism, sparked
a reinterpretation of American history that served progressives well. The
American was a new man, Turner maintained, refashioned by the transform-
ing influence of frontier life. America's development was "not simply the development of Germanic germs," but was unique and resulted in "a new product that is American." The innovative, self-reliant farmer of Turner's frontier
epitomized the democratizing effect of the westward movement, and thus
Turner's work was congenial to supporters of an aggressive, popular movement that stressed democratic means to realize political and social reform.

Equally, and perhaps more, important for progressives' attempt to break
with the past in favor of a more egalitarian polity, was the emergence of a
body of scholarly work that questioned the longstanding view of the Revolutionary generation as one motivated mostly by a sense of selfless duty to
country and commitment to natural law principles as enshrined in the Declaration of Independence. It was Charles Beard's *An Economic Interpretation
of the Constitution of the United States*, published in 1913, that undoubtedly
did the most to aid the progressive reform agenda on this front, but there were
a number of significant works by progressive scholars that preceded Beard

and, to a degree, set the stage for his dramatic interpretation of the constitutional convention. The political scientist J. Allen Smith, for example, published *The Spirit of American Government* six years before Beard's *Economic Interpretation*. Smith maintained that the delegates to the constitutional convention were best understood, not as a group of disinterested patriots pursuing the common good, but as a distinct group with definable economic interests. James Harvey Robinson, an intellectual historian and originator of the "New Historians" at Columbia University, which included a significant number of progressive luminaries such as Beard, called upon scholars to provide a usable history, one that embraced the new learning and illuminated potential solutions to the ills of industrial society. Even Turner, oftentimes considered the least radical of the leading progressive historians, criticized "Gladstone's remark that 'The American Constitution is the most wonderful work ever struck off at a given time by the brain and purpose of man.'" That statement, Turner contended, "has been shown to be misleading, for the Constitution was, with all the constructive powers of the fathers, still a growth; and our history is only to be understood as a growth from European history under the new conditions of the new world."[13]

It was Beard, however, who provided the most radical break with the standard interpretation of the proceedings at the Philadelphia convention. The *Economic Interpretation* was received like a thunderclap, with denunciations (and some praise) from many of Beard's colleagues. The delegates at Philadelphia, Beard contended, were motivated by personal economic concerns and determined to produce a document that strengthened their control of government and thus assured their continued financial success. While Beard's assertion was similar to Smith's, his methodology, which seemed to substantiate the charge of avarice in a way that Smith's had not, combined with the charge that the framers should be condemned for reprehensible self-seeking, was a direct assault on the previously sacrosanct Constitution and its authors. Jefferson may have believed that the delegates assembled in Philadelphia were "demi-gods," but Beard thought otherwise. In Beard's analysis, even Madison, perhaps especially Madison, was charged with subscribing to "the theory of economic determinism in politics."[14]

The implications of Beard's thesis were clear and significant for advocates of progressive reform: there had been no popular control of government from the founding generation to the present; a great people had been duped by the conniving of a relatively small interest group. It was, therefore, incumbent upon proponents of democracy to wrest control of government from the few and place it where, despite the rhetoric of earlier generations, it had never been, in the hands of the populace. "[O]ur fundamental law," Beard wrote, "was not the product of an abstraction known as 'the whole people,' but of a group of economic interests."[15] Though Beard, and progressive historians generally, are usually credited with positing the notion of discontinuity in America's past, there is a significant exception here. Beard sounded a clear note of continuity by maintaining that economic elites had always maintained their status by virtue of their control of the political apparatus.

Progressive interpretations of history thus supported the purposes of reformers by suggesting that America's story was one of progress, while also stressing its reliance, oftentimes, on a false understanding of the past that served to obstruct the reform agenda. Old myths and shibboleths were to be replaced with a realistic appraisal of American life, which included both an emphasis on the unique aspects of the American character and a willingness to break with an uncritical celebration of the national past.

PROGRESSIVISM AND RELIGION

History was, for the progressives, more than a series of chance events; the passing of each historical epoch marked, instead, deliberate progress on the path to genuine democracy. With this conception of history as rational and powerful, we can also see a strong religious current that runs through much of progressive thought. Like Hegel, many progressives saw the hand of God at work in the process of historical progress. History was the means by which God gradually made himself present on earth, and the end result of this divinely inspired process was to be the modern democratic state. Consequently the state, for many progressives, was a god to which all citizens owed their undivided devotion, "the Divine Idea as it exists on Earth," as Hegel had put it in his *Philosophy of History*.[16] Cooperation with history—willingness, in other words, to adjust one's politics and morality to the evolving pressures of the current age—thus becomes a kind of divine command and a test of one's faithfulness to God; those refusing to go along with the demands of historical progress were, therefore, defying the will of God itself.[17]

Such a conception of history helps to explain the remarkably explicit religious language employed by many progressive politicians. During his speech at the Progressive Party convention in 1912, Roosevelt thundered: "Our cause is based on the eternal principles of righteousness; and even though we who now lead may for a time fail, in the end the cause itself shall triumph. . . . We stand at Armageddon, and we battle for the Lord." The convention culminated with party stalwarts waving bibles and demonstrating to fervent chants of "Onward Christian Soldiers." Even with respect to issues as mundane as the gold standard, religious language was invoked, as when William Jennings Bryan famously clamored at the 1896 Democratic convention: "You shall not press down upon the brow of labor this crown of thorns, you shall not crucify mankind upon a cross of gold." This kind of language, and the fusion it represents between Hegelianism and evangelical Protestantism, calls to mind what was, in many respects, the religious arm of progressivism: Social Gospel.

Beginning in the 1880s and lasting through the first world war, Social Gospel represented the response of liberal evangelical Protestantism to the great cultural and intellectual challenges of the late nineteenth century, most notably evolution and the new science. The response of the orthodox wing of the Protestant Church was fundamentalism; going in the other direction, Social Gospel embraced evolutionary theory (although not its "survival of the fittest" determinism) and saw orthodox religion as insufficient for the times. Social Gospel posited evolution as a divine plan for rational social advancement, and suggested that it had become possible, through an empowered central state, to realize the Christian hope that "thy will be done *on earth* as it is in heaven." Social Gospel adherents considered it to be their mission to fulfill *in this life* the New Testament's call to bring about the perfect kingdom of God. Like the progressive politicians, Social Gospel theologians asserted that government, because of progress, was now in a position to bring about such an earthly utopia in the form of the modern democratic state. Walter Rauschenbusch, arguably *the* theologian of Social Gospel, criticized orthodox religion in a manner parallel to the progressive criticism of traditional constitutionalism. Orthodox religion, contended Rauschenbusch, had become too individualized; in focusing on salvation in the next life, conservative Christianity encouraged selfishness and a turning away from the world of man. Instead, Rauschenbusch urged, Christians ought to focus on salvation in this life, in the form of social goods achieved through the state. The orthodox church had encouraged what Rauschenbusch called a "religious individualism," where "there was a subtle twist of self-seeking which vitiated its Christlikeness."[18] But man would now be judged, Rauschenbusch explained, not by his individual sins, but by the degree to which he merged his will and his life with the divine purposes of the kingdom of God on earth. As a practical matter, this meant overcoming man's attachment to private property, and removing private property rights as an obstacle to social action. "We shall have to resocialize property," Rauschenbusch reasoned, by which he meant that property was to be "made to serve the public good, either by the service its uses render to the public welfare, or by the income it brings to the public treasury." "Socializing property will mean," he elaborated, "that instead of serving the welfare of a small group directly, and the public welfare only indirectly, it will be made more directly available for the service of all."[19]

To be sure, progressivism had its ardent secularists, especially among those associated with *The New Republic* and the more scientific wing of the movement. But like their more religiously inclined progressive brethren, this group saw orthodox Christianity as a great obstacle to progress. They especially resented the religious influence over education, because they saw in traditional religious education an encouragement of the young to focus on the private sphere, which detracted from the undivided devotion to the state on which progressive democracy was to depend. Thus *The New Republic* editorialized in 1916 that there had to be a "change in the meaning of tolerance." They explained that unlike eighteenth-century liberalism, "twentieth-century democracy believes that the community has certain positive ends to achieve, and if they are to be achieved the community must control the education of the young." They editorialized that "freedom and tolerance mean the development of independent powers of judgment in the young, not the freedom of older people to impose their dogmas on the young." Modern democracy, they concluded, "insists that the plasticity of the child shall not be artificially and prematurely hardened into a philosophy of life."[20] In the end, while the Social Gospel arm of progressivism seemed to speak a language quite distinct from that of the secularist arm, the same message was preached: a worship of the state as a god, and the need to overcome any attachment to the private that might stand as an obstacle to the social enterprise.

SOCIAL JUSTICE AND EDUCATION

The determination of Social Gospel advocates to remake society was part of a larger effort that originated primarily in the last twenty years of the nineteenth century. By 1900 a number of reform efforts began to coalesce around those associated with progressivism. They were a variegated group—influenced from a variety of sources including muckrakers, prohibitionists, socialists, populists, and others—though most shared the common commitment to progress through democratic education and direct social action. Advocates of social justice seemed to possess an unlimited optimism with regard to the power of public education. If they could educate the citizenry, they believed, then their reform proposals would succeed. In the language of Social Gospel, crusaders for social justice would translate the teachings of Christ into action. Jane Addams was the quintessential advocate of the social justice agenda. Her efforts in 1889 to establish Hull-House in Chicago set an example that soon spread throughout major urban centers in industrial America, resulting in the establishment of additional settlement homes such as New York's University Settlement and Boston's South End House.

Addams's "The Subjective Necessity for Social Settlements," among the most influential documents of the social justice movement, demonstrates not only the near obsession some progressives had with the democratic panacea, it also clearly reflects their determination to ally the reform agenda with "that true democracy of the early [Christian] Church." The social settlement movement, Addams maintained, must work "to make the entire social organism democratic, to extend democracy beyond its political expression." Such sentiments were molded in part by her witness to the corruption of urban "bossism" and by a "partial" democracy that bestowed the vote, but little else, on immigrants and the working poor. She appealed especially to the "fast-growing number of cultivated young people who have no recognized outlet for their active faculties" to engage in the work of social reform. Many of those same young people, she maintained, rejected "the assumption that Christianity is a set of ideas which belong to the religious consciousness" in favor of a faith that manifested itself "in the social organism."[21]

The fundamental goal of these mostly middle class reformers was to make alterations in American society in order to save it from the inevitable consequences of economic inequalities that were intensified by the combination of industrial life and the new immigration. And despite the apparent altruism of many progressive reformers, the coercive aspects of progressivism (some called it "benevolent social control") are unmistakable in its ultimately successful demands for prohibition, as well as its attempt, partly successful, to severely restrict the new immigration. Perhaps the most extreme example of coercion among some social justice crusaders is found in legislation such as Indiana's 1907 law requiring the forced sterilization of certain classes of inmates—primarily those deemed mentally deficient.

Addams believed that educators must work to universalize the experience of all, by which she meant that everyone should be enabled via progressive education and reform to participate fully and equally in society. This belief was reflected in the theories of leading progressive educationalists, including most especially the educator and philosopher John Dewey. Dewey's philosophy of education made explicit what was essentially an article of faith among progressives generally: state control and regulation of numerous aspects of public life would be required to bring about the improvements progressives sought.

Dewey's view of the purpose of education was purely democratic—education served to integrate the pupil into the larger community that was itself characterized by the universality of its experience. This approach demanded the explicit rejection of any attempt to teach transcendent principles in the classroom and thus it was ultimately hostile to religious education, which, Dewey believed, was hopelessly mired in the past. Religious education was backward-looking when the great age of democracy demanded a revolutionary change in pedagogical theory. Thus, as Dewey proclaims in his

"Pedagogic Creed," "I believe that . . . the teacher is not in the school to impose certain ideas or to form certain habits in the child, but is there as a member of the community to select the influences which shall affect the child and
to assist him in properly responding to these influences."[22] At least one irony
in Dewey's conception of education is that despite its disdain for the
"anachronistic" approach of religious education, his theory posits its own essentially religious education to replace it. The democratic faith is paramount
and the dogmatic certitude with which he proclaims the student's need to participate in the "pooled intelligence" of humanity and to be inculcated with the
universalized values of the social community suggests a substantial role for
both educationalists and for the state, which essentially replaced the function
of the church in education. This thoroughgoing elimination of a religious basis for education and its replacement with a secular faith in democracy was
the only sure means to the renewal of social life that was shared by progressive reformers and educationalists alike. As Dewey stated, "I believe that education is a regulation of the process of coming to share in the social consciousness; and that the adjustment of individual activity on the basis of this
social consciousness is the only sure method of social reconstruction."[23]

PROGRESSIVISM AND THE CONSTITUTION

In addition to its push for social reform, the progressive policy agenda included a wide array of legislative proposals to regulate private business and
property, and in many states progressives had met with considerable success
in winning their enactment. Yet the federal Constitution, undergirded by the
principle of individual property rights, continued to prove a formidable obstacle to these legislative programs, as did several of the state constitutions.
State and federal courts had, in many cases, overturned progressive legislative achievements, ruling that the new programs extended the power of government into the private sphere well beyond its constitutional limits. (The
most famous example, to be sure, was the U.S. Supreme Court's decision in
Lochner v. New York, overturning a state law regulating bakers' hours.) It was
this phenomenon that Roosevelt had in mind when he frequently railed
against the judiciary and called for the people to be given the power to over-
turn specific state judicial decisions by popular referendum. Roosevelt contended that courts had misconstrued constitutional law, "as if it prohibited the
whole people of [a] State from adopting methods of regulating the use of
property so that human life, particularly the lives of working men, shall be
safer, freer, and happier." The judiciary, argued Roosevelt, was construing the
due process clause "as if property rights, to the exclusion of human rights,

had a first mortgage on the Constitution."[24] At a more general level, the real problem, as progressives saw it, was a failure of the courts to see the Constitution as a "living" organism, one whose limitations on government ought not be read strictly or literally, but instead interpreted to fit the new demands of a new age. It was in this mode that Herbert Croly contrasted a government based on "law" to a government based on "faith." Genuine democracy, Croly argued, was grounded on faith in the people's ability to rule themselves. The founders' Constitution, by contrast, elevated law—that is, legal protection for individual rights, even against the will of the majority—over faith, and thus brought into doubt the very legitimacy of democracy. Croly asked, "does not the exaggerated value which has been attached to constitutional limitations, and the apprehensive and reactionary state of mind which has in consequence possessed many patriotic Americans, tend to undermine the foundations in human nature and human will upon which the whole superstructure of a progressive democratic society must admittedly be built?"[25]

For Wilson, the structure of the Constitution itself made it nearly impossible for progressively inclined interpreters to adapt it to their agenda. The Constitution rested, at bottom, on a system of divided powers, both between federal and state levels of government and within the national government itself. While the progressive force of history had brought about an essential unity of popular will (at least in the minds of Wilson and other progressives), the Constitution divided power in such a way as to make expression of that unified will a near impossibility. It was for this reason that Wilson detested the separation of powers, and that almost everything he wrote on the American system of government contained a sharp critique of it. The ideal model for Wilson was the parliamentary one, where the legislative and executive are essentially united, both rising or falling on the evolving popular will (indeed, many of Wilson's early writings advocated converting various facets of the American system to the parliamentary model). The separation of powers, Wilson explained, had come out of the founders' obsessive fear of majority tyranny, and thus the system was outdated for the present age, where the people were no longer a danger to themselves. As Goodnow later complained, "it was the fear of political tyranny through which liberty might be lost which led to the adoption of the theories of checks and balances and of the separation of powers."[26] The problem was outlined by Wilson on the campaign trail in 1912:

The makers of our Federal Constitution read Montesquieu with true scientific enthusiasm. They were scientists in their way—the best way of their age—those fathers of the nation. . . . They constructed a government as they would have constructed an orrery—to display the laws of nature. Politics in their thought was a variety of mechanics. The Constitution was founded on the law of gravitation. The government was to exist and move by virtue of the efficacy of "checks and balances."

The trouble with the theory is that government is not a machine, but a living thing. It falls, not under the theory of the universe, but under the theory of organic life. It is accountable to Darwin, not to Newton. It is modified by its environment, necessitated by its tasks, shaped to its functions by the sheer pressure of life. No living thing can have its organs offset against each other, as checks, and live.[27]

American government needed to be reformed so that it reflected the essential unity of the public mind that progressives believed had been brought about by history. Separation of powers, therefore, had to be discarded and replaced by a system that instead separated politics and administration. By this formulation, progressives like Wilson and Goodnow meant that the national political institutions—Congress, the presidency, and so on—ought to be democratized and unified, bringing them into much closer contact with public opinion and facilitating their expression of the general public will. At the same time, since progressives believed that the most contentious political questions had been resolved by historical development (the Civil War had been decisive in this regard), the real work of government was not in politics, but in administration—in figuring out the specific means of achieving what the people generally agreed they all wanted. Understanding the progressive vision for reforming national institutions requires a comprehension of their plan for both sides of the politics-administration dichotomy—that is, for democratizing and unifying national political institutions while separating and insulating administrative agencies.

Politics

The great problem for progressives was that American national politics suffered from a lack of accountability. As the Federalists had intended, the Constitution established an indirect form of popular rule, characterized by "the total exclusion of the people, in their collective capacity" from any direct role in governing, as James Madison put it in *Federalist* 63. For the Federalists, such a construction was an essential means to secure "the public good, and private rights, against the danger" of majority tyranny, while "at the same time to preserve the spirit and the form of popular government."[28] Likewise the separation of powers system, in failing to elevate any one branch or office above the others, denied to any one branch or office the claim of exclusively representing the people as a whole, and thus prevented any one part of the government from claiming a true position of national leadership. And this was precisely the problem from the perspective of progressives, especially for the likes of Wilson, who argued that without a clear, accountable leader, government as a whole could not be held accountable to the people's will.

For the national political institutions to be genuinely democratic, Wilson contended, there had to be an identifiable leader, to whom the public could make known its will, and whom it could hold electorally accountable for success or failure in implementing that will throughout the whole of government. "Leadership and control must be lodged somewhere," Wilson urged.[29] While Wilson's early writings looked to put Congress in this role, he ultimately concluded that only the president could serve as the kind of leader he had in mind. The president, Wilson pointed out, was the only politician who could claim to speak for the people as a whole, and thus he called upon the president to transcend the separation of powers—to consider himself not merely as chief of a single branch of government, but as the popular leader of the whole of national politics. Wilson even contrasted the "constitutional aspect" of the presidency— its constitutionally defined role as chief of one of the three coequal branches of government—to the "political" function of the president, where he could use his connection to public opinion as a tool for moving all of the branches of government in the direction called for by the people.[30] It was in this way that Wilson believed the original intention of the separation of powers system could be circumvented, and the enhanced presidency could be a means of energizing the kind of active national government that the progressive agenda required.

From the founders' perspective, the most dangerous aspect of Wilson's vision for the presidency would have been that the president's power was to come directly from the people as opposed to the Constitution. Wilson envisioned a president who, to the extent that he could claim to embody the people's will, would move the institutions of national government by the force of that popularity. Given their considerable concern about demagoguery (majority factions, *The Federalist* frequently reminds us, rarely arise spontaneously), the founders thought it paramount that the president's power be clearly understood as coming from Article II of the Constitution itself; the president, in other words, was to be both empowered by and limited by the Constitution. In this respect, Roosevelt's conception of the presidency, like Wilson's, represented a novelty in the American political tradition. In articulating what has come to be known as his "Stewardship" theory of the presidency, Roosevelt posited the idea that presidential power is not confined by the enumerated grants of power made in the Constitution. As he explained in the *Autobiography*, his presidency was defined by his

insistence upon the theory that the executive power was limited only by specific restrictions and prohibitions appearing in the Constitution or imposed by the

Congress under its Constitutional powers. My view was that every executive officer, and above all every executive officer in high position, was a steward of the people bound actively and affirmatively to do all he could for the people, and not to content himself with the negative merit of keeping his talents undamaged in a napkin. I declined to adopt the view that what was imperatively necessary for the Nation could not be done by the President unless he could find some specific authorization to do it. My belief was that it was not only his right but his duty to do anything that the needs of the Nation demanded unless such action was forbidden by the Constitution or by the laws.[31]

Roosevelt thus understood the powers of the national government, and especially those of the president, as *plenary*, not *enumerated*—defined, in other words, by the needs of the time, not by the provisions of Article II. The president was to become the interpreter of the nation's needs and was to use his position as the people's steward to keep government responsive to those needs as they evolved from one epoch to the next. It was in this way that the presidency became, for progressives, the agent of progress in national politics.

Administration

If national political institutions were to facilitate a general and unified expression of the public's will, the national administrative institutions were to translate that broad will into specific policy. And while progressives very much wanted to democratize national political institutions, their inclination in administration was just the opposite—to shield administrative agencies from political influence, so that administrators could be free to make policy on the basis of their expertise. For all their talk about historical progress and the unity of the public will, progressives complained about the corruption of politics and the dominance of special interests. Progressives took all of the contention and interest conflict in national politics not as evidence that the Federalists had been right about the perpetual factiousness of human nature, but rather as an indication that politics itself needed to be overcome so that the true, unified will of the public could emerge. The making of actual policy, then, had to be rescued from the machinations of electoral politics, and placed in the hands of those who could regulate the special interests, on the basis of expertise, for the sake of the common good. The early roots of progressive administration, therefore, can be seen in the Mugwump agitation for civil service reform. But whereas the civil service movement was a reaction to the corruption of the spoils system, the progressive vision of administration took this reaction and developed it into a much broader and more thoughtful call for reform, one that became a primary means of facilitating much of the progressive policy agenda. The role that progressives had in mind for the national government greatly exceeded the capabilities of the traditional constitutional branches. The extent of regulatory activity in which progressives wanted the national government to engage simply could not be handled by an institution like Congress. And so the establishment of a substantial bureaucratic apparatus, largely free from the influence of electoral politics, not only became a means of facilitating government by educated experts, but also provided an institutional machinery that could take on the many new tasks that progressives had in mind for the national government.

Politically, the call for an extensive, and largely independent, regulatory apparatus is most often associated with Roosevelt's campaign in 1912, where under the banner of the "New Nationalism" Roosevelt proposed extensive government supervision and regulation of the key business interests in the country. It is less well known that, in advocating the independent regulatory power of national administration, Roosevelt was actually giving concrete political shape to an idea that had long since been brought into America by Wilson, Roosevelt's opponent in the 1912 campaign. As a subsequent section of this chapter will show, Wilson's criticism of the New Nationalism reflected the essential tactics of the campaign much more than it did any principled difference between the two candidates on the question of national administrative power. For it was Wilson who pioneered the idea of separating administration from politics in the United States—an idea that was then developed into a more coherent body of work in administrative law by Goodnow.

Wilson introduced the concept of separating administration from politics in a series of essays in the 1880s, most notably "The Study of Administration," which some public administration scholars consider to have marked the founding of their discipline in this country. Goodnow, while never directly acknowledging Wilson as far as we are aware, expanded upon this Wilsonian concept in the 1890s and eventually published a book on it in 1900: *Politics and Administration*. Wilson did not assert that administration itself was a novel concept in America, but rather that the kind of administration progressives needed for their vision of the modern democratic state was clearly at odds with the principles of the founding and the traditional interpretation of the Constitution. This is because administration—as vigorous as some of the founders surely envisioned it—was confined in the original view within the executive branch. It was thus accountable to the partisan executive and confined to the exercise of executive power. Progressive administration, by contrast, was to be liberated from the influence of partisan or electoral politics and was to engage not only in executive action, but legislative and judicial action as well. If administrative agencies were to be responsible for superintending the activities of private business—a mission of such a scope that it far exceeded the capacity and expertise of Congress—then, on the basis of their expertise, administrators would need to make rules and regulations, enforce them, and adjudicate violations of them.[32] This meant, Wilson knew, that progressive administration had a big hurdle to overcome if it was to gain legitimacy in the United States.

The essence of Wilson's "Study," accordingly, is an argument that it was not right to apply constitutional analysis to the kind of administrative power he was proposing. We ought, instead, to consider constitutional and administrative questions as entirely separate and not try to drag independent administration before the bar of constitutional scrutiny. Wilson wrote of "the distinction between *constitutional* and administrative questions," and explained that "the field of administration is a field of business. It is removed from the hurry and strife of politics; it at most points stands apart even from the debatable ground of constitutional study." In particular, Wilson knew that the progressive conception of administration could not fit within the Constitution's separation of powers scheme, conceding that "one cannot easily make clear to every one just where administration resides in the various departments of any practicable government."[33] Wilson forthrightly admitted in the "Study" that his whole conception of administration was foreign—indeed, it was based on the Prussian bureaucratic state championed in Hegel's *Philosophy of Right* as the rational culmination of all of world history (Wilson even quotes from the *Philosophy of Right* in the first part of the "Study"). But, he asked, "why should we not use such parts of foreign contrivances as we want, if they be in any way serviceable? . . . If I see a murderous fellow sharpening a knife cleverly, I can borrow his way of sharpening the knife without borrowing his probable intention to commit murder with it."[34] As Goodnow helped to elaborate, the achievement of progressive policy aims would not be possible without the ability of enlightened experts to rise above the "polluted" atmosphere of special-interest politics and regulate for the common good. Administration, in contrast to politics, was about the "truth."[35] Progressives believed that administrators, unlike ordinary politicians, could be objective and could focus on the good of the whole people—oddly, their ability to do so rested primarily on being freed from electoral accountability. The salary and life tenure of administrators would take care of any self-interested inclinations that might otherwise corrupt their decision-making, Goodnow concluded, and he explained that "such a force should be free from the influence of politics because of the fact that their mission is the exercise of foresight and discretion, the pursuit of truth, the gathering of information, the maintenance of a strictly impartial attitude toward the individuals with whom they have dealings, and the provision of the most efficient possible administrative organization."[36]

Reflecting on the question of progressivism and the reform of national institutions, we come to a central irony in progressive thought: the strong democratizing argument with respect to political institutions is coupled with an argument on administration that calls for shifting policymaking power away from popular institutions and giving it to educated elites. Independent administrators are to be given significant policymaking discretion precisely to the extent that they are free from political or electoral control, and thus the progressive argument here seems to be a distinctly elitist one that proceeds under a democratic veneer. This is a characteristic of progressivism that runs consistently throughout the period—from Wilson and Goodnow in the 1880s and 1890s, through Croly and Roosevelt with the New Nationalism of 1912, and again with President Wilson as he implemented much of the New Nationalism during his own administration.

PARTIES, DIRECT DEMOCRACY, AND THE POLITICS OF REFORM

In keeping with his argument that national political institutions had become unaccountable, and that the system lacked clear leaders through whom the public could make its will manifest in national politics, Wilson advocated at one time a system of responsible party government along the parliamentary model.[37] In so doing, Wilson was trying to come up with a way to achieve a goal shared by all progressives: the democratization of national politics. His proposed remedy, however—a reformed, but vigorous, party system—was not endorsed by most others in the movement,[38] who saw the party system itself as a root problem, and thus advocated its abolition as opposed to its reform. It is important to note that this difference, while significant, was a difference in means or methods, not a difference of principle.

Croly, like Wilson, believed that the party system served to perpetuate the indirectness of American democracy, and thus stood as an obstacle to the achievement of genuine democracy. But where Wilson thought that reforms such as the direct primary could put the people in charge of the party system and thus reform it and turn it to progressive ends, Croly saw mechanisms like the primary as mere temporary steps on the road to abolishing parties altogether. At the heart of Croly's call for abolishing the party system was the conviction that partisanship itself detracted from the exclusive devotion that an individual ought to give directly to the state. When one identified as a partisan of a particular party, one could not also be a partisan of the organic whole—the state itself. The party system, Croly reasoned, "demands and obtains for a party an amount of loyal service and personal sacrifice which a public-spirited democrat should lavish only on the state."[39] With the Progressive Party of 1912, accordingly, we see a party platform to end parties

altogether. This anti-partisan attitude is also why mechanisms of direct democracy became the hallmarks of much of the progressive movement across
the country, especially at the state and local level.

Progressivism was, in many respects, a reform movement that originated
first at the local level before it emerged in state and federal government. Reforms that came to typify the progressive agenda first appeared in urban
America, as muckrakers such as Lincoln Steffens and Ida Tarbell worked to
document evidence of political corruption and vice, including prostitution
and gambling, in the pages of *McClure's*, *Cosmopolitan*, and *Success*. And in
local government a number of reform mayors such as Detroit's Hazen Pingree
(later elected governor) and Toledo's Samuel "Golden Rule" Jones supported
working class demands for greater participation in local politics via opposition to urban political machines. Among the most radical of early reformers,
Jones embraced public ownership of utilities as part of the cure for urban corruption and maintained that democracy, fully realized, would resolve the in-
equities of political and economic life.

At the city level, the progressive drive focused on the question of home
rule. Too often, it was argued, local government suffered due to restrictions
placed upon it at the state level—again by political machines often tied to
business interests. What was required, therefore, was a drive to clean up government to make it more efficient and responsive to people's needs. A few
cities in the 1890s formed citizens' associations to challenge the status quo in
municipal government. Pingree called for equitable taxation and local regulation of public utilities. He also advocated a substantial program of social
services, as did Jones, who argued that without substantial reforms such as
public ownership of utilities, competitive civil service for city government
positions, and civic improvements including taxpayer-funded parks and play-
grounds, urban America would erupt in class warfare and democracy would
be undermined. Among the most significant of the progressives' successes in
local political reform was the birth of commission government in Galveston,
Texas, in 1900. In the aftermath of a hurricane, the state legislature appointed
a commission of individuals who were responsible for specific aspects of
public life. The idea spread rapidly between 1900 and 1920. Similarly,
Staunton, Virginia (Wilson's birthplace, coincidentally), adopted the city-
manager form of government at this time.

The most significant programs, however, were found in the states. At the
turn of the century, most parties used the caucus method for choosing their
candidates for the state legislature. Political bosses dominated state capitals
as they dominated much of urban political life. The quintessential state-level
reformer, Robert M. La Follette of Wisconsin, was determined to change this
state of affairs. A member of the Republican Party, he was ostracized by the

party regulars as his reform tendencies became obvious. Undaunted, he ran for governor in 1900 and won, and was reelected two more times before moving on to the U.S. Senate. His "Wisconsin experiment" in government was praised by Roosevelt (who called it a "laboratory of democracy") for its innovative use of direct democracy devices—including the initiative, referendum, and recall—to give the people a voice in government. La Follette was convinced that his efforts in Wisconsin had, in fact, established a model that progressives could emulate throughout the country. He wrote:

> The public service of the state has been democratized by a civil service law opening it to men and women on an equal footing independent of everything excepting qualification and fitness for office. I think the passing of this law was the only case of the kind where the employees then holding office were not blanketed into the service, but were required to take the regular competitive examinations in order to retain their jobs. The law has worked to the great advantage of the service and to the general improvement of political standards. There is no longer any political pull in Wisconsin.[40]

Of course, in the same work, La Follette detailed the methods used to ensure his machine's control of the political process in Wisconsin, an irony that could scarcely have been lost on his opponents. Nonetheless, La Follette demonstrated that the progressive agenda of direct democracy and local control, accompanied by a massive regulation of industry, could be achieved at the state level. It was his goal to bring the Wisconsin example to the rest of the nation as president, though his best chance to capture the Republican nomination failed when he suffered a nervous breakdown in the 1912 primary campaign. That chapter of the progressives' story, begun by Theodore Roosevelt, was left to Woodrow Wilson to complete.

ROOSEVELT, WILSON, AND 1912

Due partly to the differences between Roosevelt and Wilson on the question of political parties, the 1912 election is often billed as a contest between the progressive Roosevelt and the conservative Wilson. Such a characterization, while inaccurate, is exacerbated by several other factors. Chief among these is that Roosevelt campaigned in 1912 on the New Nationalism—a call for a marked increase in the scope of national power and central-government supervision of private business interests—while Wilson campaigned on the New Freedom, a program critical of the paternalistic implications of Roosevelt's platform. The result has been a misleading dichotomy in the literature on the progressives, pitting the "Hamiltonian," big-government Roosevelt against the "Jeffersonian," small-government, states'-rights Wilson. Leaving aside the very important point that Hamilton and Jefferson, their differences notwithstanding, are far more akin to each other than either of them is to any progressive, the Hamiltonian-Jeffersonian dichotomy falsely portrays Wilson as a kind of anti-progressive. In fact, nothing could be further from the truth. Part of the problem comes from the fact that the Princeton collection of Wilson's papers was published and made fully available only recently, and thus much of the twentieth-century scholarship on Wilson was based upon a very incomplete look at his body of work, especially at those early works of Wilson's academic career where he was writing and thinking most seriously about the principles of politics. While the nature of this chapter prohibits any sustained examination of the question, suffice it to say that anyone who wrote "The Study of Administration" or *The State*, as Wilson did in 1887 and 1889, respectively, could not by any stretch of the imagination be characterized as a small-government, states'-rights, conservative Jeffersonian. Those works, among the many, many others like them that Wilson produced, give a conception of a centralized, bureaucratic state of such scope that even the most ardent New Nationalist could find little with which to quarrel.

What explains, then, Wilson's occasional conservative, small-government rhetoric on the 1912 campaign trail? The first thing to note is that the extent and nature of such rhetoric is often exaggerated; *The New Freedom*, even on its surface, is certainly no defense of traditional American constitutionalism or unfettered, free-market economics. But beyond this, when one considers the practical political circumstances of 1912, the campaign rhetoric is not difficult to understand. Wilson's aim, naturally, was to win the election. He had been effectively silent on the question of regulating or breaking trusts prior to 1907 and 1908, which is when he began to contemplate seriously a future in politics and the corresponding need to carve out a unique position for himself in the national debate. More importantly, Wilson's electoral fortunes rested squarely on his position within the Democratic Party. In particular, Wilson very clearly needed the William Jennings Bryan wing of the party. Consider that it took forty-six ballots for Wilson to win the party's nomination, which occurred only after Bryan intervened in Wilson's favor. Central to Bryan's populism was a fear of national executive power and a deep distrust of business interests in the northeast. By campaigning against Roosevelt's plan to maintain the business trusts by bringing them into a regulatory relationship with the national government, Wilson solidified his position with the Bryan Democrats who were essential to his victory. And consider, finally, that once Wilson was elected, he lost little time turning his back on the small-government campaign rhetoric, embarking instead on a program of expanding national government and administration very much along the lines suggested by Roosevelt's New Nationalism.

Wilson's turn to big government after 1912 was not, therefore, the "conversion" that it is often characterized to be. Rather, the anomaly was the 1912 campaign itself. Wilson was a big-government progressive long before 1912 and immediately after 1912, with the circumstances of the campaign forcing a brief detour. It is thus proper to consider both Roosevelt and Wilson as lions of the progressive movement. One of the most persuasive acknowledgments of this fact comes from Croly, who as a close advisor to Roosevelt and frequent critic of Wilson would be in a position of some authority on the question. Writing in 1914, Croly clearly considered Wilson to be a progressive. Croly characterized Wilson's progressivism as "ambiguous" and said that Wilson's "deliberate purpose seems to have been to keep progressivism vague." He later remarked that Wilson's real progressivism "poses as a higher conservatism." Why this intentional vagueness to Wilson's progressivism? Croly understood very well not just Wilson's progressivism, but also the practical politics of the day: "Be it recognized also that in Mr. Wilson's situation a certain amount of ambiguity has a manifest practical value. He is a Democrat as well as a progressive. . . . He would have good reason, consequently, for emphasizing any possible analogies between progressivism and the historic tradition of his own party."[41]

THE PROGRESSIVE PRESIDENCIES

Wilson's victory in 1912 and again in 1916 meant that progressives of both parties played a significant role in national, state, and local politics throughout the first two decades of the twentieth century. Both Roosevelt and Wilson worked to ensure that reform was brought to the forefront of American national life and, as a result of their efforts, the progressive agenda lost much of the aura of radicalism that had hobbled labor and reform efforts in the Gilded Age. Roosevelt's contribution to that achievement is immeasurable. In addition to a considerable intellect, he brought a sense of optimism to national political life. His wartime heroics and broad grin endeared him to the public, and Roosevelt had an ability to invest even seemingly mundane issues with high drama. From the time he declared his intent to enter politics—an unusual choice for somebody of his privileged background—he was clearly determined to reform the Republican Party from within. It was thus with good reason that Old Guard Republican Party bosses like Marcus Hanna were so fearful of this "cowboy" as president. And once in power, Roosevelt immediately established his determination to use the office of president more vigorously than any of his predecessors. His view of the executive as a "bully pulpit" coupled with an elastic view of the Constitution meant that Roosevelt's agenda—in both domestic and foreign policy matters—was not typically restricted by scruples over matters of constitutionality. The era of mass industry and mass immigration meant that new approaches were needed. As Roosevelt noted in his first annual message to Congress in 1901:

> The tremendous and highly complex industrial development which went on with ever accelerated rapidity during the latter half of the nineteenth century brings us face to face, at the beginning of the twentieth, with very serious social problems. The old laws, and the old customs which had almost the binding force of law, were once quite sufficient to regulate the accumulation and distribution of wealth. Since the industrial changes which have so enormously increased the productive power of mankind, they are no longer sufficient.[42]

In domestic policy, Roosevelt immediately demonstrated his willingness to intervene in industry by invoking the Sherman Antitrust Act against the Northern Securities Company, which was ultimately dissolved as an illegal monopoly. The same year (1902) he intervened to end an anthracite coal strike by the United Mine Workers that threatened a nationwide coal shortage. Roosevelt summoned representatives from the owners and the miners while he mediated an agreement. Not only was it the first time a president had acted to facilitate such talks, it was also memorable for Roosevelt's threats to bring in federal troops and nationalize the mining operations. Though the miners won only some of their demands, including higher wages and a shorter workday, Roosevelt's actions led to his reputation among many industrial workers as the protector of the common man. What followed was a substantial program to regulate numerous businesses and industries in America, including railroads and the meatpacking industry.

Similarly, Wilson viewed the president as the national leader and originator of the national political agenda. This view was reflected in his approach to Congress, where he revived the practice of delivering annual messages in person and carefully cultivated relationships with some individual members—a sign of his long-held affinity for the parliamentary model. If this approach to Congress differed in some respects from Roosevelt's, Wilson's determination to realize critical elements of the progressive reform agenda did not. Wilson already had a substantial record of reform as governor of New Jersey. Once inaugurated as president, he moved quickly to reduce the tariff, a measure which most progressives sought and, even more directly related to the progressive agenda, the lost revenues were to be recovered by making use of the recently ratified Sixteenth Amendment that levied an income tax on American workers. He also took measures to reorganize and regulate the banking system by signing the Federal Reserve Act (1913) and sought support for stronger anti-trust legislation that ultimately resulted in the Clayton Antitrust Act (1914). Wilson also supported the creation of the Federal Trade Commission, an independent regulatory agency authorized to investigate corporations engaged in interstate commerce and violations of antitrust laws.

Through the realization of their agendas, Roosevelt and Wilson had made reform respectable. Federal regulation of numerous aspects of public life had become commonplace. Americans may have tired of their crusading zeal, but the progressive presidents and their supporters had inaugurated a new era in American government.

PROGRESSIVISM, WAR, AND PEACE

The energy that Presidents Roosevelt and Wilson showed in pursuing progressive goals was not confined to domestic reform measures. Both men supported active foreign policies that, if justified and applied differently, demonstrated nonetheless a similarity in the idealism that underwrote them. Both believed that a well conceived foreign policy could spread American ideals abroad even as it enhanced the American economy. This is not to say, however, that they recommended comparable courses of action in a given situation—quite the opposite was oftentimes true. Roosevelt, for example, could scarcely restrain his scathing criticism of Wilson's policy of neutrality when, Roosevelt believed, the situation in Europe demanded American intervention in World War I. And Wilson clearly rejected Roosevelt's colonialist aspirations that resulted in the acquisition of the Philippine Islands after the Spanish-American War. Still, there was an aggressive strain in many progressives' foreign policy, including that of Roosevelt and Wilson, which mirrored the forcefulness of their determination in matters of domestic social and political reform.

Beginning in the 1890s, America embarked upon a course of foreign intervention that clearly rejected cherished principles of American foreign policy as established both in Washington's Farewell Address and the Monroe Doctrine. The decision to embrace imperialism in the interest of establishing a network of colonial outposts and overseas holdings reflected the belief among some that America must look to a "new manifest destiny" to secure its future. If America did not expand abroad, it was argued, the ability to compete with other colonial powers would be lost. Among the most ardent of the leading progressive expansionists was Indiana senator Albert J. Beveridge. Like Roosevelt, Beveridge was convinced that America must expand in order to sustain its national greatness and, since the continental frontier was closed according to the 1890 census and Turner's recent thesis, the logical place to look was the Pacific basin. Virtually all progressives who believed such expansion should be raised to the level of a national imperative were influenced to at least some degree by the writings of Alfred Thayer Mahan, whose publication of *The Influence of Sea Power upon History, 1660–1783* in 1890 staunchly supported overseas expansion. Indeed, Mahan's call for a canal across the isthmus of Central America, the possession of overseas coaling stations in the Pacific, and a navy powerful enough to carry such an ambitious program to completion fit perfectly with Roosevelt's energetic nationalism.

Though Wilson's foreign policy is distinguished from Roosevelt's by a clear disdain for colonialist expansion, he quickly demonstrated that, as president, he was willing to intervene forcefully to spread his vision of ideal government. The revolutions in Mexico and the instability they bred reportedly elicited from Wilson the promise to "teach the South American republics to elect good men." And Wilson twice intervened militarily in Mexico, ostensibly to uphold American rights there, but also to shape the outcome of the revolutionary contest. Before the United States entered World War I, he also dispatched marines to Haiti and the Dominican Republic.

It was, however, Wilson's decisions regarding World War I that left an indelible mark on his presidency and caused substantial divisions among leading progressives, including Roosevelt, La Follette, and Wilson's Secretary of State, William Jennings Bryan. Wilson had steadfastly maintained his determination to keep the United States out of the calamitous war in Europe. Seeking reelection in 1916 he continued, despite the infamous sinking of the *Lusitania* and the loss of 128 American lives, to speak the language of neutrality and to offer the good offices of the United States to negotiate an end to the war. However, Germany, as an act of military desperation, resumed unrestricted submarine warfare on February 1, 1917, which soon meant the loss of more American lives and Wilson's request for a declaration of war. Echoing the sentiments of Bryan, La Follette argued that Wilson had, in fact, not been impartial in thought or in action as he had called upon Americans to be at the outset of the war. Rather, Wilson demanded that Germany observe neutral rights, warning that it would be held to "strict accountability" for violations of American neutrality, but did not require the same of Britain.

America's entry into the war was ultimately more than Germany could withstand. It sought an armistice based on Wilson's Fourteen Points, and Wilson headed for Europe to negotiate a treaty that, he believed, would usher in a new age of international peace. Wilson's progressive idealism was reflected in his calls for a "peace without victory" and a "war to end all wars." Such language was, however, lost on the victors in the peace negotiations at Versailles. When presented with Wilson's original fourteen points, British and French representatives balked. The result was a peace very different from the one Wilson had envisioned; not only did his call for the national self-determination of all peoples go unrealized, but his hope for American participation in a League of Nations was defeated in the Senate.

Wilson had called in 1917 for Congress to declare war in order to "make the world safe for democracy." In so doing, he departed from the more nationalistic views of Roosevelt and also laid the foundation for one of most enduring legacies of progressivism in our own time. In promoting worldwide democracy, Wilson made clear, America was not a self-interested actor but was instead "one of the champions of the rights of mankind." He elaborated that "we have no selfish ends to serve, we desire no conquest, no dominion. We seek no indemnities for ourselves, no material compensation for the sacrifices we shall freely make."[43] His fourteen-point program of peace called for a "general association of nations" founded on the "principle of justice" for "all peoples and nationalities."[44] The connections between this rhetoric and American pronouncements to this day are manifest (President George W. Bush has recently declared that the goal of American foreign policy is "the global expansion of democracy"). We can see in the case of foreign policy, therefore, why the importance of progressivism to understanding the politics of contemporary America is widely acknowledged. What we have endeavored to show in this chapter is its continuing relevance on other fronts as well.

NOTES

1. This introduction is intended to be a concise overview of the essential tenets of progressivism. That such an endeavor may simplify the many complexities involved goes without saying. It is certainly not intended to break new scholarly ground, but rather to provide a resource for students and scholars making use of the selections in the book. As such, we do not cite the many relevant scholarly articles on progressivism since our priority is to familiarize students with the primary texts. Readers interested in the interpretative debates on the progressives should, of course, consult the literature where those debates can be found. Some of the interpretive issues pertaining to the Progressive Era are treated in Ronald J. Pestritto's *Woodrow Wilson and the Roots of Modern Liberalism* (Rowman & Littlefield, 2005).

2. See, for example, Franklin D. Roosevelt, "Campaign Address on Progressive Government, September 23, 1932," in *Public Papers and Addresses of Franklin D. Roosevelt*, ed. Samuel I. Rosenman (New York: Random House, 1938), 1:742–56. Emphasis in all citations will be in the original unless otherwise specified. In most cases, citations to Progressive-Era works are from the standard sources. In those cases where the work cited is also excerpted in this collection, we direct readers to the appropriate page number in this collection.

3. Woodrow Wilson, "An Address to the Jefferson Club of Los Angeles, May 12, 1911," in *The Papers of Woodrow Wilson* (hereafter cited as *PWW*), 69 vols., ed. Arthur S. Link (Princeton, N.J.: Princeton University Press, 1966–1993), 23:34.

4. Woodrow Wilson, "The Author and Signers of the Declaration of Independence, July 1907," in *PWW*, 17:251.

5. Frank J. Goodnow, *Social Reform and the Constitution* (New York: The Macmillan Company, 1911), 1, 3.

6. Frank J. Goodnow, *The American Conception of Liberty and Government* (Brown University Colver Lectures, 1916), 11. See also *American Progressivism*, 57.

7. Abraham Lincoln to Henry L. Pierce and Others, April 6, 1859, in *Speeches and Writings, 1859–1865: Speeches, Letters, and Miscellaneous Writings, the Lincoln-Douglas Debates*, ed. Don E. Fehrenbacher, Library of America (New York: Literary Classics of the United States, distributed by the Viking Press, 1989), 19.

8. John Dewey, *Liberalism and Social Action* (Amherst, N.Y.: Prometheus Books, 2000), 40–41.

9. Woodrow Wilson, *The New Freedom* (New York: Doubleday, Page & Company, 1913), 46–47. See also *American Progressivism*, 50.

10. Theodore Roosevelt, "The New Nationalism," in *The New Nationalism* (New York: The Outlook Company, 1910), 17–18. See also *American Progressivism*, 217.

11. Woodrow Wilson, "Socialism and Democracy, August 22, 1887," in *PWW*, 5:561. Emphasis added.

12. Frederick Jackson Turner, "The Significance of History," in *American Historians: A Selection*, ed. Harvey Wish (New York: Oxford University Press, 1962 [orig. pub. 1891]), 299.

13. Turner, "The Significance of History," 299.

14. Charles Beard, *An Economic Interpretation of the Constitution of the United States* (New York: The Macmillan Company, 1935), 15. See also *American Progressivism*, 94.

15. Beard, *Economic Interpretation*, 17. See also *American Progressivism*, 94.

16. G. W. F. Hegel, *The Philosophy of History*, trans. J. Sibree (New York: Dover Publications, 1956), 39. The divinity of the state, Hegel explained, meant that "all worth which the human being possesses—all spiritual reality, he possesses only through the State" (p. 39).

17. For some good examples of this mode of thinking, see two of Wilson's early religious essays: "Christ's Army, August 17, 1876," in *PWW*, 1:180–81; "Christian Progress, December 20, 1876," in *PWW*, 1:235.

18. Walter Rauschenbusch, *Christianizing the Social Order* (New York: The Macmillan Company, 1913), 111. See also *American Progressivism*, 113.

19. Rauschenbusch, *Christianizing the Social Order*, 419–20. See also *American Progressivism*, 118.

20. "Father Blakely States the Issue," unsigned editorial in *The New Republic*, July 29, 1916, 320. See also *American Progressivism*, 137.

21. Jane Addams, *Twenty Years at Hull-House* (New York: Macmillan, 1910), 94, 98. See also *American Progressivism*, 104.

22. John Dewey, "My Pedagogic Creed," *School Journal* 54 (January 1897): Article II. See also *American Progressivism*, 129.

23. Dewey, "My Pedagogic Creed," Article V. See also *American Progressivism*, 133.

24. Theodore Roosevelt, "The Right of the People to Rule," *The Outlook*, March 23, 1912, 619, 620. See also *American Progressivism*, 254.

25. Herbert Croly, *Progressive Democracy* (New York: The Macmillan Company, 1914), 167.

26. Goodnow, *The American Conception of Liberty and Government*, 41.

27. Wilson, *The New Freedom*, 46–47. See also *American Progressivism*, 50. In this particular part of the speech Wilson closely paraphrased from his book, *Constitutional Government in the United States* (New York: Columbia University Press, 1908), 56. See also *American Progressivism*, 155.

28. Publius, *The Federalist*, ed. Charles R. Kesler and Clinton Rossiter (New York: Signet Classic, 2003), 63:385, 10:75.

29. Wilson, *Constitutional Government*, 54. See also *American Progressivism*, 153.

30. Wilson, *Constitutional Government*, 66. See also *American Progressivism*, 160.

31. Theodore Roosevelt, *An Autobiography* (New York: The Macmillan Company, 1913), 388–89. See also *American Progressivism*, 181.

32. This is why the majority opinion for the U.S. Supreme Court in *Humphrey's Executor v. United States*—a central case in the legitimization of independent regulatory agencies—refers to the function of agencies as not only executive, but also "quasi-legislative" and "quasi-judicial." Indeed, the Court uses the legislative and judicial nature of agency decision making to justify agency independence from presidential control. 295 U.S. 602 (1935).

33. Woodrow Wilson, "The Study of Administration" in *Woodrow Wilson: Essential Political Writings*, Ronald J. Pestritto (Lanham, Md.: Lexington Books, 2005), 240–41. See also *American Progressivism*, 202.

34. Wilson, "Study of Administration," 246–47. See also *American Progressivism*, 209.

35. Frank J. Goodnow, *Politics and Administration* (New York: Macmillan, 1900), 82.

36. Goodnow, *Politics and Administration*, 85.

37. See, for example, Woodrow Wilson, "Government By Debate, December 1882," in *PWW*, 2:159–275; "Wanted—A Party, September 1, 1886," in *PWW*, 5:342; "Leaderless Government, August 5, 1897," in *PWW*, 10:288–304.

38. The exception here would be Goodnow, who makes his own call for a responsible party model in *Politics and Administration*, 199–254.

39. Croly, *Progressive Democracy*, 341. See also *American Progressivism*, 267.

40. Robert M. La Follette, *La Follette's Autobiography: A Personal Narrative of Political Experiences* (Madison, Wis.: The Robert M. La Follette Co., 1911), 365–66.

41. Croly, *Progressive Democracy*, 15–18. See also *American Progressivism*, 293.

42. Theodore Roosevelt, "First Annual Message, December 3, 1901," in *Messages and Papers of the Presidents* (Washington, D.C.: Bureau of National Literature, 1917), 6645.

43. Woodrow Wilson, "An Address to a Joint Session of Congress, April 2, 1917," in *PWW*, 41:525.

44. Woodrow Wilson, "An Address to a Joint Session of Congress, January 8, 1918," in *PWW*, 45:538–39.

1

THE PRINCIPLES OF PROGRESSIVISM

2

Who Is a Progressive?*

Theodore Roosevelt

Upon his return to the United States in 1910 from his travels abroad, former President Theodore Roosevelt (1858–1919) was beseeched by his supporters to run for the Republican nomination in 1912. Disappointed with the "betrayal" of progressive principles by his handpicked successor, William Howard Taft, Roosevelt, though he did not immediately break with Taft, nonetheless spoke widely on the need for a dramatic program of reform legislation. Taft's 1911 attempt to break, rather than regulate, United States Steel, resulted in public attacks by Roosevelt on this "archaic" and outmoded attempt to handle the trusts. Buoyed by a groundswell of support, Roosevelt entered the race in February 1912. In the following speech, delivered in Louisville in April, he identifies Taft with the forces of privilege arrayed against authentic progressives who champion the measures of direct democracy necessary to restore popular control of government.

In his recent speech at Philadelphia President Taft stated that he was a Progressive, and this raises the question as to what a Progressive is. More is involved than any man's say-so as to himself.

A well-meaning man may vaguely think of himself as a Progressive without having even the faintest conception of what a Progressive is. Both vision and intensity of conviction must go to the make-up of any man who is to lead the forward movement, and mildly good intentions are utterly useless as substitutes.

---

* Editors' Note: Theodore Roosevelt, "Who Is a Progressive?" *The Outlook* 100, April 1912, 809–14.

The essential difference, as old as civilized history, is between the men who, with fervor and broad sympathy and imagination, stand for the forward movement, the men who stand for the uplift and betterment of mankind, and who have faith in the people, on the one hand; and, on the other hand, the men of narrow vision and small sympathy, who are not stirred by the wrongs of others. With these latter stand also those other men who distrust the people, and many of whom not merely distrust the people, but wish to keep them helpless so as to exploit them for their own benefit.

The difference has never been more accurately set forth than in a lecture by the great English writer, Mr. J. A. Froude, delivered some forty-five years ago, and running as follows:

> Two kinds of men . . . appear as leaders in time of change. . . . On one side there are the . . . men who have no confidence in the people—who have no passionate convictions—men who believe that all wholesome reforms proceed downward from the educated to the multitudes; who regard with contempt, qualified by terror, appeals to the popular conscience or to popular intelligence.
>
> Opposite to these are the men of faith—and by faith I do not mean belief in dogmas, but belief in goodness, belief in justice, in righteousness. . . . They are not contented with looking for what may be useful or pleasant to themselves; they look by quite other methods for what is honorable, for what is good, for what is just. They believe that if they can find out that, then at all hazards, and in spite of all present consequences to themselves, that is to be preferred.
>
> When the air is heavy with impostors, and men live only to make money, . . . and the kingdom of heaven is bought and sold, and all that is high and pure in man is smothered by corruption, fire of the same kind bursts out in higher natures with a fierceness which cannot be controlled; and, confident in truth and right, they call fearlessly on the seven thousand in Israel who have not bowed the knee to Baal to rise and stand by them.
>
> They do not ask whether those whom they address have wide knowledge of history or science or philosophy; they ask rather that they shall be honest, that they shall be brave. . . . They know well that conscience is no exceptional privilege of the great or the cultivated, that to be generous and unselfish is no prerogative of rank or intellect.

We of to-day who stand for the Progressive movement here in the United States are not wedded to any particular kind of machinery, save solely as means to the end desired. Our aim is to secure the real and not the nominal rule of the people. With this purpose in view, we propose to do away with whatever in our government tends to secure to privilege, and to the great sinister special interests, a rampart from behind which they can beat back the forces that strive for social and industrial justice, and frustrate the will of the people.

For this purpose we believe in securing for the people the direct election of United States Senators, exactly as the people have already secured in actual practice the direct election of the President. We believe in securing for the people the right of nominating candidates for office, from the President down, by direct primaries, because the convention system, good in its day, has been twisted from its purpose, so that the delegates to the conventions, when chosen under the present methods by pressure of money and patronage, often deliberately misrepresent instead of representing the popular will. We believe in securing to the people the exercise of a real and not merely a nominal control over their representatives in office, this control to include the power to secure the enactment of laws which the people demand, and the rejection of laws to which the people are opposed, if, after due effort, it is found impossible to get from the Legislature and the courts a real representation of the deliberate popular judgment in these matters.

But these and kindred measures are merely machinery, and each community must judge for itself as to the machinery which its needs make necessary. The object, however, must be the same everywhere; that is, to give the people real control, and to have the people exercise this control in a spirit of the broadest sympathy and broadest desire to secure social and industrial justice for every man and woman, so that the work of all of us may be done and the lives of all of us lived under conditions which will tend to increase the dignity, the worth, and the efficiency of each individual.

If in any State the courts, in addition to doing justice in the ordinary cases between man and man, have striven to help and not hamper the people in their efforts to secure social and industrial justice in a far broader sense for the people as a whole, then in that community there may be no need for change as regards them. But where, in any community, as in my own State of New York, for instance, the highest court of the State, because of its adherence to outworn, to dead and gone systems of philosophy, and its lack of understanding of and sympathy with the living, the vital needs of those in the community whose needs are greatest, becomes a bulwark of privilege and the most effective of all means for preventing the people from working in efficient fashion for true justice, then I hold that the people must themselves be given the power, after due deliberation and in Constitutional fashion, to have their judgment made efficient and their interpretation of the Constitution made binding upon their servants the judges no less than upon their servants the legislators and executives.

Every man who fights fearlessly and effectively against special privilege in any form is to that extent a Progressive. Every man who, directly or indirectly, upholds privilege and favors the special interests, whether he acts from evil motives or merely because he is puzzle-headed or dull of mental vision or lacking in social sympathy, or whether he simply lacks interest in the subject, is a reactionary.

Every man is to that extent a Progressive if he stands for any form of social justice, whether it be securing proper protection for factory girls against dangerous machinery, for securing a proper limitation of hours of labor for women and children in industry, for securing proper living conditions for those who dwell in the thickly crowded regions of our great cities, for helping, so far as legislators can help, all the conditions of work and life for wage-workers in great centers of industry, or for helping by the action both of the National and State governments, so far as conditions will permit, the men and women who dwell in the open country to increase their efficiency both in production on their farms and in business arrangements for the marketing of their produce, and also to increase the opportunities to give the best possible expression to their social life. The man is a reactionary, whatever may be his professions and no matter how excellent his intentions, who opposes these movements, or who, if in high place, takes no interest in them and does not earnestly lead them forward.

When, in deference to the reactionaries in Congress, the President put a stop to the work of the Country Life Commission, so that for three years the National Government has done little but mark time, or indeed to step backward, as regards this movement, then, no matter how good his intentions, his actions ranged him against the Progressive side. When the President supports those courts which declare that the people have no power to do social justice by enacting laws such as those I have above outlined, and when he opposes the effort to give to the sober judgment of the people due effect, as against the decisions of a reactionary court, then he shows himself a reactionary.

When the President characterizes a moderate proposal to render effective the sober judgment of the American people, as against indefensible and reactionary court decisions in favor of the privileged classes, as "laying the ax at the foot of the tree of well-ordered freedom," then the President is standing against the sane and moderate movement for social justice; he is standing in favor of privilege; and he thereby ranks himself against the Progressives, against the cause of justice for the helpless and the wronged, and on the side of the reactionaries, on the side of the beneficiaries of privilege and injustice.

Four years ago the Progressives supported Mr. Taft for President, and he was opposed by such representatives of special privilege as Mr. Penrose of Pennsylvania, Mr. Aldrich of Rhode Island, Mr. Gallinger of New Hampshire, and Messrs. Lorimer, Cannon, and McKinley of Illinois; and he was opposed by practically all the men of the stamp of Messrs. Guggenheim and Evans in Colorado, Mr. Cox in Ohio, and Mr. Patrick Calhoun of San Francisco. These men were not Progressives then, and they do not pretend to be Progressives now. But, unlike the President, they know who is a Progressive and who is not. They know that he is not a Progressive. Their judgment in this matter is good. After three and a half years of association with and knowledge of the President, these and their fellows are now the President's chief supporters; and they and the men who feel and act as they do in business and in politics give him the great bulk of his strength. The President says that he is a Progressive. These men know him well and have studied his actions for three years, and they regard him as being precisely the kind of Progressive whom they approve—that is, as not a Progressive at all.

Now, the progressiveness that meets and merits the cordial approval of these gentlemen is not the kind of progressiveness which we on our side champion. However good the President's intentions, I believe that his actions have shown that he is entitled to the support of precisely these men. Take the most important bit of legislation enacted by the last Republican Congress— the Rate Bill. When this bill was submitted by the Administration, it was a thoroughly mischievous measure, which would have undone the good work that has been accomplished in the control of the great railways during the last twenty years. In that shape it was reported out of the Senate committee by its ardent champion, Senator Aldrich. In that shape it was championed by all the representatives of privilege and special interest, and it received the earnest support of all those gentlemen whom I have mentioned who had it in their power to give such support.

But the Progressives in the Senate amended the bill, against the determined opposition of the reactionary friends of the Administration. They made it a good bill by striking out the chief features of the bill as the reactionaries framed it. They made but one mistake. They left in the bill the provision for a Commerce Court; and in its actual workings this feature of the bill has proved thoroughly mischievous, and should be repealed.

The gentlemen in question and their allies cordially approve the administration of the Pure Food and Drugs Bill during the last three years, which has resulted in Dr. Wiley's resigning, because, as he says in print, the situation has become intolerable, and "the fundamental principles of the Food and Drugs Act had one by one been paralyzed and discredited." He specifically mentioned among the interests engaged in the manufacture of misbranded or adulterated foods which had escaped from the control of the Bureau the interests engaged in "the manufacture of so-called whisky from alcohol, colors, and flavors." The gentlemen I have named and the great interests back of them, and their allies, like Mr. Tawney, of Minnesota, were responsible for the President's abandoning the Country Life and Conservation Commissions, which had cost the Government nothing and had rendered invaluable service to the country; and they also cordially approved the nomination of Mr. Ballinger to the position of Secretary of the Interior.

For two years the Administration did everything in its power to undo the most valuable work that had been done in Conservation, especially in securing to the people the right to regulate water power franchise in the public interest. This effort became so flagrant and the criticism so universal that it was finally abandoned even by the Administration itself. As for the efforts to secure social justice in industrial matters, by securing child labor legislation, for instance, the Administration simply abandoned them completely.

Alike in its action and in its inaction, the conduct of the Administration during the last three years has been such as to merit the support and approval of Messrs. Aldrich, Gallinger, Penrose, Lorimer, Cox, Guggenheim, and the other gentlemen I have mentioned. I do not wonder that they support it, but I do not regard an Administration which has merited and which receives such support as being entitled to call itself Progressive, no matter with what elasticity the word may be stretched.

No men have been closer or more interested students of the career of President Taft than these men, no men better understand its real significance, no men better appreciate what the effect of the continuance of this Administration for another four years would mean. I believe that their judgment upon the Administration and upon what its continuance would mean to the people can be accepted, and I think that their judgment, as shown by the extreme recklessness of their actions in trying to secure the President's renomination, gives us an accurate gauge as to what the Administration merits from the people, and what the action of the people should be.

There is no question that in many States these gentlemen and those now allied with them are well aware that the majority of the people are against them, but they have set themselves to work by hook or by crook to overcome that majority. Under ordinary circumstances, in an ordinary political contest among politicians of substantially the same stamp, they would undoubtedly prefer to follow the majority of the people. They do not do so in this instance because they realize fully that the interests they champion are antagonistic to the interests of the people, and that on this occasion the line-up is clean-cut between the people on one side, and on the other the political bosses and all who represent special privilege and the evil alliance of big business with politics.

The Republican party is now facing a great crisis. It is to decide whether it will be, as in the days of Lincoln, the party of the plain people, the party of progress, the party of social and industrial justice; or whether it will be the party of privilege and of special interests, the heir to those who were Lincoln's most bitter opponents, the party that represents the great interests within and without Wall Street which desire through their control over the servants of the public to be kept immune from punishment when they do wrong and to be given privileges to which they are not entitled.

The big business concern that is both honest and far-sighted will, I believe, in the end favor our effort to secure thorough-going supervision and control over industrial big business, just as we have now secured it over the business of inter-State transportation and the business of banking under the National law. We do not propose to do injustice to any man, but we do propose adequately to guarantee the people against injustice by the mighty corporations which make up the predominant and characteristic feature of modern industrial life.

Prosperity can permanently come to this country only on a basis of honesty and of fair treatment for all. Those men of enormous wealth who bitterly oppose every species of effective control by the people, through their Governmental agents, over the business use of that wealth are, I verily believe, most short-sighted as to their own ultimate interests. They should welcome such effort, they should welcome every effort to make them observe and to assist them in observing the law, so that their activities shall be helpful and not harmful to the American people. Most surely if the wise and moderate control we advocate does not come, then some day these men or their descendants will have to face the chance of some movement of really dangerous and drastic character being directed against them.

The very wealthy men who oppose this action illustrate the undoubted truth that some of the men who have the money touch, some of the men who can amass enormous fortunes, possess an ability as specialized and non-indicative of other forms of ability as the ability to play chess exceptionally well, or to add up four columns of figures at once. The men of wealth of this type are not only hostile to the interests of the country, but hostile to their own interests; their great business ability is unaccompanied by even the slightest ability to read the signs of the times or understand the temper of the American people.

I stand for the adequate control, the real control, of all big business, and especially of all monopolistic big business where it proves unwise or impossible to break up the monopoly.

There is a grim irony in the effect that has been produced upon Wall Street by the complete breakdown of the prosecutions against various trusts, notably the Standard Oil and Tobacco Trusts, under the Sherman Law. I have always insisted that, while the Sherman Law should be kept upon the books so as to be used wherever possible against monopoly, yet that it is by itself wholly unable to afford the relief demanded by the American people as against all the great corporations actually or potentially guilty of anti-social practices. Wall Street was at first flurried by decisions in the Oil and Tobacco Trust cases. But as regards the Sherman Anti-Trust Law, Wall Street has now caught up with the Administration.

The President has expressed his entire satisfaction with the Anti-Trust Law, and now that the result of the prosecutions under it has been to strengthen the Standard Oil and Tobacco Trusts, to increase the value of their stocks, and, at least in the case of the Standard Oil, to increase the price to the consumer, Wall Street is also showing in practical fashion its satisfaction with the workings of the law, by its antagonism to us who intend to establish a real control of big business which shall not harm legitimate business, but shall really, and not nominally, put a stop to the evil practices of evil combinations.

The President has stated that he distrusts "impulsive action" by the public. I certainly greatly prefer deliberate action by the public, and in every proposal I have ever made I have always provided for such deliberate action. But I prefer even impulsive action by the public to action by the politicians against the interests of the public, whether this action be taken in tricky haste or with tricky deliberation. The President has warned us against soap-box primaries. At least these primaries are better than the primaries which represented the "impulsive action" of the postmasters in States like Georgia, Florida, and South Carolina, when these "impulsive" postmasters held their conventions at the earliest possible date, so as to affect the result in other States of the Union where there is a genuine Republican party.

I see by the press that in your own State [Kentucky] the postmasters have been warned to resign their leadership in the party committees; but, if the statements in the press are correct, the resignations are not demanded with any "impulsiveness." On the contrary, they have been asked with such leisurely deliberation that the day for holding the primaries will have passed before the request becomes effective. Now, gentlemen, if the newspaper reports are correct, such a request is a good deal worse than a sham.

We are in a period of change; we are fronting a great period of further change. Never was the need more imperative for men of vision who are also men of action. Disaster is ahead of us if we trust to the leadership of the men whose hearts are seared and whose eyes are blinded, who believe that we can find safety in dull timidity and dull action. The unrest cannot be quieted by the ingenious trickery of those who profess to advance by merely marking time. It cannot be quieted by demanding only the prosperity which is to come to those who have much, in such quantity that some will drift through to those who have little. There must be material prosperity; they are enemies of all of us who wantonly or unwisely interfere with or disregard it; but it can come in permanent shape only if obtained in accordance with and not against the spirit of justice and of righteousness.

Clouds hover about the horizon throughout the civilized world. But here in America the fault is our own if the sky above us is not clear. We have a continent on which to work out our destiny. Our people, our men and women, are fit to face the mighty days. If we fail, the failure will be lamentable; for not only shall we fail for ourselves, but our failure will wreck the fond desires of all throughout the world who look toward us with the eager hope that here, in this great Republic, it shall be proved, from ocean to ocean, that the people can rule themselves, and, thus ruling, can give liberty and do justice both to themselves and to others.

The present contest is but a phase of the larger struggle. Assuredly the fight will go on. Our opponents, representing the brute power of ceded privilege, can win only by using the led captains of mercenary politics, and the crooked financiers who stand behind those led captains, and those newspapers which those financiers and politicians own, influence, or control. They can win only by playing upon the timidity or the short-sightedness or the mere lack of knowledge of worthy citizens, and by misleading them into supporting for the moment the powers that prey, the powers of pillage, the dread powers that exploit the people for their own purpose, and that turn popular government into a sinister sham.

Certain big men, who, alas! have sometimes perverted the courts to their own uses, now tell us that it is impious to speak of the people's insisting upon justice being done by the courts. We answer that with all our might we will uphold the courts against lawlessness; and that we also intend to see that in their turn the courts give justice to all. We say, in the words of Lincoln, that we must prevent wrong "being done either by Congress or courts. The people of these United States are rightful masters of both Congress and courts, not to overthrow the Constitution, but to overthrow the men who pervert the Constitution."

Again, Lincoln stated our case to-day when he said, in the course of his joint debate with Douglas, "That is the real issue. That is the issue which will continue in this country when these poor tongues of Judge Douglas and myself shall be silent. It is the eternal struggle between these two principles—right and wrong—throughout the world. They are the two principles that have stood face to face from the beginning of time. The one is the common right of humanity, the other 'the divine right of kings.' It is the same principle in whatever shape it develops itself. It is the same spirit that says, 'You toil and work and earn bread and I'll eat it.' No matter in what shape it comes, whether from the mouth of a king who bestrides the people of his own nation and lives from the fruit of their labor, or from one race of men as an apology for enslaving another race, it is the same tyrannical principle."

And of course this applies no more to the slave-owner or to the foreign despot than to the present-day American citizen who oppresses others by the abuse of special privilege, be his wealth great or little, be he the multi-millionaire owner of railways and mines and factories who forgets his duties to those who earn him his bread while earning their own, or be he only the owner of a foul little sweatshop in which he grinds dollars from the excessive and underpaid labor of haggard women.

We who stand for the cause of progress, for the cause of the uplift of humanity and the betterment of mankind, are pledged to eternal war against tyranny and wrong, by the few or by the many, by a plutocracy or by a mob. We stand for justice and for fair play; fearless and confident we face the coming years, for we know that ours are the banners of justice and that all men who wish well to the people must fight under them. We fight to make this country a better place to live in for those who have been harshly treated by fate; and if we succeed, it will also be a better place to live in for those who have been well treated. None of us can really prosper permanently if masses of our fellows are debased and degraded, if masses of men and women are ground down and forced to lead starved and sordid lives, so that their souls are crippled like their bodies and the fine edge of their every feeling is blunted.

I ask that those of us to whom Providence, to whom fate, has been kind, remember that each must be his brother's keeper, and that all must feel their obligation to the less fortunate who work beside us in the strain and press of our eager modern life. I ask justice for the weak for their sakes, and I ask it also for the sake of our own children, and of our children's children who are to come after us. This country will not be a good place for any of us to live in if it is not a reasonably good place for all of us to live in. When I plead the cause of the crippled brakeman on a railway, of the overworked girl in a factory, of the stunted child toiling at inhuman labor, of all who work excessively or in unhealthy surroundings, of the family dwelling in the squalor of a noisome tenement, of the worn-out farmer in regions where the farms are worn out also; when I protest against the unfair profits of unscrupulous and conscienceless men, or against the greedy exploitation of the helpless by the beneficiaries of privilege—in all these cases I am not only fighting for the weak, I am also fighting for the strong. The sons of all of us will pay in the future if we of the present do not do justice in the present. If the fathers cause others to eat bitter bread, the teeth of their own sons shall be set on edge. Our cause is the cause of justice for all, in the interest of all. Surely there was never a more noble cause; surely there was never a cause in which it was better worth while to spend and be spent.

3

What Is Progress?*

From *The New Freedom*, Chapter 2

Woodrow Wilson

The twenty-eighth president of the United States who also served as governor of New Jersey, Woodrow Wilson (1856–1924), is known best for his public life and especially for his leadership during and after World War I. But Wilson was also a prolific academic long before he became a politician, having held professorships at Bryn Mawr, Wesleyan, and finally Princeton (his alma mater). His many academic books and essays, in addition to his political speeches, are a rich source for those interested in both the theory and practice of American progressivism. In the following chapter from *The New Freedom*—an edited collection of his campaign speeches from 1912—Wilson critiques the limited constitutionalism of the American founders and identifies progressivism with an evolutionary interpretation of American government.

In that sage and veracious chronicle, "Alice Through the Looking-Glass," it is recounted how, on a noteworthy occasion, the little heroine is seized by the Red Chess Queen, who races her off at a terrific pace. They run until both of them are out of breath; then they stop, and Alice looks around her and says, "Why, we are just where we were when we started!" "Oh, yes," says the Red Queen; "you have to run twice as fast as that to get anywhere else."

That is a parable of progress. The laws of this country have not kept up with the change of economic circumstances in this country; they have not kept up with the change of political circumstances; and therefore we are not even where we were when we started. We shall have to run, not until we are

---

* Editors' Note: Woodrow Wilson, *The New Freedom* (New York: Doubleday, Page and Company, 1913), 33–54.

out of breath, but until we have caught up with our own conditions, before we shall be where we were when we started; when we started this great experiment which has been the hope and the beacon of the world. And we should have to run twice as fast as any rational program I have seen in order to get anywhere else.

I am, therefore, forced to be a progressive, if for no other reason, because we have not kept up with our changes of conditions, either in the economic field or in the political field. We have not kept up as well as other nations have. We have not kept our practices adjusted to the facts of the case, and until we do, and unless we do, the facts of the case will always have the better of the argument; because if you do not adjust your laws to the facts, so much the worse for the laws, not for the facts, because law trails along after the facts. Only that law is unsafe which runs ahead of the facts and beckons to it and makes it follow the will-o'-the-wisps of imaginative projects.

Business is in a situation in America which it was never in before; it is in a situation to which we have not adjusted our laws. Our laws are still meant for business done by individuals; they have not been satisfactorily adjusted to business done by great combinations, and we have got to adjust them. I do not say we may or may not; I say we must; there is no choice. If your laws do not fit your facts, the facts are not injured, the law is damaged; because the law, unless I have studied it amiss, is the expression of the facts in legal relationships. Laws have never altered the facts; laws have always necessarily expressed the facts; adjusted interests as they have arisen and have changed toward one another.

Politics in America is in a case which sadly requires attention. The system set up by our law and our usage doesn't work,—or at least it can't be depended on; it is made to work only by a most unreasonable expenditure of labor and pains. The government, which was designed for the people, has got into the hands of bosses and their employers, the special interests. An invisible empire has been set up above the forms of democracy.

There are serious things to do. Does any man doubt the great discontent in this country? Does any man doubt that there are grounds and justifications for discontent? Do we dare stand still? Within the past few months we have witnessed (along with other strange political phenomena, eloquently significant of popular uneasiness) on one side a doubling of the Socialist vote and on the other the posting on dead walls and hoardings all over the country of certain very attractive and diverting bills warning citizens that it was "better to be safe than sorry" and advising them to "let well enough alone." Apparently a good many citizens doubted whether the situation they were advised to let alone was really well enough, and concluded that they would take a chance of being sorry. To me, these counsels of do-nothingism, these counsels of sitting still for fear something would happen, these counsels addressed to the hopeful, energetic people of the United States, telling them that they are not wise enough to touch their own affairs without marring them, constitute the most extraordinary argument of fatuous ignorance I ever heard. Americans are not yet cowards. True, their self-reliance has been sapped by years of submission to the doctrine that prosperity is something that benevolent magnates provide for them with the aid of the government; their self-reliance has been weakened, but not so utterly destroyed that you can twit them about it. The American people are not naturally stand-patters. Progress is the word that charms their ears and stirs their hearts.

There are, of course, Americans who have not yet heard that anything is going on. The circus might come to town, have the big parade and go, without their catching a sight of the camels or a note of the calliope. There are people, even Americans, who never move themselves or know that anything else is moving.

A friend of mine who had heard of the Florida "cracker," as they call a certain ne'er-do-weel portion of the population down there, when passing through the State in a train, asked some one to point out a "cracker" to him. The man asked replied, "Well, if you see something off in the woods that looks brown, like a stump, you will know it is either a stump or a cracker; if it moves, it is a stump."

Now, movement has no virtue in itself. Change is not worth while for its own sake. I am not one of those who love variety for its own sake. If a thing is good to-day, I should like to have it stay that way to-morrow. Most of our calculations in life are dependent upon things staying the way they are. For example, if, when you got up this morning, you had forgotten how to dress, if you had forgotten all about those ordinary things which you do almost automatically, which you can almost do half awake, you would have to find out what you did yesterday. I am told by the psychologists that if I did not remember who I was yesterday, I should not know who I am to-day, and that, therefore, my very identity depends upon my being able to tally to-day with yesterday. If they do not tally, then I am confused; I do not know who I am, and I have to go around and ask somebody to tell me my name and where I came from.

I am not one of those who wish to break connection with the past; I am not one of those who wish to change for the mere sake of variety. The only men who do that are the men who want to forget something, the men who filled yesterday with something they would rather not recollect to-day, and so go about seeking diversion, seeking abstraction in something that will blot out recollection, or seeking to put something into them which will blot out all recollection. Change is not worth while unless it is improvement. If I move out of my present house because I do not like it, then I have got to choose a better house, or build a better house, to justify the change.

It would seem a waste of time to point out that ancient distinction,—between mere change and improvement. Yet there is a class of mind that is prone to confuse them. We have had political leaders whose conception of greatness was to be forever frantically doing something,—it mattered little what; restless, vociferous men, without sense of the energy of concentration, knowing only the energy of succession. Now, life does not consist of eternally running to a fire. There is no virtue in going anywhere unless you will gain something by being there. The direction is just as important as the impetus of motion.

All progress depends on how fast you are going, and where you are going, and I fear there has been too much of this thing of knowing neither how fast we were going or where we were going. I have my private belief that we have been doing most of our progressiveness after the fashion of those things that in my boyhood days we called "treadmills," a treadmill being a moving platform, with cleats on it, on which some poor devil of a mule was forced to walk forever without getting anywhere. Elephants and even other animals have been known to turn treadmills, making a good deal of noise, and causing certain wheels to go round, and I daresay grinding out some sort of product for somebody, but without achieving much progress. Lately, in an effort to persuade the elephant to move, really, his friends tried dynamite. It moved,—in separate and scattered parts, but it moved.

A cynical but witty Englishman said, in a book, not long ago, that it was a mistake to say of a conspicuously successful man, eminent in his line of business, that you could not bribe a man like that, because, he said, the point about such men is that they have been bribed—not in the ordinary meaning of that word, not in any gross, corrupt sense, but they have achieved their great success by means of the existing order of things and therefore they have been put under bonds to see that that existing order of things is not changed; they are bribed to maintain the *status quo*.

It was for that reason that I used to say, when I had to do with the administration of an educational institution, that I should like to make the young gentlemen of the rising generation as unlike their fathers as possible. Not because their fathers lacked character or intelligence or knowledge or patriotism, but because their fathers, by reason of their advancing years and their established position in society, had lost touch with the processes of life; they had forgotten what it was to begin; they had forgotten what it was to rise; they had forgotten what it was to be dominated by the circumstances of their life on their way up from the bottom to the top, and, therefore, they were out of sympathy with the creative, formative and progressive forces of society.

Progress! Did you ever reflect that that word is almost a new one? No word comes more often or more naturally to the lips of modern man, as if the thing it stands for were almost synonymous with life itself, and yet men through many thousand years never talked or thought of progress. They thought in the other direction. Their stories of heroisms and glory were tales of the past. The ancestor wore the heavier armor and carried the larger spear. "There were giants in those days." Now all that has altered. We think of the future, not the past, as the more glorious time in comparison with which the present is nothing. Progress, development,—those are modern words. The modern idea is to leave the past and press onward to something new.

But what is progress going to do with the past, and with the present? How is it going to treat them? With ignominy, or respect? Should it break with them altogether, or rise out of them, with its roots still deep in the older time? What attitude shall progressives take toward the existing order, toward those institutions of conservatism, the Constitution, the laws, and the courts?

Are those thoughtful men who fear that we are now about to disturb the ancient foundations of our institutions justified in their fear? If they are, we ought to go very slowly about the processes of change. If it is indeed true that we have grown tired of the institutions which we have so carefully and sedulously built up, then we ought to go very slowly and very carefully about the very dangerous task of altering them. We ought, therefore, to ask ourselves, first of all, whether thought in this country is tending to do anything by which we shall retrace our steps, or by which we shall change the whole direction of our development?

I believe, for one, that you cannot tear up ancient rootages and safely plant the tree of liberty in soil which is not native to it. I believe that the ancient traditions of a people are its ballast; you cannot make a *tabula rasa* upon which to write a political program. You cannot take a new sheet of paper and determine what your life shall be to-morrow. You must knit the new into the old. You cannot put a new patch on an old garment without ruining it; it must be not a patch, but something woven into the old fabric, of practically the same pattern, of the same texture and intention. If I did not believe that to be progressive was to preserve the essentials of our institutions, I for one could not be a progressive.

One of the chief benefits I used to derive from being president of a university was that I had the pleasure of entertaining thoughtful men from all over the world. I cannot tell you how much has dropped into my granary by their presence. I had been casting around in my mind for something by which to draw several parts of my political thought together when it was my good fortune to entertain a very interesting Scotsman who had been devoting himself to the philosophical thought of the seventeenth century. His talk was so engaging that it was delightful to hear him speak of anything, and presently there came out of the unexpected region of his thought the thing I had been waiting for. He called my attention to the fact that in every generation all sorts of speculation and thinking tend to fall under the formula of the dominant thought of the age. For example, after the Newtonian Theory of the universe had been developed, almost all thinking tended to express itself in the analogies of the Newtonian Theory, and since the Darwinian Theory has reigned amongst us, everybody is likely to express whatever he wishes to expound in terms of development and accommodation to environment.

Now, it came to me, as this interesting man talked, that the Constitution of the United States had been made under the dominion of the Newtonian Theory. You have only to read the papers of *The Federalist* to see that fact written on every page. They speak of the "checks and balances" of the Constitution, and use to express their idea the simile of the organization of the universe, and particularly of the solar system,—how by the attraction of gravitation the various parts are held in their orbits; and then they proceed to represent Congress, the Judiciary, and the President as a sort of imitation of the solar system.

They were only following the English Whigs, who gave Great Britain its modern constitution. Not that those Englishmen analyzed the matter, or had any theory about it; Englishmen care little for theories. It was a Frenchman, Montesquieu, who pointed out to them how faithfully they had copied Newton's description of the mechanism of the heavens.

The makers of our Federal Constitution read Montesquieu with true scientific enthusiasm. They were scientists in their way,—the best way of their age,—those fathers of the nation. Jefferson wrote of "the laws of Nature,"—and then by way of afterthought,—"and of Nature's God." And they constructed a government as they would have constructed an orrery,—to display the laws of nature. Politics in their thought was a variety of mechanics. The Constitution was founded on the law of gravitation. The government was to exist and move by virtue of the efficacy of "checks and balances."

The trouble with the theory is that government is not a machine, but a living thing. It falls, not under the theory of the universe, but under the theory of organic life. It is accountable to Darwin, not to Newton. It is modified by its environment, necessitated by its tasks, shaped to its functions by the sheer pressure of life. No living thing can have its organs offset against each other, as checks, and live. On the contrary, its life is dependent upon their quick cooperation, their ready response to the commands of instinct or intelligence, their amicable community of purpose. Government is not a body of blind forces; it is a body of men, with highly differentiated functions, no doubt, in our modern day, of specialization, with a common task and purpose. Their co-operation is indispensable, their warfare fatal. There can be no successful government without the intimate, instinctive co-ordination of the organs of life and action. This is not theory, but fact, and displays its force as fact, whatever theories may be thrown across its track. Living political constitutions must be Darwinian in structure and in practice. Society is a living organism and must obey the laws of life, not of mechanics; it must develop.

All that progressives ask or desire is permission—in an era when "development," "evolution," is the scientific word—to interpret the Constitution according to the Darwinian principle; all they ask is recognition of the fact that a nation is a living thing and not a machine.

Some citizens of this country have never got beyond the Declaration of Independence, signed in Philadelphia, July 4th, 1776. Their bosoms swell against George III, but they have no consciousness of the war for freedom that is going on to-day.

The Declaration of Independence did not mention the questions of our day. It is of no consequence to us unless we can translate its general terms into examples of the present day and substitute them in some vital way for the examples it itself gives, so concrete, so intimately involved in the circumstanc[e]s of the day in which it was conceived and written. It is an eminently practical document, meant for the use of practical men; not a thesis for philosophers, but a whip for tyrants; not a theory of government, but a program of action. Unless we can translate it into the questions of our own day, we are not worthy of it, we are not the sons of the sires who acted in response to its challenge.

What form does the contest between tyranny and freedom take to-day? What is the special form of tyranny we now fight? How does it endanger the rights of the people, and what do we mean to do in order to make our contest against it effectual? What are to be the items of our new declaration of independence?

By tyranny, as we now fight it, we mean control of the law, of legislation and adjudication, by organizations which do not represent the people, by means which are private and selfish. We mean, specifically, the conduct of our affairs and the shaping of our legislation in the interest of special bodies of capital and those who organize their use. We mean the alliance, for this purpose, of political machines with selfish business. We mean the exploitation of the people by legal and political means. We have seen many of our governments under these influences cease to be representative governments, cease to be governments representative of the people, and become governments representative of special interests, controlled by machines, which in their turn are not controlled by the people.

Sometimes, when I think of the growth of our economic system, it seems to me as if, leaving our law just about where it was before any of the modern inventions or developments took place, we had simply at haphazard extended the family residence, added an office here and a workroom there, and a new set of sleeping rooms there, built up higher on our foundations, and put out little lean-tos on the side, until we have a structure that has no character whatever. Now, the problem is to continue to live in the house and yet change it.

Well, we are architects in our time, and our architects are also engineers. We don't have to stop using a railroad terminal because a new station is being built. We don't have to stop any of the processes of our lives because we are rearranging the structures in which we conduct those processes. What we have to undertake is to systematize the foundations of the house, then to thread all the old parts of the structure with the steel which will be laced together in modern fashion, accommodated to all the modern knowledge of structural strength and elasticity, and then slowly change the partitions, relay the walls, let in the light through new apertures, improve the ventilation; until finally, a generation or two from now, the scaffolding will be taken away, and there will be the family in a great building whose noble architecture will at last be disclosed, where men can live as a single community, co-operative as in a perfected, co-ordinated beehive, not afraid of any storm of nature, not afraid of any artificial storm, any imitation of thunder and lightning, knowing that the foundations go down to the bedrock of principle, and knowing that whenever they please they can change that plan again and accommodate it as they please to the altering necessities of their lives.

But there are a great many men who don't like the idea. Some wit recently said, in view of the fact that most of our American architects are trained in a certain *École* in Paris, that all American architecture in recent years was either bizarre or "Beaux Arts." I think that our economic architecture is decidedly bizarre; and I am afraid that there is a good deal to learn about matters other than architecture from the same source from which our architects have learned a great many things. I don't mean the School of Fine Arts at Paris, but the experience of France; for from the other side of the water men can now hold up against us the reproach that we have not adjusted our lives to modern conditions to the same extent that they have adjusted theirs. I was very much interested in some of the reasons given by our friends across the Canadian border for being very shy about the reciprocity arrangements. They said: "We are not sure whither these arrangements will lead, and we don't care to associate too closely with the economic conditions of the United States until those conditions are as modern as ours." And when I resented it, and asked for particulars, I had, in regard to many matters, to retire from the debate. Because I found that they had adjusted their regulations of economic development to conditions we had not yet found a way to meet in the United States.

Well, we have started now at all events. The procession is under way. The stand-patter doesn't know there is a procession. He is asleep in the back part of his house. He doesn't know that the road is resounding with the tramp of men going to the front. And when he wakes up, the country will be empty. He will be deserted, and he will wonder what has happened. Nothing has happened. The world has been going on. The world has a habit of going on. The world has a habit of leaving those behind who won't go with it. The world has always neglected stand-patters. And, therefore, the stand-patter does not excite my indignation; he excites my sympathy. He is going to be so lonely before it is all over. And we are good fellows, we are good company; why doesn't he come along? We are not going to do him any harm. We are going to show him a good time. We are going to climb the slow road until it reaches some upland where the air is fresher, where the whole talk of mere politicians is stilled, where men can look in each other's faces and see that there is nothing to conceal, that all they have to talk about they are willing to talk about in the open and talk about with each other; and whence, looking back over the road, we shall see at last that we have fulfilled our promise to mankind. We had said to all the world, "America was created to break every kind of monopoly, and to set men free, upon a footing of equality, upon a footing of opportunity, to match their brains and their energies." [A]nd now we have proved that we meant it.

4

The American Conception of Liberty*

Frank Johnson Goodnow

Frank Johnson Goodnow (1859–1939) was the first president of the American Political Science Association. A student of John Burgess, he taught at Columbia University prior to his term as president of Johns Hopkins University. Most of Goodnow's work came in the field of administrative law, where he pioneered (along with Woodrow Wilson) a science of administration separated from the limits of constitutional government. His most comprehensive work in this regard was *Politics and Administration* (1900). In the following lecture, given at Brown University in 1916, Goodnow promotes this separation of politics and administration by way of critiquing the natural-rights theory of the Declaration of Independence and its influence on the practice of American government.

The end of the eighteenth century was marked by the formulation and general acceptance by thinking men in Europe of a political philosophy which laid great emphasis on individual private rights. Man was by this philosophy conceived of as endowed at the time of his birth with certain inalienable rights. Thus, Rousseau in his "Social Contract" treated man as primarily an individual and only secondarily as a member of human society. Society itself was regarded as based upon a contract made between the individuals by whose union it was formed. At the time of making this contract these individuals were deemed to have reserved certain rights spoken of as "natural"

* Editors' Note: Frank Johnson Goodnow, *The American Conception of Liberty and Government*, Brown University: The Colver Lectures (Providence, R.I.: Standard printing company, 1916), 9–21, 29–31. Excerpt.

rights. These rights could neither be taken away nor be limited without the consent of the individual affected.

Such a theory, of course, had no historical justification. There was no record of the making of any such contract as was postulated. It was impossible to assert, as a matter of fact even, that man existed first as an individual and that later he became, as the result of any act of volition on his part, a member of human society. But at a time when truth was sought usually through speculation rather than observation, the absence of proof of the facts which lay at the basis of the theory did not seriously trouble those by whom it was formulated or accepted.

While there was no justification in fact for this social contract theory and this doctrine of natural rights, their acceptance by thinking men did nevertheless have an important influence upon the development of thought and in that way upon the actual conditions of human life. For these theories were not only a philosophical explanation of the organization of society; they were at the same time the result of the then existing social conditions, and like most such theories were also an attempt to justify a course of conduct which was believed to be expedient.

At the end of the eighteenth century a great change was beginning in Western Europe. The enlargement of the field of commercial transactions, due to the discovery and colonization of America and to the contact of Europe with Asia, particularly with India, had opened new spheres of activity to those minded for adventure. The invention of the steam engine and its application to manufacturing were rapidly changing industrial conditions. The factory system was in process of establishment and had already begun to displace domestic industry.

The new possibilities of reward for individual endeavor made men impatient of the restrictions on private initiative incident to an industrial and commercial system which was fast passing away. They therefore welcomed with eagerness a political philosophy which, owing to the emphasis it placed upon private rights, would if acted upon have the effect of freeing them from what they regarded as hampering limitations on individual initiative.

This political philosophy was incorporated into the celebrated Declaration of the Rights of Man and of the Citizen promulgated in France on the eve of the Revolution. A perusal of this remarkable document reveals the fact, however, that the reformers of France had not altogether emancipated themselves from the influences of their historical development. For almost every clause of the Declaration refers to rights under the law rather than to rights which were natural to and inherent in man.

The subsequent development in Europe of this private rights philosophy is along the lines thus marked out by the Declaration. The rights which men have been recognized as possessing have not been considered to be inherent rights, attaching to man at the time of his birth, so much as rights which find their origin in the law as adopted by that organ of government regarded as representative of the society of which the individual man is a member.

In a word, man is regarded now throughout Europe, contrary to the view expressed by Rousseau, as primarily a member of society and secondarily as an individual. The rights which he possesses are, it is believed, conferred upon him, not by his Creator, but rather by the society to which he belongs. What they are is to be determined by the legislative authority in view of the needs of that society. Social expediency, rather than natural right, is thus to determine the sphere of individual freedom of action.

The development of this private rights philosophy has been, however, somewhat different in the United States. The philosophy of Rousseau was accepted in this country probably with even greater enthusiasm than was the case in Europe. The social and economic conditions of the Western World were, in the first place, more favorable than in Europe for its acceptance. There was at the time no well-developed social organization in this country. America was the land of the pioneer, who had to rely for most of his success upon his strong right arm. Such communities as did exist were loosely organized and separated one from another. Roads worthy of the name hardly existed and communication was possible only by rivers which were imperfectly navigable or over a sea which, when account is taken of the vessels then in use, was tempestuous in character.

Furthermore, the religious and moral influences in this country, which owed much to the Protestant Reformation, all favored the development of an extreme individualism. They emphasized personal responsibility and the salvation of the individual soul. It was the fate of the individual rather than that of the social group which appealed to the preacher or aroused the anxiety of the theologian. It was individual rather than social morality which was emphasized by the ethical teacher and received attention in moral codes. Everything, in a word, favored the acceptance of the theory of individual natural rights.

The result was the adoption in this country of a doctrine of unadulterated individualism. Every one had rights. Social duties were hardly recognized, or if recognized little emphasis was laid upon them. It was apparently thought that every one was able and willing to protect his rights, and that as a result of the struggle between men for their rights and of the compromise of what appeared to be conflicting rights would arise an effective social organization.

The rights with which it was believed that man was endowed by his Creator were, as was the case in France, set forth in bills of rights which formed an important part of American constitutions. The form in which they were stated in American bills of rights was subject to fewer qualifications than was the case in France. Their origin was found in nature rather than in the law. The development of these rights, further, has been quite different from the European development which has been noted. American courts, early in the history of the country, claimed and secured the general recognition of a power to declare unconstitutional and therefore void acts of legislation which, in their opinion, were not in conformity with these bills of rights. In their determination of these questions, American courts appear to have been largely influenced by the private rights conception of the prevalent political philosophy. The result has been that the private individual rights of American citizens have come to be formulated and defined, not by representative legislative bodies, as is now the rule in Europe, but by courts which have in the past been much under the influence of the political philosophy of the eighteenth century.

In thus adopting the Continental political philosophy of the eighteenth century, American judges modified greatly the conception of individual liberty which was the basis of English political practice. The most important modifications were two in number: —

In the first place, the rights of men, of which their liberty consisted, were, as natural rights, regarded in a measure—and in no small measure—as independent of the law. This modification of the original English idea was an almost necessary result of the fact that these rights were set forth in written constitutions, which were placed under the protection of courts. The written constitution was considered to be the act of the sovereign people. It therefore was superior to any mere laws which might be passed by the representatives of the people in the lawmaking bodies. These bodies being simply delegates of the people were not authorized to do anything not within the powers granted to them. If a written constitution provided that a man had a certain right, it was evident that the legislature could not take it away from him. When the courts assumed in the United States the power to declare unconstitutional acts of the legislature, they did so because their duty was to apply the law as they found it. They might not, therefore, apply as law an act of the legislature which in their opinion was in conflict with the Constitution, since, being in conflict with the Constitution, the highest law of all, such an act could not be law.

In this way natural rights came to have an existence apart from the law, or, at any rate, apart from the law as it had up to that time been understood.

The importance which was attributed by the Americans of those days to this idea of natural rather than legal rights will be appreciated when we recall that the Constitution of the United States, which in its original form contained few if any provisions relative to these natural rights, was ultimately adopted only on condition that they should be enumerated in a bill of rights to be appended to the Constitution. This was subsequently done in Amendments I to IX. The Ninth Amendment to the United States Constitution in particular is a characteristic expression of the feeling of the time that these natural rights existed independently of all law. It reads: "The enumeration in the Constitution of certain rights shall not be construed to deny or disparage others retained by the people."

In the second place, our American courts emphasized substantive rights rather than the right to particular methods of procedure. Most of the historic rights of Englishmen had been rights to particular methods of action. Thus, the right to a special kind of trial for crime—that is, the right to trial by jury— was regarded as one of the most sacred rights of an Englishman.

The English insistence on particular methods of procedure was due to the belief that these methods had shown themselves, as the result of a long experience, to be valuable aids in securing the end desired. This end was freedom from arbitrary autocratic action on the part of those to whom political power had been entrusted. It was the rule of law—that is, the rule of a principle of general application as opposed to the rule of a person arbitrary and capricious— which the Englishman sought. It was to secure his rights through this rule of law that he originated the form of government which has been called "constitutional." The Englishman, as a matter of fact, never claimed that he had any natural rights; that is, rights to which he was entitled by reason of the fact that he is a man, a human being. He was perfectly satisfied if it was recognized in his political and legal system that no attempt might be made, except in the manner by law provided, to take away what he might think were his rights. This claim being admitted, he felt that in some way or other he would be able to have the law so formulated that he could secure the recognition of all substantive rights which he ought at any particular time to possess. To secure the recognition in the law of these substantive rights he insisted upon the grant to more and more of the people of the land of the power to control legislation. For through the control of legislation was obtained the power to determine what are his rights.

The rights of Englishmen were, therefore, so far as they were defined at all, to be found in acts of legislation and in judicial decisions. One of the earliest and most important of these acts of legislation is what is known as the Great Charter, which was originally forced from a reluctant king in 1215. The most notable clauses of the Great Charter deal not so much with what have been called "substantive" as with procedural rights. Thus, in section 12 the Crown enacts that "no scutage or aid (i.e., no tax) shall be imposed in our kingdom unless by the General Council of our kingdom." Section 14 provides how the General Council shall be composed and called together. Section 39, probably the most important section of all, provides that "no freeman shall be taken or imprisoned or disseized or outlawed or banished or anyways destroyed, nor will we pass upon him nor will we send upon him, unless by the lawful judgment of his peers, or by the law of the land."

It will be noticed that this famous provision of the Great Charter accords hardly any recognition to a substantive right. It is not said that a freeman has any right not to be "taken or imprisoned or disseized or outlawed or banished." Indeed it is clearly implied that such a right does not exist. What the section does say is that these things shall not be done to the freeman except in a specified way, which is, according to law. It is the rule of law which the Great Charter emphasizes. It was to the rule of law then that the Englishmen of the beginning of the thirteenth century were striving to attain.

The power of the American courts to determine in the concrete and in detail,—which after all is the only thing that amounts to much in this life,—the content of private rights was very large because of the fact that these rights were often stated in very general terms in the Constitution. The most marked instance of such vagueness is perhaps to be found in the almost universal provision that no one shall be deprived of life, liberty or property without due process of law. The Constitution does not define property nor liberty nor due process of law. All of these matters have had to be "pricked out," as Mr. Justice Holmes of the United States Supreme Court has said in decisions which are almost too numerous to be counted.

The following are some of the conclusions characteristic of American ideas of private rights which the courts have reached:

The clause providing that private property shall not be taken for public use without just compensation has been interpreted as prohibiting inferentially the taking of property for private use. The interpretation is really due to the recognition in the individual of a natural inherent substantive right of property which may be taken from him by the government only in the case mentioned in the Constitution, viz., by taking property for public use. It is therefore altogether probable that the American courts would have held unconstitutional an act of the legislature similar to the recent act of the British Parliament apportioning the property which had been held to belong to what was known as the "Scotch Wee Kirk" between that church and the "Free Kirk."

Again the clause providing that no person shall "be deprived of life, liberty or property without due process of law" has been held by some of the State courts, under the influence of the idea of inherent absolute individual substantive rights to prevent the legislature from passing an act which changes the basis of the liability of employer to employed. The old basis of the liability was negligence. The act declared unconstitutional provided in the case of accident a liability on the part of the employer regardless of the question whether he was negligent or not. Other acts of legislation have been declared unconstitutional as violating this due process clause, because they imposed upon an employer the duty to pay employees in money, or at stated periods, or because they forbade an employer to work his men more than a certain number of hours a week or a day. These acts were held unconstitutional as depriving either the employer or the employed of his property or his liberty.

Such decisions have been reached as a result of the fact that the American courts have emphasized the idea of a substantive right and have lost sight of the fact that the right granted in the Constitution if defined in the light of its history was a right not under all conceivable circumstances to liberty or property, but merely a right not to be deprived of liberty or property except in a certain way, that is, by due process of law. The fact that in all these cases an act of the legislature, that is, a law in the historic English sense, provided that liberty or property should be taken away was not regarded by the courts as due process of law. In fact the courts of the United States have really taken the position that there is no due process of law by which the individual may be deprived of some of these absolute substantive inherent natural rights.

Furthermore and partly as a consequence of the acceptance of the conception of private rights as inherent and not based upon law the content and character of private rights specifically provided for by legislation have been fixed, not so much as the result of an inquiry into their social expediency but rather because it has been believed that the individual has rights with which he has been endowed by his Creator, rights which it would be improper to take away or to limit even in the interest of society.

Take for example the qualifications required for entrance into the legal profession. What they shall be is, in large if not in controlling degree, determined in view of the assumed existence in every respectable and reasonably intelligent individual of a right to practise law. Such considerations as the evil influence upon the community of a superabundance of lawyers are given very little weight. Although it might easily be shown that the overcrowding of the legal profession almost inevitably leads to an increase of litigation which has evil effects upon the community, that fact is not permitted to have much influence on the determination of the qualifications of lawyers since an encroachment might as a consequence be made upon the inborn and inherent right of every man to become a lawyer.

This general attitude towards private rights is, it seems to me, at the present time in process of modification. Whatever may have been formerly the advantages attaching to a private rights political philosophy—and that they were many I should be the last person to deny—this question of private rights has been reexamined with the idea of ascertaining whether, under the conditions of modern life, our traditional political philosophy should be retained.

The political philosophy of the eighteenth century was formulated before the announcement and acceptance of the theory of evolutionary development. The natural rights doctrine presupposed almost that society was static or stationary rather than dynamic or progressive in character. It was generally believed at the end of the eighteenth century that there was a social state which under all conditions and at all times would be absolutely ideal. The rights which man had were believed to come from his Creator. These rights consequently were the same then as they once had been and would always remain the same. Natural rights were in theory thus permanent and immutable. Natural rights being conceived of as eternal and immutable, the theory of natural rights did not permit of their amendment in view of a change in conditions.

The actual rights which at the close of the eighteenth century were recognized were, however, as a matter of fact influenced in large measure by the social and economic conditions of the time when the recognition was made. Those conditions have certainly been subjected to great modifications. The pioneer can no longer rely upon himself alone. Indeed with the increase of population and the conquest of the wilderness the pioneer has almost disappeared. The improvement in the means of communication, which has been one of the most marked changes that have occurred, has placed in close contact and relationship once separated and unrelated communities. The canal and the railway, the steamship and the locomotive, the telegraph and the telephone, we might add the motor car and the aëroplane have all contributed to the formation of a social organization such as our forefathers never saw in their wildest dreams. The accumulation of capital, the concentration of industry with the accompanying increase in the size of the industrial unit and the loss of personal relations between employer and employed, have all brought about a constitution of society very different from that which was to be found a century and a quarter ago. Changed conditions, it has been thought, must bring in their train different conceptions of private rights if society is to be advantageously carried on. In other words, while insistence on individual rights may have been of great advantage at a time when the social organization was not highly developed, it may become a menace when social rather than individual efficiency is the necessary prerequisite of progress. For social efficiency probably owes more to the common realization of social duties than to the general insistence on privileges based on individual private rights. As our conditions have changed, as the importance of the social group has been realized, as it has been perceived that social efficiency must be secured if we are to attain and retain our place in the field of national competition which is practically coterminous with the world, the attitude of our courts on the one hand towards private rights and on the other hand towards social duties has gradually been changing. The general theory remains the same.

Man is still said to be possessed of inherent natural rights of which he may not be deprived without his consent. The courts still now and then hold unconstitutional acts of legislature which appear to encroach upon those rights. At the same time the sphere of governmental action is continually widening and the actual content of individual private rights is being increasingly narrowed.

. . .

We no longer believe as we once believed that a good social organization can be secured merely through stressing our rights. The emphasis is being laid more and more on social duties. The efficiency of the social group is taking on in our eyes a greater importance than it once had. We are not, it is true, taking the view that the individual man lives for the state of which he is a member and that state efficiency is in some mysterious way an admirable end in and of itself.

But we have come to the conclusion that man under modern conditions is primarily a member of society and that only as he recognizes his duties as a member of society can he secure the greatest opportunities as an individual. While we do not regard society as an end in itself we do consider it as one of the most important means through which many may come into his own.

You are probably asking yourselves: What is the purpose of saying these things in this place? What connection have they with a great educational institution? My answer to these questions is this. Those who are in charge of such an institution are under a very solemn obligation. They are in some measure at any rate responsible for the beliefs of the coming generation of thinkers and of moulders of public opinion. We teachers perhaps take ourselves too seriously at times. That I am willing to admit. We may not have nearly the influence which we think we have. Changes in economic conditions for which we are in no way responsible bring in their train regardless of what we teach changes in beliefs and opinions. But if we are unable to exercise great influence in the institution of positive changes, we can by acquainting ourselves with the changes in conditions and by endeavoring to accommodate our teaching to those changes, certainly refrain from impeding progress. This may be an over-modest estimate of the function of a teacher. At the same time it is an ideal the realization of which is not to be despised. For many universities have in the past been the homes of conservatism. New ideas have often knocked for a long time on the gates of learning before they have been permitted to enter. Even after they have passed the portal they are sometimes the object of a suspicion which it has taken years to allay.

So I repeat we teachers are in a measure responsible for the thoughts of the coming generation. This being the case, if under the conditions of modern life it is the social group rather than the individual which is increasing in importance, if it is true that greater emphasis should be laid on social duties and less on individual rights, it is the duty of the University to call the attention of the student to this fact and it is the duty of the student when he goes out into the world to do what in him lies to bring this truth home to his fellows.

II

PROGRESSIVE INTERPRETATIONS OF HISTORY

5

The Significance of the Frontier in American History*

Frederick Jackson Turner

Among the most influential of American historians, Frederick Jackson Turner (1861–1932) largely rejected the "germ theory" of his mentor, Herbert Baxter Adams, which held that American institutions were derivatives of Germanic origin, and formulated his own "frontier thesis" as a means of explaining American development. Central to Turner's methodology was his willingness to make use of multiple disciplines such as sociology, statistics, and geography in his work. Though he wrote a number of important works including *The Rise of the New West* (1906) and the posthumously published *The Significance of Sections in American History* (1932), which was awarded a Pulitzer prize, none equaled the influence of his 1893 essay "The Significance of the Frontier in American History." Turner's argument that historical research, properly conducted, would lead inevitably to reform legislation resonated with progressives, as did his emphasis on the democratic ideal of the frontier examined in the following selection.

In a recent bulletin of the Superintendent of the Census for 1890 appear these significant words: "Up to and including 1880 the country had a frontier of settlement, but at present the unsettled area has been so broken into by isolated bodies of settlement that there can hardly be said to be a frontier line. In the discussion of its extent, its westward movement, etc., it can not, therefore, any longer have a place in the census reports." This brief official statement marks the closing of a great historic movement. Up to our own day American

* Editors' Note: Frederick Jackson Turner, "The Significance of the Frontier in American History," *Annual Report of the American Historical Association for 1893* (Washington, D.C., 1894), 199–227. The author's footnotes have been omitted.

history has been in a large degree the history of the colonization of the Great West. The existence of an area of free land, its continuous recession, and the advance of American settlement westward, explain American development.

Behind institutions, behind constitutional forms and modifications, lie the vital forces that call these organs into life and shape them to meet changing conditions. The peculiarity of American institutions is, the fact that they have been compelled to adapt themselves to the changes of an expanding people— to the changes involved in crossing a continent, in winning a wilderness, and in developing at each area of this progress out of the primitive economic and political conditions of the frontier into the complexity of city life. Said Calhoun in 1817, "We are great, and rapidly—I was about to say fearfully—growing!" So saying, he touched the distinguishing feature of American life. All peoples show development; the germ theory of politics has been sufficiently emphasized. In the case of most nations, however, the development has occurred in a limited area; and if the nation has expanded, it has met other growing peoples whom it has conquered. But in the case of the United States we have a different phenomenon. Limiting our attention to the Atlantic coast, we have the familiar phenomenon of the evolution of institutions in a limited area, such as the rise of representative government; the differentiation of simple colonial governments into complex organs; the progress from primitive industrial society, without division of labor, up to manufacturing civilization. But we have in addition to this a recurrence of the process of evolution in each western area reached in the process of expansion. Thus American development has exhibited not merely advance along a single line, but a return to primitive conditions on a continually advancing frontier line, and a new development for that area. American social development has been continually beginning over again on the frontier. This perennial rebirth, this fluidity of American life, this expansion westward with its new opportunities, its continuous touch with the simplicity of primitive society, furnish the forces dominating American character. The true point of view in the history of this nation is not the Atlantic coast, it is the great West. Even the slavery struggle, which is made so exclusive an object of attention by writers like Prof. Von Holst, occupies its important place in American history because of its relation to westward expansion.

In this advance, the frontier is the outer edge of the wave—the meeting point between savagery and civilization. Much has been written about the frontier from the point of view of border warfare and the chase, but as a field for the serious study of the economist and the historian it has been neglected.

The American frontier is sharply distinguished from the European frontier— a fortified boundary line running through dense populations. The most significant thing about the American frontier is, that it lies at the hither edge of free land. In the census reports it is treated as the margin of that settlement which has a density of two or more to the square mile. The term is an elastic one, and for our purposes does not need sharp definition. We shall consider the whole frontier belt, including the Indian country and the outer margin of the "settled area" of the census reports. This paper will make no attempt to treat the subject exhaustively; its aim is simply to call attention to the frontier as a fertile field for investigation, and to suggest some of the problems which arise in connection with it.

In the settlement of America we have to observe how European life entered the continent, and how America modified and developed that life and reacted on Europe. Our early history is the study of European germs developing in an American environment. Too exclusive attention has been paid by institutional students to the Germanic origins, too little to the American factors. The frontier is the line of most rapid and effective Americanization. The wilderness masters the colonist. It finds him a European in dress, industries, tools, modes of travel, and thought. It takes him from the railroad car and puts him in the birch canoe. It strips off the garments of civilization and arrays him in the hunting shirt and the moccasin. It puts him in the log cabin of the Cherokee and Iroquois and runs an Indian palisade around him. Before long he has gone to planting Indian corn and plowing with a sharp stick; he shouts the war cry and takes the scalp in orthodox Indian fashion. In short, at the frontier the environment is at first too strong for the man. He must accept the conditions which it furnishes, or perish, and so he fits himself into the Indian clearings and follows the Indian trails. Little by little he transforms the wilderness, but the outcome is not the old Europe, not simply the development of Germanic germs, any more than the first phenomenon was a case of reversion to the Germanic mark. The fact is, that here is a new product that is American. At first, the frontier was the Atlantic coast. It was the frontier of Europe in a very real sense. Moving westward, the frontier became more and more American. As successive terminal moraines result from successive glaciations, so each frontier leaves its traces behind it, and when it becomes a settled area the region still partakes of the frontier characteristics. Thus the advance of the frontier has meant a steady movement away from the influence of Europe, a steady growth of independence on American lines. And to study this advance, the men who grew up under these conditions, and the political, economic, and social results of it, is to study the really American part of our history.

STAGES OF FRONTIER ADVANCE

In the course of the seventeenth century the frontier was advanced up the Atlantic river courses, just beyond the "fall line," and the tidewater region became the settled area. In the first half of the eighteenth century another advance occurred. Traders followed the Delaware and Shawnese Indians to the Ohio as early as the end of the first quarter of the century. Gov. Spotswood, of Virginia, made an expedition in 1714 across the Blue Ridge. The end of the first quarter of the century saw the advance of the Scotch-Irish and the Palatine Germans up the Shenandoah Valley into the western part of Virginia, and along the Piedmont region of the Carolinas. The Germans in New York pushed the frontier settlement up the Mohawk to German Flats. In Pennsylvania the town of Bedford indicates the line of settlement. Settlements had begun on New River, a branch of the Kanawha, and on the sources of the Yadkin and French Broad. The King attempted to arrest the advance by his proclamation of 1763, forbidding settlements beyond the sources of the rivers flowing into the Atlantic; but in vain. In the period of the Revolution the frontier crossed the Alleghanies into Kentucky and Tennessee, and the upper waters of the Ohio were settled. When the first census was taken in 1790, the continuous settled area was bounded by a line which ran near the coast of Maine, and included New England except a portion of Vermont and New Hampshire, New York along the Hudson and up the Mohawk about Schenectady, eastern and southern Pennsylvania, Virginia well across the Shenandoah Valley, and the Carolinas and eastern Georgia. Beyond this region of continuous settlement were the small settled areas of Kentucky and Tennessee, and the Ohio, with the mountains intervening between them and the Atlantic area, thus giving a new and important character to the frontier. The isolation of the region increased its peculiarly American tendencies, and the need of transportation facilities to connect it with the East called out important schemes of internal improvement, which will be noted farther on. The "West," as a self-conscious section, began to evolve.

From decade to decade distinct advances of the frontier occurred. By the census of 1820 the settled area included Ohio, southern Indiana and Illinois, southeastern Missouri, and about one-half of Louisiana. This settled area had surrounded Indians areas, and the management of these tribes became an object of political concern. The frontier region of the time lay along the Great Lakes, where Astor's American Fur Company operated in the Indian trade, and beyond the Mississippi, where Indian traders extended their activity even to the Rocky Mountains; Florida also furnished frontier conditions. The Mississippi River region was the scene of typical frontier settlements.

The rising steam navigation on western waters, the opening of the Erie Canal, and the westward extension of cotton culture added five frontier states to the Union in this period. Grund, writing in 1836, declares: "It appears then that the universal disposition of Americans to emigrate to the western wilderness, in order to enlarge their dominion over inanimate nature, is the actual result of an expansive power which is inherent in them, and which by continually agitating all classes of society is constantly throwing a large portion of the whole population on the extreme confines of the State, in order to gain space for its development. Hardly is a new State or Territory formed before the same principle manifests itself again and gives rise to a further emigration; and so is it destined to go on until a physical barrier must finally obstruct its progress."

In the middle of this century the line indicated by the present eastern boundary of Indian Territory, Nebraska, and Kansas marked the frontier of the Indian country. Minnesota and Wisconsin still exhibited frontier conditions, but the distinctive frontier of the period is found in California, where the gold discoveries had sent a sudden tide of adventurous miners, and in Oregon, and the settlements in Utah. As the frontier had leaped over the Alleghanies, so now it skipped the Great Plains and the Rocky Mountains; and in the same way that the advance of the frontiersmen beyond the Alleghanies had caused the rise of important questions of transportation and internal improvement, so now the settlers beyond the Rocky Mountains needed means of communication with the East, and in the furnishing of these arose the settlement of the Great Plains and the development of still another kind of frontier life. Railroads, fostered by land grants, sent an increasing tide of immigrants into the far West. The United States Army fought a series of Indian wars in Minnesota, Dakota, and the Indian Territory.

By 1880 the settled area had been pushed into northern Michigan, Wisconsin, and Minnesota, along Dakota rivers, and in the Black Hills region, and was ascending the rivers of Kansas and Nebraska. The development of mines in Colorado had drawn isolated frontier settlements into that region, and Montana and Idaho were receiving settlers. The frontier was found in these mining camps and the ranches of the Great Plains. The superintendent of the census for 1890 reports, as previously stated, that the settlements of the West lie so scattered over the region that there can no longer be said to be a frontier line.

In these successive frontiers we find natural boundary lines which have served to mark and to affect the characteristics of the frontiers, namely: The "fall line"; the Alleghany Mountains; the Mississippi; the Missouri, where its direction approximates north and south; the line of the arid lands, approximately the ninety-ninth meridian; and the Rocky Mountains. The fall line marked the frontier of the seventeenth century; the Alleghanies that of the eighteenth; the Mississippi that of the first quarter of the nineteenth; the Missouri that of the middle of this century (omitting the California movement); and the belt of the Rocky Mountains and the arid tract, the present frontier. Each was won by a series of Indian wars.

THE FRONTIER FURNISHES A FIELD FOR
COMPARATIVE STUDY OF SOCIAL DEVELOPMENT

At the Atlantic frontier one can study the germs of processes repeated at each
successive frontier. We have the complex European life sharply precipitated
by the wilderness into the simplicity of primitive conditions. The first frontier had to meet its Indian question, its question of the disposition of the public domain, of the means of intercourse with older settlements, of the extension of political organization, of religious and educational activity. And the
settlement of these and similar questions for one frontier served as a guide for
the next. The American student needs not to go to the "prim little townships
of Sleswick" for illustration of the law of continuity and development. For example, he may study the origin of our land policies in the colonial land policy: he may see how the system grew by adapting the statutes to the customs
of the successive frontiers. He may see how the mining experience in the lead
regions of Wisconsin, Illinois, and Iowa was applied to the mining laws of the
Rockies, and how our Indian policy has been a series of experimentations on
successive frontiers. Each tier of new States has found in the older ones material for its constitutions. Each frontier has made similar contributions to
American character, as will be discussed farther on.

But with all these similarities there are essential differences, due to the
place element and the time element. It is evident that the farming frontier of
the Mississippi Valley presents different conditions from the mining frontier
of the Rocky Mountains. The frontier reached by the Pacific Railroad, sur-
veyed into rectangles, guarded by the United States Army, and recruited by
the daily immigrant ship, moves forward at a swifter pace and in a different
way than the frontier reached by the birch canoe or the pack horse. The geol-
ogist traces patiently the shores of ancient seas, maps their areas, and compares the older and the newer. It would be a work worth the historian's labors
to mark these various frontiers and in detail compare one with another. Not
only would there result a more adequate conception of American development and characteristics, but invaluable additions would be made to the history of society.

Loria, the Italian economist, has urged the study of colonial life as an aid
in understanding the stages of European development, affirming that colonial
settlement is for economic science what the mountain is for geology, bringing to light primitive stratifications. "America," he says, "has the key to the
historical enigma which Europe has sought for centuries in vain, and the land
which has no history reveals luminously the course of universal history."
There is much truth in this. The United States lies like a huge page in the history of society. Line by line as we read this continental page from west to east

we find the record of social evolution. It begins with the Indian and the hunter; it goes on to tell of the disintegration of savagery by the entrance of the trader, the pathfinder of civilization; we read the annals of the pastoral stage in ranch life; the exploitation of the soil by the raising of unrotated crops of corn and wheat in sparsely settled farming communities; the intensive culture of the denser farm settlement; and finally the manufacturing organization with city and factory system. This page is familiar to the student of census statistics, but how little of it has been used by our historians. Particularly in eastern States this page is a palimpsest. What is now a manufacturing State was in an earlier decade an area of intensive farming. Earlier yet it had been a wheat area, and still earlier the "range" had attracted the cattle-herder. Thus Wisconsin, now developing manufacture, is a State with varied agricultural interests. But earlier it was given over to almost exclusive grain-raising, like North Dakota at the present time.

Each of these areas has had an influence in our economic and political history; the evolution of each into a higher stage has worked political transformations. But what constitutional historian has made any adequate attempt to interpret political facts by the light of these social areas and changes?

The Atlantic frontier was compounded of fisherman, fur-trader, miner, cattle-raiser, and farmer. Excepting the fisherman, each type of industry was on the march toward the West, impelled by an irresistible attraction. Each passed in successive waves across the continent. Stand at Cumberland Gap and watch the procession of civilization, marching single file—the buffalo following the trail to the salt springs, the Indian, the fur-trader and hunter, the cattle-raiser, the pioneer farmer—and the frontier has passed by. Stand at South Pass in the Rockies a century later and see the same procession with wider intervals between. The unequal rate of advance compels us to distinguish the frontier into the trader's frontier, the rancher's frontier, or the miner's frontier, and the farmer's frontier. When the mines and the cow pens were still near the fall line the traders' pack trains were tinkling across the Alleghanies, and the French on the Great Lakes were fortifying their posts, alarmed by the British trader's birch canoe. When the trappers scaled the Rockies, the farmer was still near the mouth of the Missouri.

THE INDIAN TRADER'S FRONTIER

Why was it that the Indian trader passed so rapidly across the continent? What effects followed from the trader's frontier? The trade was coeval with American discovery. The Norsemen, Vespuccius, Verrazani, Hudson, John Smith, all trafficked for furs. The Plymouth pilgrims settled in Indian cornfields, and their first return cargo was of beaver and lumber. The records of the various New England colonies show how steadily exploration was carried into the wilderness by this trade. What is true for New England is, as would be expected, even plainer for the rest of the colonies. All along the coast from Maine to Georgia the Indian trade opened up the river courses. Steadily the trader passed westward, utilizing the older lines of French trade. The Ohio, the Great Lakes, the Mississippi, the Missouri, and the Platte, the lines of western advance, were ascended by traders. They found the passes in the Rocky Mountains and guided Lewis and Clarke, Fremont, and Bidwell. The explanation of the rapidity of this advance is connected with the effects of the trader on the Indian. The trading post left the unarmed tribes at the mercy of those that had purchased fire-arms—a truth which the Iroquois Indians wrote in blood, and so the remote and unvisited tribes gave eager welcome to the trader. "The savages," wrote La Salle, "take better care of us French than of their own children; from us only can they get guns and goods." This accounts for the trader's power and the rapidity of his advance. Thus the disintegrating forces of civilization entered the wilderness. Every river valley and Indian trail became a fissure in Indian society, and so that society became honeycombed. Long before the pioneer farmer appeared on the scene, primitive Indian life had passed away. The farmers met Indians armed with guns. The trading frontier, while steadily undermining Indian power by making the tribes ultimately dependent on the whites, yet, through its sale of guns, gave to the Indians increased power of resistance to the farming frontier. French colonization was dominated by its trading frontier; English colonization by its farming frontier. There was an antagonism between the two frontiers as between the two nations. Said Duquesne to the Iroquois, "Are you ignorant of the difference between the king of England and the king of France? Go see the forts that our king has established and you will see that you can still hunt under their very walls. They have been placed for your advantage in places which you frequent. The English, on the contrary, are no sooner in possession of a place than the game is driven away. The forest falls before them as they advance, and the soil is laid bare so that you can scarce find the wherewithal to erect a shelter for the night."

And yet, in spite of this opposition of the interests of the trader and the farmer, the Indian trade pioneered the way for civilization. The buffalo trail became the Indian trail, and this became the trader's "trace"; the trails widened into roads, and the roads into turnpikes, and these in turn were transformed into railroads. The same origin can be shown for the railroads of the South, the far West, and the Dominion of Canada. The trading posts reached by these trails were on the sites of Indian villages which had been placed in positions suggested by nature; and these trading posts, situated so as to command the water systems of the country, have grown into such cities as Albany, Pittsburgh, Detroit, Chicago, St. Louis, Council Bluffs, and Kansas City. Thus civilization in America has followed the arteries made by geology, pouring an ever richer tide through them, until at last the slender paths of aboriginal intercourse have been broadened and interwoven into the complex mazes of modern commercial lines; the wilderness has been interpenetrated by lines of civilization growing ever more numerous. It is like the steady growth of a complex nervous system for the originally simple, inert continent. If one would understand why we are to-day one nation, rather than a collection of isolated states, he must study this economic and social consolidation of the country. In this progress from savage conditions lie topics for the evolutionist.

The effect of the Indian frontier as a consolidating agent in our history is important. From the close of the seventeenth century various intercolonial congresses have been called to treat with Indians and establish common measures of defense. Particularism was strongest in colonies with no Indian frontier. This frontier stretched along the western border like a cord of union. The Indian was a common danger, demanding united action. Most celebrated of these conferences was the Albany congress of 1754, called to treat with the Six Nations, and to consider plans of union. Even a cursory reading of the plan proposed by the congress reveals the importance of the frontier. The powers of the general council and the officers were, chiefly, the determination of peace and war with the Indians, the regulation of Indian trade, the purchase of Indian lands, and the creation and government of new settlements as a security against the Indians. It is evident that the unifying tendencies of the Revolutionary period were facilitated by the previous cooperation in the regulation of the frontier. In this connection may be mentioned the importance of the frontier, from that day to this, as a military training school, keeping alive the power of resistance to aggression, and developing the stalwart and rugged qualities of the frontiersman.

THE RANCHER'S FRONTIER

It would not be possible in the limits of this paper to trace the other frontiers across the continent. Travelers of the eighteenth century found the "cowpens" among the canebrakes and peavine pastures of the South, and the "cow drivers" took their droves to Charleston, Philadelphia, and New York. Travelers at the close of the War of 1812 met droves of more than a thousand cattle and swine from the interior of Ohio going to Pennsylvania to fatten for the Philadelphia market. The ranges of the Great Plains, with ranch and cowboy and nomadic life, are things of yesterday and of to-day. The experience of the Carolina cowpens guided the ranchers of Texas. One element favoring the rapid extension of the rancher's frontier is the fact that in a remote country lacking transportation facilities the product must be in small bulk, or must be able to transport itself, and the cattle raiser could easily drive his product to market. The effect of these great ranches on the subsequent agrarian history of the localities in which they existed should be studied.

THE FARMER'S FRONTIER

The maps of the census reports show an uneven advance of the farmer's frontier, with tongues of settlement pushed forward and with indentations of wilderness. In part this is due to Indian resistance, in part to the location of river valleys and passes, in part to the unequal force of the centers of frontier attraction. Among the important centers of attraction may be mentioned the following: fertile and favorably situated soils, salt springs, mines, and army posts.

ARMY POSTS

The frontier army post, serving to protect the settlers from the Indians, has also acted as a wedge to open the Indian country, and has been a nucleus for settlement. In this connection mention should also be made of the Government military and exploring expeditions in determining the lines of settlement. But all the more important expeditions were greatly indebted to the earliest pathmakers, the Indian guides, the traders and trappers, and the French voyageurs, who were inevitable parts of governmental expeditions from the day of Lewis and Clarke. Each expedition was an epitome of the previous factors in western advance.

SALT SPRINGS

In an interesting monograph, Victor Hehn has traced the effect of salt upon early European development, and has pointed out how it affected the lines of settlement and the form of administration. A similar study might be made for the salt springs of the United States. The early settlers were tied to the coast by the need of salt, without which they could not preserve their meats or live in comfort. Writing in 1752, Bishop Spangenburg says of a colony for which he was seeking lands in North Carolina, "They will require salt & other necessaries which they can neither manufacture nor raise. Either they must go to Charleston, which is 300 miles distant . . . Or else they must go to Boling's Point in V^a on a branch of the James & is also 300 miles from here . . . Or else they must go down the Roanoke—I know not how many miles—where salt is brought up from the Cape Fear." This may serve as a typical illustration. An annual pilgrimage to the coast for salt thus became essential. Taking flocks or furs and ginseng root, the early settlers sent their pack trains after seeding time each year to the coast. This proved to be an important educational influence, since it was almost the only way in which the pioneer learned what was going on in the East. But when discovery was made of the salt springs of the Kanawha, and the Holston, and Kentucky, and central New York, the West began to be freed from dependence on the coast. It was in part the effect of finding these salt springs that enabled settlement to cross the mountains.

From the time the mountains rose between the pioneer and the seaboard, a new order of Americanism arose. The West and the East began to get out of touch of each other. The settlements from the sea to the mountains kept connection with the rear and had a certain solidarity. But the over-mountain men grew more and more independent. The East took a narrow view of American advance, and nearly lost these men. Kentucky and Tennessee history bears abundant witness to the truth of this statement. The East began to try to hedge and limit westward expansion. Though Webster could declare that there were no Alleghanies in his politics, yet in politics in general they were a very solid factor.

LAND

The exploitation of the beasts took hunter and trader to the west, the exploitation of the grasses took the rancher west, and the exploitation of the virgin soil of the river valleys and prairies attracted the farmer. Good soils have been the most continuous attraction to the farmer's frontier. The land hunger of the Virginians drew them down the rivers into Carolina, in early colonial days; the search for soils took the Massachusetts men to Pennsylvania and to New York. As the eastern lands were taken up migration flowed across them to the west. Daniel Boone, the great backwoodsman, who combined the occupations of hunter, trader, cattle-raiser, farmer, and surveyor—learning, probably from the traders, of the fertility of the lands on the upper Yadkin, where the traders were wont to rest as they took their way to the Indians, left his Pennsylvania home with his father, and passed down the Great Valley road to that stream. Learning from a trader whose posts were on the Red River in

Kentucky of its game and rich pastures, he pioneered the way for the farmers to that region. Thence he passed to the frontier of Missouri, where his settlement was long a landmark on the frontier. Here again he helped to open the way for civilization, finding salt licks, and trails, and land. His son was among the earliest trappers in the passes of the Rocky Mountains, and his party are said to have been the first to camp on the present site of Denver. His grandson, Col. A. J. Boone, of Colorado, was a power among the Indians of the Rocky Mountains, and was appointed an agent by the Government. Kit Carson's mother was a Boone. Thus this family epitomizes the backwoodsman's advance across the continent.

The farmer's advance came in a distinct series of waves. In Peck's New Guide to the West, published in Boston in 1837, occurs this suggestive passage:

Generally, in all the western settlements, three classes, like the waves of the ocean, have rolled one after the other. First comes the pioneer, who depends for the subsistence of his family chiefly upon the natural growth of vegetation, called the "range," and the proceeds of hunting. His implements of agriculture are rude, chiefly of his own make, and his efforts directed mainly to a crop of corn and a "truck patch." The last is a rude garden for growing cabbage, beans, corn for roasting ears, cucumbers, and potatoes. A log cabin, and, occasionally, a stable and corn-crib, and a field of a dozen acres, the timber girdled or "deadened," and fenced, are enough for his occupancy. It is quite immaterial whether he ever becomes the owner of the soil. He is the occupant for the time being, pays no rent, and feels as independent as the "lord of the manor." With a horse, cow, and one or two breeders of swine, he strikes into the woods with his family, and becomes the founder of a new county, or perhaps state. He builds his cabin, gathers around him a few other families of similar tastes and habits, and occupies till the range is somewhat subdued, and hunting a little precarious, or, which is more frequently the case, till the neighbors crowd around, roads, bridges, and fields annoy him, and he lacks elbow room. The preemption law enables him to dispose of his cabin and cornfield to the next class of emigrants; and, to employ his own figures, he "breaks for the high timber," "clears out for the New Purchase," or migrates to Arkansas or Texas, to work the same process over.

The next class of emigrants purchase the lands, add field to field, clear out the roads, throw rough bridges over the streams, put up hewn log houses with glass windows and brick or stone chimneys, occasionally plant orchards, build mills, schoolhouses, court-houses, etc., and exhibit the picture and forms of plain, frugal, civilized life.

Another wave rolls on. The men of capital and enterprise come. The settler is ready to sell out and take the advantage of the rise in property, push farther into the interior and become, himself, a man of capital and enterprise in turn. The small village rises to a spacious town or city; substantial edifices of brick, extensive fields, orchards, gardens, colleges, and churches are seen. Broadcloths, silks, leghorns, crapes, and all the refinements, luxuries, elegancies, frivolities, and fashions are in vogue. Thus wave after wave is rolling westward; the real Eldorado is still farther on.

A portion of the two first classes remain stationary amidst the general movement, improve their habits and condition, and rise in the scale of society.

The writer has traveled much amongst the first class, the real pioneers. He has lived many years in connection with the second grade; and now the third wave is sweeping over large districts of Indiana, Illinois, and Missouri. Migration has become almost a habit in the West. Hundreds of men can be found, not over 50 years of age, who have settled for the fourth, fifth, or sixth time on a new spot. To sell out and remove only a few hundred miles makes up a portion of the variety of backwoods life and manners.

Omitting those of the pioneer farmers who move from the love of adventure, the advance of the more steady farmer is easy to understand. Obviously the immigrant was attracted by the cheap lands of the frontier, and even the native farmer felt their influence strongly. Year by year the farmers who lived on soil whose returns were diminished by unrotated crops were offered the virgin soil of the frontier at nominal prices. Their growing families demanded more lands, and these were dear. The competition of the unexhausted, cheap, and easily tilled prairie lands compelled the farmer either to go west and continue the exhaustion of the soil on a new frontier, or to adopt intensive culture. Thus the census of 1890 shows, in the Northwest, many counties in which there is an absolute or a relative decrease of population. These States have been sending farmers to advance the frontier on the plains, and have themselves begun to turn to intensive farming and to manufacture. A decade before this, Ohio had shown the same transition stage. Thus the demand for land and the love of wilderness freedom drew the frontier ever onward.

Having now roughly outlined the various kinds of frontiers, and their modes of advance, chiefly from the point of view of the frontier itself, we may next inquire what were the influences on the East and on the Old World. A rapid enumeration of some of the more noteworthy effects is all that I have time for.

COMPOSITE NATIONALITY

First, we note that the frontier promoted the formation of a composite nationality for the American people. The coast was preponderantly English, but the later tides of continental immigration flowed across to the free lands. This was the case from the early colonial days. The Scotch Irish and the Palatine

Germans, or "Pennsylvania Dutch," furnished the dominant element in the stock of the colonial frontier. With these peoples were also the freed indented servants, or redemptioners, who at the expiration of their time of service passed to the frontier. Governor Spotswood of Virginia writes in 1717, "The inhabitants of our frontiers are composed generally of such as have been transported hither as servants, and, being out of their time, settle themselves where land is to be taken up and that will produce the necessarys of life with little labour." Very generally these redemptioners were of non-English stock. In the crucible of the frontier the immigrants were Americanized, liberated, and fused into a mixed race, English in neither nationality nor characteristics. The process has gone on from the early days to our own. Burke and other writers in the middle of the eighteenth century believed that Pennsylvania was "threatened with the danger of being wholly foreign in language, manners, and perhaps even inclinations." The German and Scotch-Irish elements in the frontier of the South were only less great. In the middle of the present century the German element in Wisconsin was already so considerable that leading publicists looked to the creation of a German state out of the commonwealth by concentrating their colonization. Such examples teach us to beware of misinterpreting the fact that there is a common English speech in America into a belief that the stock is also English.

INDUSTRIAL INDEPENDENCE

In another way the advance of the frontier decreased our dependence on England. The coast, particularly of the South, lacked diversified industries, and was dependent on England for the bulk of its supplies. In the South there was even a dependence on the Northern colonies for articles of food. Governor Glenn, of South Carolina, writes in the middle of the eighteenth century: "Our trade with New York and Philadelphia was of this sort, draining us of all the little money and bills we could gather from other places for their bread, flour, beer, hams, bacon, and other things of their produce, all which, except beer, our new townships began to supply us with, which are settled with very industrious and thriving Germans. This no doubt diminishes the number of shipping and the appearance of our trade, but it is far from being a detriment to us." Before long the frontier created a demand for merchants. As it retreated from the coast it became less and less possible for England to bring her supplies directly to the consumer's wharfs, and carry away staple crops, and staple crops began to give way to diversified agriculture for a time. The effect of this phase of the frontier action upon the northern section is perceived when we realize how the advance of the frontier aroused seaboard cities like Boston, New York, and Baltimore, to engage in rivalry for what Washington called "the extensive and valuable trade of a rising empire."

EFFECTS ON NATIONAL LEGISLATION

The legislation which most developed the powers of the National Government, and played the largest part in its activity, was conditioned on the frontier. Writers have discussed the subjects of tariff, land, and internal improvement, as subsidiary to the slavery question. But when American history comes to be rightly viewed it will be seen that the slavery question is an incident. In the period from the end of the first half of the present century to the close of the civil war slavery rose to primary, but far from exclusive, importance. But this does not justify Dr. von Holst (to take an example) in treating our constitutional history in its formative period down to 1828 in a single volume, giving six volumes chiefly to the history of slavery from 1828 to 1861, under the title "Constitutional History of the United States." The growth of nationalism and the evolution of American political institutions were dependent on the advance of the frontier. Even so recent a writer as Rhodes, in his "History of the United States Since the Compromise of 1850," has treated the legislation called out by the western advance as incidental to the slavery struggle.

This is a wrong perspective. The pioneer needed the goods of the coast, and so the grand series of internal improvement and railroad legislation began, with potent nationalizing effects. Over internal improvements occurred great debates, in which grave constitutional questions were discussed. Sectional groupings appear in the votes, profoundly significant for the historian. Loose construction increased as the nation marched westward. But the West was not content with bringing the farm to the factory. Under the lead of Clay—"Harry of the West"—protective tariffs were passed, with the cry of bringing the factory to the farm. The disposition of the public lands was a third important subject of national legislation influenced by the frontier.

THE PUBLIC DOMAIN

The public domain has been a force of profound importance in the nationalization and development of the Government. The effects of the struggle of the landed and the landless States, and of the ordinance of 1787, need no discussion. Administratively the frontier called out some of the highest and most vitalizing activities of the General Government. The purchase of Louisiana was perhaps the constitutional turning point in the history of the Republic, inasmuch as it afforded both a new area for national legislation and the occasion of the downfall of the policy of strict construction. But the purchase of Louisiana was called out by frontier needs and demands. As frontier States accrued to the Union the national power grew. In a speech on the dedication of the Calhoun monument Mr. Lamar explained: "In 1789 the States were the creators of the Federal Government; in 1861 the Federal Government was the creator of a large majority of the States."

When we consider the public domain from the point of view of the sale and disposal of the public lands we are again brought face to face with the frontier. The policy of the United States in dealing with its lands is in sharp contrast with the European system of scientific administration. Efforts to make this domain a source of revenue, and to withhold it from emigrants in order that settlement might be compact, were in vain. The jealousy and the fears of the East were powerless in the face of the demands of the frontiersman. John Quincy Adams was obliged to confess: "My own system of administration, which was to make the national domain the inexhaustible fund for progressive and unceasing internal improvement, has failed." The reason is obvious; a system of administration was not what the West demanded; it wanted land. Adams states the situation as follows: "The slaveholders of the South have bought the cooperation of the western country by the bribe of western lands, abandoning to the new Western States their own proportion of the public property and aiding them in the design of grasping all the lands into their own hands. Thomas H. Benton was the author of this system, which he brought forward as a substitute for the American system of Mr. Clay, and to supplant him as the leading statesman of the West. Mr. Clay, by his tariff compromise with Mr. Calhoun, abandoned his own American system. At the same time he brought forward a plan for distributing among all the States of the Union the proceeds of the sales of the public lands. His bill for that purpose passed both Houses of Congress, but was vetoed by President Jackson, who, in his annual message of December, 1832, formally recommended that all public lands should be gratuitously given away to individual adventurers and to the States in which the lands are situated.

"No subject," said Henry Clay, "which has presented itself to the present, or perhaps any preceding, Congress, is of greater magnitude than that of the public lands." When we consider the far-reaching effects of the Government's land policy upon political, economic, and social aspects of American life, we are disposed to agree with him. But this legislation was framed under frontier influences, and under the lead of Western statesmen like Benton and Jackson. Said Senator Scott of Indiana in 1841: "I consider the preemption law merely declaratory of the custom or common law of the settlers."

NATIONAL TENDENCIES OF THE FRONTIER

It is safe to say that the legislation with regard to land, tariff, and internal improvements—the American system of the nationalizing Whig party—was conditioned on frontier ideas and needs. But it was not merely in legislative action that the frontier worked against the sectionalism of the coast. The economic and social characteristics of the frontier worked against sectionalism. The men of the frontier had closer resemblances to the Middle region than to either of the other sections. Pennsylvania had been the seed-plot of frontier emigration, and, although she passed on her settlers along the Great Valley into the West of Virginia and the Carolinas, yet the industrial society of these Southern frontiersmen was always more like that of the Middle region than like that of the tide-water portion of the South, which later came to spread its industrial type throughout the South.

The Middle region, entered by New York harbor, was an open door to all Europe. The tide-water part of the South represented typical Englishmen, modified by a warm climate and servile labor, and living in baronial fashion on great plantations; New England stood for a special English movement— Puritanism. The Middle region was less English than the other sections. It has a wide mixture of nationalities, a varied society, the mixed town and county system of local government, a varied economic life, many religious sects. In short, it was a region mediating between New England and the South, and the East and the West. It represented that composite nationality which the contemporary United States exhibits, that juxtaposition of non-English groups, occupying a valley or a little settlement, and presenting reflections of the map of Europe in their variety. It was democratic and nonsectional, if not national; "easy, tolerant, and contented"; rooted strongly in material prosperity. It was typical of the modern United States. It was least sectional, not only because it lay between North and South, but also because with no barriers to shut out its frontiers from its settled region, and with a system of connecting waterways, the Middle region mediated between East and West as well as between North and South. Thus it became the typically American region. Even the New Englander, who was shut out from the frontier by the Middle region, tarrying in New York or Pennsylvania on his westward march, lost the acuteness of his sectionalism on the way.

The spread of cotton culture into the interior of the South finally broke down the contrast between the "tide-water" region and the rest of the State, and based Southern interests on slavery. Before this process revealed its results the western portion of the South, which was akin to Pennsylvania in stock, society, and industry, showed tendencies to fall away from the faith of the fathers into internal improvement legislation and nationalism. In the Virginia convention of

1829–'30, called to revise the constitution, Mr. Leigh, of Chesterfield, one of the tide-water counties, declared:

> One of the main causes of discontent which led to this convention, that which had the strongest influence in overcoming our veneration for the work of our fathers, which taught us to contemn the sentiments of Henry and Mason and Pendleton, which weaned us from our reverence for the constituted authorities of the State, was an overweening passion for internal improvement. I say this with perfect knowledge, for it has been avowed to me by gentlemen from the West over and over again. And let me tell the gentleman from Albemarle (Mr. Gordon) that it has been another principal object of those who set this ball of revolution in motion, to overturn the doctrine of State rights, of which Virginia has been the very pillar, and to remove the barrier she has interposed to the interference of the Federal Government in that same work of internal improvement, by so reorganizing the legislature that Virginia, too, may be hitched to the Federal car.

It was this nationalizing tendency of the West that transformed the democracy of Jefferson into the national republicanism of Monroe and the democracy of Andrew Jackson. The West of the war of 1812, the West of Clay, and Benton, and Harrison, and Andrew Jackson, shut off by the Middle States and the mountains from the coast sections, had a solidarity of its own with national tendencies. On the tide of the Father of Waters, North and South met and mingled into a nation. Interstate migration went steadily on—a process of crossfertilization of ideas and institutions. The fierce struggle of the sections over slavery on the western frontier does not diminish the truth of this statement; it proves the truth of it. Slavery was a sectional trait that would not down, but in the West it could not remain sectional. It was the greatest of frontiersmen who declared: "I believe this Government can not endure permanently half slave and half free. It will become all of one thing or all of the other." Nothing works for nationalism like intercourse within the nation. Mobility of population is death to localism, and the western frontier worked irresistibly in unsettling population. The effects reached back from the frontier and affected profoundly the Atlantic coast and even the Old World.

GROWTH OF DEMOCRACY

But the most important effect of the frontier has been in the promotion of democracy here and in Europe. As has been indicated, the frontier is productive of individualism. Complex society is precipitated by the wilderness into a kind of primitive organization based on the family. The tendency is anti-social. It produces antipathy to control, and particularly to any direct control. The tax-gatherer is viewed as a representative of oppression. Prof. Osgood, in an able article, has pointed out that the frontier conditions prevalent in the colonies are important factors in the explanation of the American Revolution, where individual liberty was sometimes confused with absence of all effective government. The same conditions aid in explaining the difficulty of instituting a strong government in the period of the confederacy. The frontier individualism has from the beginning promoted democracy.

The frontier States that came into the Union in the first quarter of a century of its existence came in with democratic suffrage provisions, and had reactive effects of the highest importance upon the older States whose peoples were being attracted there. An extension of the franchise became essential. It was *western* New York that forced an extension of suffrage in the constitutional convention of that State in 1821; and it was *western* Virginia that compelled the tide-water region to put a more liberal suffrage provision in the constitution framed in 1830, and to give to the frontier region a more nearly proportionate representation with the tide-water aristocracy. The rise of democracy as an effective force in the nation came in with western preponderance under Jackson and William Henry Harrison, and it meant the triumph of the frontier—with all of its good and with all of its evil elements. An interesting illustration of the tone of frontier democracy in 1830 comes from the same debates in the Virginia convention already referred to. A representative from western Virginia declared:

> But, sir, it is not the increase of population in the West which this gentleman ought to fear. It is the energy which the mountain breeze and western habits impart to those emigrants. They are regenerated, politically I mean, sir. They soon become *working politicians*; and the difference, sir, between a *talking* and a *working* politician is immense. The Old Dominion has long been celebrated for producing great orators; the ablest metaphysicians in policy; men that can split hairs in all abstruse questions of political economy. But at home, or when they return from Congress, they have Negroes to fan them asleep. But a Pennsylvania, a New York, an Ohio, and a western Virginia statesman, though far inferior in logic, metaphysics, and rhetoric to an old Virginia statesman, has this advantage, that when he returns home he takes off his coat and takes hold of the plow. This gives him bone and muscle, sir, and preserves his republican principles pure and uncontaminated.

So long as free land exists, the opportunity for a competency exists, and economic power secures political power. But the democracy born of free land, strong in selfishness and individualism, intolerant of administrative experience and education, and pressing individual liberty beyond its proper bounds, has its dangers as well as its benefits. Individualism in America has allowed a laxity in regard to governmental affairs which has rendered possible the spoils system and all the manifest evils that follow from the lack of a highly developed civic spirit. In this connection may be noted also the influence of frontier conditions in permitting lax business honor, inflated paper currency and wild-cat banking. The colonial revolutionary frontier was the region whence emanated many of the worst forms of an evil currency. The West in the war of 1812 repeated the phenomenon on the frontier of that day, while the speculation and wild-cat banking of the period of the crisis of 1837 occurred on the new frontier belt of the next tier of States. Thus each one of the periods of lax financial integrity coincides with periods when a new set of frontier communities had arisen, and coincides in area with these successive frontiers, for the most part. The recent Populist agitation is a case in point. Many a State that now declines any connection with the tenets of the Populists, itself adhered to such ideas in an earlier stage of the development of the State. A primitive society can hardly be expected to show the intelligent appreciation of the complexity of business interests in a developed society. The continual recurrence of these areas of paper-money agitation is another evidence that the frontier can be isolated and studied as a factor in American history of the highest importance.

ATTEMPTS TO CHECK AND REGULATE THE FRONTIER

The East has always feared the result of an unregulated advance of the frontier, and has tried to check and guide it. The English authorities would have checked settlement at the headwaters of the Atlantic tributaries and allowed the "savages to enjoy their deserts in quiet lest the peltry trade should decrease." This called out Burke's splendid protest:

> If you stopped your grants, what would be the consequence? The people would occupy without grants. They have already so occupied in many places. You can not station garrisons in every part of these deserts. If you drive the people from one place, they will carry on their annual tillage and remove with their flocks and herds to another. Many of the people in the back settlements are already little attached to particular situations. Already they have topped the Appalachian mountains. From thence they behold before them an immense plain, one vast, rich, level meadow; a square of five hundred miles. Over this they would wander without a possibility of restraint; they would change their manners with their habits of life; would soon forget a government by which they were disowned; would become hordes of English Tartars; and, pouring down upon your unfortified frontiers a fierce and irresistible cavalry, become masters of your governors,

and your counselors, your collectors and comptrollers, and of all the slaves that adhered to them. Such would, and in no long time must, be the effect of attempting to forbid as a crime and to suppress as an evil the command and blessing of Providence, "Increase and multiply." Such would be the happy result of an endeavor to keep as a lair of wild beasts that earth which God, by an express charter, has given to the children of men.

But the English Government was not alone in its desire to limit the advance of the frontier and guide its destinies. Tide-water Virginia and South Carolina gerrymandered those colonies to insure the dominance of the coast in their legislatures. Washington desired to settle a State at a time in the Northwest; Jefferson would reserve from settlement the territory of his Louisiana purchase north of the thirty-second parallel, in order to offer it to the Indians in exchange for their settlements east of the Mississippi. "When we shall be full on this side," he writes, "we may lay off a range of States on the western bank from the head to the mouth, and so range after range, advancing compactly as we multiply." Madison went so far as to argue to the French minister that the United States had no interest in seeing population extend itself on the right bank of the Mississippi, but should rather fear it. When the Oregon question was under debate, in 1824, Smyth, of Virginia, would draw an unchangeable line for the limits of the United States at the outer limit of two tiers of States beyond the Mississippi, complaining that the seaboard States were being drained of the flower of their population by the bringing of too much land into market. Even Thomas Benton, the man of widest views of the destiny of the West, at this stage of his career declared that along the ridge of the Rocky mountains "the western limits of the Republic should be drawn, and the statue of the fabled god Terminus should be raised upon its highest peak, never to be thrown down." But the attempts to limit the boundaries, to restrict land sales and settlement, and to deprive the West of its share of political power were all in vain. Steadily the frontier of settlement advanced and carried with it individualism, democracy, and nationalism, and powerfully affected the East and the Old World.

MISSIONARY ACTIVITY

The most effective efforts of the East to regulate the frontier came through its educational and religious activity, exerted by interstate migration and by organized societies. Speaking in 1835, Dr. Lyman Beecher declared: "It is equally plain that the religious and political destiny of our nation is to be decided in the West," and he pointed out that the population of the West "is assembled from all the States of the Union and from all the nations of Europe, and is rushing in like the waters of the flood, demanding for its moral preservation the immediate and universal action of those institutions which discipline the mind and arm the conscience and the heart. And so various are the opinions and habits, and so recent and imperfect is the acquaintance, and so sparse are the settlements of the West, that no homogeneous public sentiment can be formed to legislate immediately into being the requisite institutions. And yet they are all needed immediately in their utmost perfection and power. A nation is being 'born in a day.' . . . But what will become of the West if her prosperity rushes up to such a majesty of power, while those great institutions linger which are necessary to form the mind and the conscience and the heart of that vast world. It must not be permitted. . . . Let no man at the East quiet himself and dream of liberty, whatever may become of the West. . . . Her destiny is our destiny."

With the appeal to the conscience of New England, he adds appeals to her fears lest other religious sects anticipate her own. The New England preacher and school-teacher left their mark on the West. The dread of Western emancipation from New England's political and economic control was paralleled by her fears lest the West cut loose from her religion. Commenting in 1850 on reports that settlement was rapidly extending northward in Wisconsin, the editor of the Home Missionary writes: "We scarcely know whether to rejoice or mourn over this extension of our settlements. While we sympathize in whatever tends to increase the physical resources and prosperity of our country, we can not forget that with all these dispersions into remote and still remoter corners of the land the supply of the means of grace is becoming relatively less and less." Acting in accordance with such ideas, home missions were established and Western colleges were erected. As seaboard cities like Philadelphia, New York, and Baltimore strove for the mastery of Western trade, so the various denominations strove for the possession of the West. Thus an intellectual stream from New England sources fertilized the West. Other sections sent their missionaries; but the real struggle was between sects. The contest for power and the expansive tendency furnished to the various sects by the existence of a moving frontier must have had important results on the character of religious organization in the United States. The multiplication of rival churches in the little frontier towns had deep and lasting social effects. The religious aspects of the frontier make a chapter in our history which needs study.

INTELLECTUAL TRAITS

From the conditions of frontier life came intellectual traits of profound importance. The works of travelers along each frontier from colonial days onward describe certain common traits, and these traits have, while softening down, still persisted as survivals in the place of their origin, even when a higher social organization succeeded. The result is that to the frontier the American intellect owes its striking characteristics. That coarseness and strength combined with acuteness and inquisitiveness; that practical, inventive turn of mind, quick to find expedients; that masterful grasp of material things, lacking in the artistic but powerful to effect great ends; that restless, nervous energy; that dominant individualism, working for good and for evil, and withal that buoyancy and exuberance which comes with freedom — these are traits of the frontier, or traits called out elsewhere because of the existence of the frontier. Since the days when the fleet of Columbus sailed into the waters of the New World, America has been another name for opportunity, and the people of the United States have taken their tone from the incessant expansion which has not only been open but has even been forced upon them. He would be a rash prophet who should assert that the expansive character of American life has now entirely ceased. Movement has been its dominant fact, and, unless this training has no effect upon a people, the American energy will continually demand a wider field for its exercise. But never again will such gifts of free land offer themselves. For a moment, at the frontier, the bonds of custom are broken and unrestraint is triumphant. There is not *tabula rasa*. The stubborn American environment is there with its imperious summons to accept its conditions; the inherited ways of doing things are also there; and yet, in spite of environment, and in spite of custom, each frontier did indeed furnish a new field of opportunity, a gate of escape from the bondage of the past; and freshness, and confidence, and scorn of older society, impatience of its restraints and its ideas, and indifference to its lessons, have accompanied the frontier. What the Mediterranean Sea was to the Greeks, breaking the bond of custom, offering new experiences, calling out new institutions and activities, that, and more, the ever retreating frontier has been to the United States directly, and to the nations of Europe more remotely. And now, four centuries from the discovery of America, at the end of a hundred years of life under the Constitution, the frontier has gone, and with its going has closed the first period of American history.

6

Historical Interpretation in the United States*

From *An Economic Interpretation of the Constitution of the United States*, Chapter 1

Charles Beard

Through his controversial writings on the Constitution, the Civil War, and American foreign policy during Franklin Roosevelt's presidency, Charles Beard (1874–1948) established his reputation as a maverick in the disciplines of political science and history. He completed his doctorate in political science at Columbia University in 1904 and held professorships there and at several other universities during his career. A prolific author, his most important works included *An Economic Interpretation of the Constitution of the United States* (1913); *Rise of American Civilization* (1927), coauthored with his wife Mary; and *President Roosevelt and the Coming of War, 1941* (1948). In the following passage, reminiscent of the "muckraking" of early progressive writers, Beard asserts that the personal economic interest of the framers and ratifiers of the Constitution was their most important motive for action.

In the juristic view, the Constitution is not only the work of the whole people, but it also bears in it no traces of the party conflict from which it emerged. Take, for example, any of the traditional legal definitions of the Constitution; Miller's will suffice: "A constitution, in the American sense of the word, is any instrument by which the fundamental powers of the government are established, limited, and defined, and by which these powers are distributed among the several departments for their more safe and useful exercise, for the benefit of the body politic. . . . It is not, however, the origin of

* Editors' Note: Charles Beard, *An Economic Interpretation of the Constitution of the United States* (New York: The Macmillan Company, 1913), 11–18. Excerpt. The author's footnotes have been omitted.

private rights, nor the foundation of laws. It is not the cause, but the consequence of personal and political freedom. It declares those natural and fundamental rights of individuals, for the security and common enjoyment of
which governments are established."

Nowhere in the commentaries is there any evidence of the fact that the
rules of our fundamental law are designed to protect any class in its rights, or
secure the property of one group against the assaults of another. "The Constitution," declares Bancroft, "establishes nothing that interferes with equality and individuality. It knows nothing of differences by descent, or opinions,
of favored classes, or legalized religion, or the political power of property. It
leaves the individual along-side of the individual. . . . As the sea is made up
of drops, American society is composed of separate, free, and constantly
moving atoms, ever in reciprocal action . . . so that the institutions and laws
of the country rise out of the masses of individual thought, which, like the waters of the ocean, are rolling evermore."

In turning from the vague phraseology of Bancroft to an economic interpretation of constitutional history, it is necessary to realize at the outset that
law is not an abstract thing, a printed page, a volume of statutes, a statement
by a judge. So far as it becomes of any consequence to the observer it must
take on a real form; it must govern actions; it must determine positive relations between men; it must prescribe processes and juxtapositions. A statute
may be on the books for an age, but unless, under its provisions, a determi-
nate arrangement of human relations is brought about or maintained, it exists
only in the imagination. Separated from the social and economic fabric by
which it is, in part, conditioned and which, in turn, it helps to condition, it has
no reality.

Now, most of the law (except the elemental law of community defence) is
concerned with the property relations of men, which reduced to their simple
terms mean the processes by which the ownership of concrete forms of property is determined or passes from one person to another. As society becomes
more settled and industrial in character, mere defence against violence (a very
considerable portion of which originates in forcible attempts to change the
ownership of property) becomes of relatively less importance; and property
relations increase in complexity and subtlety.

But it may be said that constitutional law is a peculiar branch of the law;
that it is not concerned primarily with property or with property relations, but
with organs of government, the suffrage, administration. The superficiality of
this view becomes apparent at a second glance. Inasmuch as the primary object of a government, beyond the mere repression of physical violence, is the
making of the rules which determine the property relations of members of society, the dominant classes whose rights are thus to be determined must per-

force obtain from the government such rules as are consonant with the larger interests necessary to the continuance of their economic processes, or they must themselves control the organs of government. In a stable despotism the former takes place; under any other system of government, where political power is shared by any portion of the population, the methods and nature of this control become the problem of prime importance—in fact, the fundamental problem in constitutional law. The social structure by which one type of legislation is secured and another prevented—that is, the constitution—is a secondary or derivative feature arising from the nature of the economic groups seeking positive action and negative restraint.

In what has just been said there is nothing new to scholars who have given any attention to European writings on jurisprudence. It is based in the first instance on the doctrine advanced by Jhering that law does not "grow," but is, in fact, "made"—adapted to precise interests which may be objectively determined. It was not original with Jhering. Long before he worked out the concept in his epoch-making book, *Der Zweck im Recht*, Lassalle had set it forth in his elaborate *Das System der erworbenen Rechte*, and long before Lassalle had thought it through, our own Madison had formulated it, after the most wide-reaching researches in history and politics.

In fact, the inquiry which follows is based upon the political science of James Madison, the father of the Constitution and later President of the Union he had done so much to create. This political science runs through all of his really serious writings and is formulated in its most precise fashion in *The Federalist* as follows: "The diversity in the faculties of men, from which the rights of property originate, is not less an insuperable obstacle to a uniformity of interests. The protection of these faculties is the first object of government. From the protection of different and unequal faculties of acquiring property, the possession of different degrees and kinds of property immediately results; and from the influence of these on the sentiments and views of the respective proprietors, ensues a division of society into different interests and parties. . . . The most common and durable source of factions has been the various and unequal distribution of property. Those who hold and those who are without property have ever formed distinct interests in society. Those who are creditors, and those who are debtors, fall under a like discrimination. A landed interest, a manufacturing interest, a mercantile interest, a moneyed interest, with many lesser interests, grow up of necessity in civilized nations and divide them into different classes, actuated by different sentiments and views. The regulation of these various and interfering interests forms the principal task of modern legislation, and involves the spirit of party and faction in the necessary and ordinary operations of the government."

Here we have a masterly statement of the theory of economic determinism in politics. Different degrees and kinds of property inevitably exist in modern society; party doctrines and "principles" originate in the sentiments and views which the possession of various kinds of property creates in the minds of he possessors; class and group divisions based on property lie at the basis of modern government; and politics and constitutional law are inevitably a reflex of these contending interests. Those who are inclined to repudiate the hypothesis of economic determinism as a European importation must, therefore, revise their views, on learning that one of the earliest, and certainly one of the clearest, statements of it came from a profound student of politics who sat in the Convention that framed our fundamental law.

. . .

The requirements for an economic interpretation of the formation and adoption of the Constitution may be stated in a hypothetical proposition which, although it cannot be verified absolutely from ascertainable data, will at once illustrate the problem and furnish a guide to research and generalization.

It will be admitted without controversy that the Constitution was the creation of a certain number of men, and it was opposed by a certain number of men. Now, if it were possible to have an economic biography of all those connected with its framing and adoption,—perhaps about 160,000 men altogether,—the materials for scientific analysis and classification would be available. Such an economic biography would include a list of the real and personal property owned by all of these men and their families: lands and houses, with incumbrances, money at interest, slaves, capital invested in shipping and manufacturing, and in state and continental securities.

Suppose it could be shown from the classification of the men who supported and opposed the Constitution that there was no line of property division at all; that is, that men owning substantially the same amounts of the same kinds of property were equally divided on the matter of adoption or rejection—it would then become apparent that the Constitution had no ascertainable relation to economic groups or classes, but was the product of some abstract causes remote from the chief business of life—gaining a livelihood.

Suppose, on the other hand, that substantially all of the merchants, money lenders, security holders, manufacturers, shippers, capitalists, and financiers and their professional associates are to be found on one side in support of the Constitution and that substantially all or the major portion of the opposition came from the non-slaveholding farmers and the debtors—would it not be pretty conclusively demonstrated that our fundamental law was not the product of an abstraction known as "the whole people," but of a group of economic interests which must have expected beneficial results from its adoption? Obviously all the facts here desired cannot be discovered, but the data presented in the following chapters bear out the latter hypothesis, and thus a reasonable presumption in favor of the theory is created.

Of course, it may be shown (and perhaps can be shown) that the farmers and debtors who opposed the Constitution were, in fact, benefited by the general improvement which resulted from its adoption. It may likewise be shown, to take an extreme case, that the English nation derived immense advantages from the Norman Conquest and the orderly administrative processes which were introduced, as it undoubtedly did; nevertheless, it does not follow that the vague thing known as "the advancement of general welfare" or some abstraction known as "justice" was the immediate, guiding purpose of the leaders in either of these great historic changes. The point is, that the direct, impelling motive in both cases was the economic advantages which the beneficiaries expected would accrue to themselves first, from their action. Further than this, economic interpretation cannot go. It may be that some larger world-process is working through each series of historical events; but ultimate causes lie beyond our horizon.

III

SOCIAL JUSTICE, SOCIAL GOSPEL, AND EDUCATION

7

Subjective Necessity for Social Settlements*

From *Twenty Years at Hull-House*, Chapter 6

Jane Addams

A progressive leader of the social justice movement in America, Jane Addams (1860–1935) is remembered chiefly for her establishment of Hull-House in Chicago, a settlement house modeled partly on Toynbee Hall in London and devoted to poor relief and aid to urban immigrants. While much of her time was spent at Hull-House, Addams took an active role in securing progressive legislation, including the Child Labor Law of 1903. She actively campaigned for Theodore Roosevelt's Progressive ticket in 1912 and shared the Nobel Peace Prize in 1931. Though she published a number of works on political thought and social reform, including *Democracy and Social Ethics* (1902) and *The Spirit of Youth and the City Streets* (1909), her best-known work remains *Twenty Years at Hull-House* (1910). The following selection was originally delivered as an address at Plymouth, Massachusetts, in 1892. Addams calls for a renewed effort to unite the purposes of the Settlement Movement with the social teachings of the early Christian Church.

This paper is an attempt to analyze the motives which underlie a movement based, not only upon conviction, but upon genuine emotion, wherever educated young people are seeking an outlet for that sentiment of universal brotherhood, which the best spirit of our times is forcing from an emotion into a motive. These young people accomplish little toward the solution of this social problem, and bear the brunt of being cultivated into unnourished, oversensitive lives. They have been shut off from the common labor by which

* Editors' Note: Jane Addams, *Twenty Years at Hull-House* (New York: MacMillan, 1910), 91–100. Excerpt.

they live which is a great source of moral and physical health. They feel a fatal want of harmony between their theory and their lives, a lack of coördination between thought and action. I think it is hard for us to realize how seriously many of them are taking to the notion of human brotherhood, how eagerly they long to give tangible expression to the democratic ideal. These young men and women, longing to socialize their democracy, are animated by certain hopes which may be thus loosely formulated; that if in a democratic country nothing can be permanently achieved save through the masses of the people, it will be impossible to establish a higher political life than the people themselves crave; that it is difficult to see how the notion of a higher civic life can be fostered save through common intercourse; that the blessings which we associate with a life of refinement and cultivation can be made universal and must be made universal if they are to be permanent; that the good we secure for ourselves is precarious and uncertain, is floating in mid-air, until it is secured for all of us and incorporated into our common life. It is easier to state these hopes than to formulate the line of motives, which I believe to constitute the trend of the subjective pressure toward the Settlement. There is something primordial about these motives, but I am perhaps overbold in designating them as a great desire to share the race life. We all bear traces of the starvation struggle which for so long made up the life of the race. Our very organism holds memories and glimpses of that long life of our ancestors which still goes on among so many of our contemporaries. Nothing so deadens the sympathies and shrivels the power of enjoyment, as the persistent keeping away from the great opportunities for helpfulness and a continual ignoring of the starvation struggle which makes up the life of at least half the race. To shut one's self away from that half of the race life is to shut one's self away from the most vital part of it; it is to live out but half the humanity to which we have been born heir and to use but half our faculties. We have all had longings for a fuller life which should include the use of these faculties. These longings are the physical complement of the "Intimations of Immortality," on which no ode has yet been written. To portray these would be the work of a poet, and it is hazardous for any but a poet to attempt it.

You may remember the forlorn feeling which occasionally seizes you when you arrive early in the morning a stranger in a great city: the stream of laboring people goes past you as you gaze through the plate-glass window of your hotel; you see hard working men lifting great burdens; you hear the driving and jostling of huge carts and your heart sinks with a sudden sense of futility. The door opens behind you and you turn to the man who brings you in your breakfast with a quick sense of human fellowship. You find yourself praying that you may never lose your hold on it all. A more poetic prayer would be that the great mother breasts of our common humanity, with its labor and suffering and its homely comforts, may never be withheld from you. You turn helplessly to the waiter and feel that it would be almost grotesque to claim from him the sympathy you crave because civilization has placed you apart, but you resent your position with a sudden sense of snobbery. Literature is full of portrayal of these glimpses: they come to shipwrecked men on rafts; they overcome the differences of an incongruous multitude when in the presence of a great danger or when moved by a common enthusiasm. They are not, however, confined to such moments, and if we were in the habit of telling them to each other, the recital would be as long as the tales of children are, when they sit down on the green grass and confide to each other how many times they have remembered that they lived once before. If these childish tales are the stirring of inherited impressions, just so surely is the other the striving of inherited powers.

"It is true that there is nothing after disease, indigence and a sense of guilt, so fatal to health and to life itself as the want of a proper outlet for active faculties." I have seen young girls suffer and grow sensibly lowered in vitality in the first years after they leave school. In our attempt then to give a girl pleasure and freedom from care we succeed, for the most part, in making her pitifully miserable. She finds "life" so different from what she expected it to be. She is besotted with innocent little ambitions, and does not understand this apparent waste of herself, this elaborate preparation, if no work is provided for her. There is a heritage of noble obligation which young people accept and long to perpetuate. The desire for action, the wish to right wrong and alleviate suffering haunts them daily. Society smiles at it indulgently instead of making it of value to itself. The wrong to them begins even farther back, when we restrain the first childish desires for "doing good" and tell them that they must wait until they are older and better fitted. We intimate that social obligation begins at a fixed date, forgetting that it begins with birth itself. We treat them as children who, with strong-growing limbs, are allowed to use their legs but not their arms, or whose legs are daily carefully exercised that after a while their arms may be put to high use. We do this in spite of the protest of the best educators, Locke and Pestalozzi. We are fortunate in the meantime if their unused members do not weaken and disappear. They do sometimes. There are a few girls who, by the time they are "educated," forget their old childish desires to help the world and to play with poor little girls "who haven't playthings." Parents are often inconsistent: they deliberately expose their daughters to knowledge of the distress in the world; they send them to hear missionary addresses on famines in India and China; they accompany them to lectures on the suffering in Siberia; they agitate together over the forgotten region of East London. In addition to this, from babyhood the altruistic tendencies of these daughters are persistently cultivated. They are taught to be self-forgetting and self-sacrificing, to consider the good of the whole before the good of the ego. But when all this information and culture show results, when the daughter comes back from college and begins to recognize her social claim to the "submerged tenth," and to evince a disposition to fulfill it, the family claim is strenuously asserted; she is told that she is unjustified, ill-advised in her efforts. If she persists, the family too often are injured and unhappy unless the efforts are called missionary and the religious zeal of the family carry them over their sense of abuse. When this zeal does not exist, the result is perplexing. It is a curious violation of what we would fain believe a fundamental law—that the final return of the deed is upon the head of the doer. The deed is that of exclusiveness and caution, but the return, instead of falling upon the head of the exclusive and cautious, falls upon a young head full of generous and unselfish plans. The girl loses something vital out of her life to which she is entitled. She is restricted and unhappy; her elders, meanwhile, are unconscious of the situation and we have all the elements of a tragedy.

We have in America a fast-growing number of cultivated young people who have no recognized outlet for their active faculties. They hear constantly of the great social maladjustment, but no way is provided for them to change it, and their uselessness hangs about them heavily. Huxley declares that the sense of uselessness is the severest shock which the human system can sustain, and that if persistently sustained, it results in atrophy of function. These young people have had advantages of college, of European travel, and of economic study, but they are sustaining this shock of inaction. They have pet phrases, and they tell you that the things that make us all alike are stronger than the things that make us different. They say that all men are united by needs and sympathies far more permanent and radical than anything that temporarily divides them and sets them in opposition to each other. If they affect art, they say that the decay in artistic expression is due to the decay in ethics, that art when shut away from the human interests and from the great mass of humanity is self-destructive. They tell their elders with all the bitterness of youth that if they expect success from them in business or politics or in whatever lines their ambition for them has run, they must let them consult all of humanity; that they must let them find out what the people want and how they want it. It is only the stronger young people, however, who formulate this. Many of them dissipate their energies in so-called enjoyment. Others not content with that, go on studying and go back to college for their second degrees; not that they are especially fond of study, but because they want something definite to do, and their powers have been trained in the direction of mental accumulation. Many are buried beneath this mental accumulation with lowered vitality and discontent. Walter Besant says they have had the vision that

Peter had when he saw the great sheet let down from heaven, wherein was neither clean nor unclean. He calls it the sense of humanity. It is not philanthropy nor benevolence, but a thing fuller and wider than either of these.

This young life, so sincere in its emotion and good phrases and yet so undirected, seems to me as pitiful as the other great mass of destitute lives. One is supplementary to the other, and some method of communication can surely be devised. Mr. Barnett, who urged the first Settlement,—Toynbee Hall, in East London,—recognized this need of outlet for the young men of Oxford and Cambridge, and hoped that the Settlement would supply the communication. It is easy to see why the Settlement movement originated in England, where the years of education are more constrained and definite than they are here, where class distinctions are more rigid. The necessity of it was greater there, but we are fast feeling the pressure of the need and meeting the necessity for Settlements in America. Our young people feel nervously the need of putting theory into action, and respond quickly to the Settlement form of activity.

Other motives which I believe make toward the Settlement are the result of a certain renaissance going forward in Christianity. The impulse to share the lives of the poor, the desire to make social service, irrespective of propaganda, express the spirit of Christ, is as old as Christianity itself. We have no proof from the records themselves that the early Roman Christians, who strained their simple art to the point of grotesqueness in their eagerness to record a "good news" on the walls of the catacombs, considered this good news a religion. Jesus had no set of truths labeled Religious. On the contrary, his doctrine was that all truth is one, that the appropriation of it is freedom. His teaching had no dogma to mark it off from truth and action in general. He himself called it a revelation—a life. These early Roman Christians received the Gospel message, a command to love all men, with a certain joyous simplicity. The image of the Good Shepherd is blithe and gay beyond the gentlest shepherd of Greek mythology; the hart no longer pants, but rushes to the water brooks. The Christians looked for the continuous revelation, but believed what Jesus said, that this revelation, to be retained and made manifest, must be put into terms of action; that action is the only medium man has for receiving and appropriating truth; that the doctrine must be known through the will.

That Christianity has to be revealed and embodied in the line of social progress is a corollary to the simple proposition, that man's action is found in his social relationships in the way in which he connects with his fellows; that his motives for action are the zeal and affection with which he regards his fellows. By this simple process was created a deep enthusiasm for humanity, which regarded man as at once the organ and the object of revelation; and by this process came about the wonderful fellowship, the true democracy of the early Church, that so captivates the imagination. The early Christians were preeminently nonresistant. They believed in love as a cosmic force. There was no iconoclasm during the minor peace of the Church. They did not yet denounce nor tear down temples, nor preach the end of the world. They grew to a mighty number, but it never occurred to them, either in their weakness or in their strength, to regard other men for an instant as their foes or as aliens. The spectacle of the Christians loving all men was the most astounding Rome had ever seen. They were eager to sacrifice themselves for the weak, for children, and for the aged; they identified themselves with slaves and did not avoid the plague; they longed to share the common lot that they might receive the constant revelation. It was a new treasure which the early Christians added to the sum of all treasures, a joy hitherto unknown in the world—the joy of finding the Christ which lieth in each man, but which no man can unfold save in fellowship. A happiness ranging from the heroic to the pastoral enveloped them. They were to possess a revelation as long as life had new meaning to unfold, new action to propose.

I believe that there is a distinct turning among many young men and women toward this simple acceptance of Christ's message. They resent the assumption that Christianity is a set of ideas which belong to the religious consciousness, whatever that may be. They insist that it cannot be proclaimed and instituted apart from the social life of the community and that it must seek a simple and natural expression in the social organism itself. The Settlement movement is only one manifestation of that wider humanitarian movement which throughout Christendom, but preeminently in England, is endeavoring to embody itself, not in a sect, but in society itself.

I believe that this turning, this renaissance of the early Christian humanitarianism, is going on in America, in Chicago, if you please, without leaders who write or philosophize, without much speaking, but with a bent to express in social service and in terms of action the spirit of Christ. Certain it is that spiritual force is found in the Settlement movement, and it is also true that this force must be evoked and must be called into play before the success of any Settlement is assured. There must be the overmastering belief that all that is noblest in life is common to men as men, in order to accentuate the likenesses and ignore the differences which are found among the people whom the Settlement constantly brings into juxtaposition. It may be true, as the Positivists insist, that the very religious fervor of man can be turned into love for his race, and his desire for a future life into content to live in the echo of his deeds; Paul's formula of seeking for the Christ which lieth in each man and founding our likenesses on him, seems a simpler formula to many of us.

In a thousand voices singing the Hallelujah Chorus in Handel's "Messiah," it is possible to distinguish the leading voices, but the differences of training and cultivation between them and the voices of the chorus, are lost in the unity of purpose and in the fact that they are all human voices lifted by a high motive. This is a weak illustration of what a Settlement attempts to do. It aims, in a measure, to develop whatever of social life its neighborhood may afford, to focus and give form to that life, to bring to bear upon it the results of cultivation and training; but it receives in exchange for the music of isolated voices the volume and strength of the chorus. It is quite impossible for me to say in what proportion or degree the subjective necessity which led to the opening of Hull-House combined the three trends: first, the desire to interpret democracy in social terms; secondly, the impulse beating at the very source of our lives, urging us to aid in the race progress; and, thirdly, the Christian movement toward humanitarianism. It is difficult to analyze a living thing; the analysis is at best imperfect. Many more motives may blend with the three trends; possibly the desire for a new form of social success due to the nicety of imagination, which refuses worldly pleasures unmixed with the joys of self-sacrifice; possibly a love of approbation, so vast that it is not content with the treble clapping of delicate hands, but wishes also to hear the bass notes from toughened palms, may mingle with these.

The Settlement, then, is an experimental effort to aid in the solution of the social and industrial problems which are engendered by the modern conditions of life in a great city. It insists that these problems are not confined to any one portion of a city. It is an attempt to relieve, at the same time, the overaccumulation at one end of society and the destitution at the other; but it assumes that this overaccumulation and destitution is most sorely felt in the things that pertain to social and educational advantages. From its very nature it can stand for no political or social propaganda. It must, in a sense, give the warm welcome of an inn to all such propaganda, if perchance one of them be found an angel. The one thing to be dreaded in the Settlement is that it lose its flexibility, its power of quick adaptation, its readiness to change its methods as its environment may demand. It must be open to conviction and must have a deep and abiding sense of tolerance. It must be hospitable and ready for experiment. It should demand from its residents a scientific patience in the accumulation of facts and the steady holding of their sympathies as one of the best instruments for that accumulation. It must be grounded in a philosophy whose foundation is on the solidarity of the human race, a philosophy which will not waver when the race happens to be represented by a drunken woman or an idiot boy. Its residents must be emptied of all conceit of opinion and all self-assertion, and ready to arouse and interpret the public opinion of their neighborhood. They must be content to live quietly side by side with their neighbors, until they grow into a sense of relationship and mutual interests. Their neighbors are held apart by differences of race and language which the residents can more easily overcome. They are bound to see the needs of their neighborhood as a whole, to furnish data for legislation, and to use their influence to secure it. In short, residents are pledged to devote themselves to the duties of good citizenship and to the arousing of the social energies which too largely lie dormant in every neighborhood given over to industrialism. They are bound to regard the entire life of their city as organic, to make an effort to unify it, and to protest against its over-differentiation.

It is always easy to make all philosophy point one particular moral and all history adorn one particular tale; but I may be forgiven the reminder that the best speculative philosophy sets forth the solidarity of the human race; that the highest moralists have taught that without the advance and improvement of the whole, no man can hope for any lasting improvement in his own moral or material individual condition; and that the subjective necessity for Social Settlements is therefore identical with that necessity, which urges us on toward social and individual salvation.

8

Social Christianity and Personal Religion*

From *Christianizing the Social Order,* Part II, Chapter 6

Walter Rauschenbusch

Beginning in the 1880s and lasting through the First World War, the Social Gospel movement was the theological and institutional response of liberal evangelical Protestantism to the challenge brought forth by evolutionary science. The Baptist minister Walter Rauschenbusch (1861–1918) was, more than any other figure, the theologian of Social Gospel. Heavily influenced by his experience as a pastor in New York City's Hell's Kitchen, Rauschenbusch advocated Christian socialism as the means for achieving the kingdom of God here on earth. In the following selection from *Christianizing the Social Order* (1912), he argues that traditional religion was too individualized—selfishly emphasizing individual salvation in the next life, instead of salvation in this life achieved through social action.

We who know personal religion by experience know that there is nothing on earth to compare with the moral force exerted by it. It has demonstrated its social efficiency in our own lives. It was personal religion which first set us our tasks of service in youth, and which now holds us to them when our body droops and our spirit flags. Religion can turn diffident, humble men like Shaftesbury into invincible champions of the poor. All social movements would gain immensely in enthusiasm, persuasiveness, and wisdom, if the hearts of their advocates were cleansed and warmed by religious faith. Even those who know religious power only by observation on others will concede that.

---

* Editors' Note: Walter Rauschenbusch, *Christianizing the Social Order* (New York: The Macmillan Company, 1912), 103–13, 120–22. Excerpt. The author's footnotes have been omitted.

But will the reënforcement work the other way, also? Religion strengthens the social spirit; will the social spirit strengthen personal religion? When a minister gets hot about child labor and wage slavery, is he not apt to get cold about prayer meetings and evangelistic efforts? When young women become interested in social work, do they not often lose their taste for the culture of the spiritual life and the peace of religious meditation? A hot breakfast is an event devoutly to be desired, but is it wise to chop up your precious old set of colonial furniture to cook the breakfast? Would the reënforcement of the social spirit be worth while if we lost our personal religion in the process?

If this is indeed the alternative, we are in a tragic situation, compelled to choose between social righteousness and communion with God.

Personal religion has a supreme value for its own sake not merely as a feeder of social morality, but as the highest unfolding of life itself, as the blossoming of our spiritual nature. Spiritual regeneration is the most important fact in any life history. A living experience of God is the crowning knowledge attainable to a human mind. Each one of us needs the redemptive power of religion for his own sake, for on the tiny stage of the human soul all the vast world tragedy of good and evil is reënacted. In the best social order that is conceivable men will still smolder with lust and ambition, and be lashed by hate and jealousy as with the whip of a slave driver. No material comfort and plenty can satisfy the restless soul in us and give us peace with ourselves. All who have made test of it agree that religion alone holds the key to the ultimate meaning of life, and each of us must find his way into the inner mysteries alone. The day will come when all life on this planet will be extinct, and what meaning will our social evolution have had if that is all? Religion is eternal life in the midst of time and transcending time. The explanations of religion have often been the worst possible, God knows, but the fact of religion is the biggest thing there is.

If, therefore, our personal religious life is likely to be sapped by our devotion to social work, it would be a calamity second to none. But is it really likely that this will happen? The great aim underlying the whole social movement is the creation of a free, just, and brotherly social order. This is the greatest moral task conceivable. Its accomplishment is the manifest will of God for this generation. Every Christian motive is calling us to it. If it is left undone, millions of lives will be condemned to a deepening moral degradation and to spiritual starvation. Does it look probable that we shall lose our contact with God if we plunge too deeply into this work? Does it stand to reason that we shall go astray from Jesus Christ if we engage in the unequal conflict with organized wrong? What kind of "spirituality" is it which is likely to get hurt by being put to work for justice and our fellow-men?

Some of the anxiety about personal religion is due to a subtle lack of faith in religion. Men think it is a fragile thing that will break up and vanish when the customs and formulas which have hitherto incased and protected it are broken and cast aside. Most of us have known religion under one form, and we suppose it can have no other. But religion is the life of God in the soul of man, and is God really so fragile? Will the tongue of fire sputter and go out unless we shelter it under a bushel? Let the winds of God roar through it, and watch it! Religion unites a great variability of form with an amazing constancy of power. The Protestant Reformation changed the entire outward complexion of religion in the nations of northern Europe. All the most characteristic forms in which Christianity had expressed itself and by which its strength had hitherto been gauged were swept away. No pope, no priest, no monk, no mass, no confessional, no rosary, no saints, no images, no processions, no pilgrimages, no indulgences! It was a clean sweep. What was left of religion? Religion itself! At least your Puritans and Huguenots seemed to think they had personal religion; more, in fact, than ever before. Catholics thought it was the destruction of personal religion; really it was the rise of a new type of religion. In the same way the social Christianity of to-day is not a dilution of personal religion, but a new form of experimental Christianity, and its religious testimony will have to be heard henceforth when "the varieties of religious experience" are described.

Nevertheless, conservative Christian men are not frightened by their own imaginings when they fear that the progress of the social interest will mean a receding of personal religion. They usually have definite cases in mind in which that seemed to be the effect, and it is well worth while to examine these more closely.

In the first place, personal religion collapses with some individuals, because in their case it had long been growing hollow and thin. Not all who begin the study of music or poetry in youth remain lovers of art and literature to the end, and not all who begin a religious life in the ardor of youth keep up its emotional intimacy as life goes on. Take any group of one hundred religious people, laymen or ministers, and it is a safe guess that in a considerable fraction of them the fire of vital religion is merely flickering in the ashes. As long as their life goes on in the accustomed way, they maintain their religious connections and expressions, and so do sincerely, but if they move to another part of the country, or if a new interest turns their minds forcibly in some other direction, the frayed bond parts and they turn from their Church and religion. If it is the social interest which attracts them, it may seem to them and others that this has extinguished their devotional life. In reality there was little personal religion to lose, and that little would probably have been lost in some other way. This would cover the inner history of some ministers as well as of church members.

In other cases we must recognize that men become apathetic about church activities in which they have been interested, because they have found something better. The Hebrew prophets turned in anger from the sacrificial doings of their people; Jesus turned away from the long prayers of the Pharisees, who were the most pious people of his day; the Reformers repudiated many of the most devout activities of medieval Catholicism. Wherever there is a new awakening of spiritual life, there is a discarding of old religious forms, and it is to the interest of personal religion that there should be. Is there nothing petty, useless, and insipid in the Catholic or Protestant church life of our day from which a soul awakened to larger purposes ought really to turn away? Is it reprehensible if some drop out of a dress parade when they hear the sound of actual fighting just across the hills?

It is also true that in this tremendous awakening and unsettlement some turn away in haste from things which have lasting value. Few men and few movements have such poise that they never overshoot the mark. When the Reformation turned its back on medieval superstition, it also smashed the painted windows of the cathedrals and almost banished art and music from its services. When mystics feel the compelling power of the inner word of God, they are apt to slight the written word. So when religious souls who have been shut away from social ideals and interests and pent up within a fine but contracted religious habitation get the new outlook of the social awakening, it sweeps them away with new enthusiasms. Their life rushes in to fill the empty spaces. Their mind is busy with a religious comprehension of a hundred new facts and problems, and the old questions of personal religion drop out of sight. In such cases we can safely trust to experience to restore the equilibrium. In a number of my younger friends the balancing is now going on. As they work their way in life and realize the real needs of men and the real values of life, they get a new comprehension of the power and preciousness of personal and intimate religion, and they turn back to the old truths of Christianity with a fresh relish and a firmer accent of conviction. We shall see that rediscovery in thousands within a few years. No doubt they are to blame for their temporary one-sidedness, but their blame will have to be shared by generations of religious individualists whose own persistent one-sidedness had distorted the rounded perfection of Christianity and caused the present excessive reaction.

The question takes a wider meaning when we turn to the alienation of entire classes from religion. There is no doubt that in all the industrialized nations of Europe, and in our own country, the working classes are dropping out of connection with their churches and synagogues, and to a large extent are

transferring their devotion to social movements, so that it looks as if the social interest displaced religion. But here, too, we must remember that solid
masses of the population of continental Europe have never had much vital religion to lose. Their religion was taught by rote and performed by rote. It was
gregarious and not personal. Detailed investigations have been made of the
religious thought world of the peasantry or industrial population of limited
districts, and the result always is that the centuries of indoctrination by the
Church have left only a very thin crust of fertile religious conviction and experience behind. This is not strange, for whenever any spontaneous and democratic religion has arisen among the people, the established churches have
done their best to wet-blanket and suppress it, and they have succeeded finely.
When these people cut loose from their churches, they may not be getting
much farther away from God. Usually these unchurched people still have a
strong native instinct for religion, and when the vital issues and convictions
of their own life are lifted into the purer light of Jesus Christ and set on fire
by religious faith, they respond.

A new factor enters the situation when we encounter the influence of "scientific socialism." It is true, the party platform declares that "religion is a
private affair." The saving of souls is the only industry that socialism distinctly relegates to private enterprise. If that meant simply separation of
Church and State, Americans could heartily assent. If it meant that the Socialist Party proposes to be the political organization of the working class for
the attainment of economic ends and to be neutral in all other questions, it
would be prudent tactics. But in practice it means more. The socialism of
continental Europe, taking it by and large, is actively hostile, not only to bad
forms of organized religion, but to religion itself. Churchmen feel that a man
is lost to religion when he joins the Socialist Party, and socialist leaders feel
that a socialist who is still an active Christian is only half baked. When
French and German socialists learn that men trained in the democracy and
vitality of the free churches of England and America combine genuine piety
and ardent devotion to the Socialist Party, it comes to them as a shock of sur-
prise. In May, 1910, about 260 delegates of the English "Brotherhoods" visited Lille in France and were received by the French trades-unionists and socialists with parades and public meetings. The crowds on the streets did not
know what to make of it when they saw the Englishmen marching under the
red flag of socialism and yet bearing banners with the inscriptions: "We represent 500,000 English workmen;" "We proclaim the Fatherhood of God and
the Brotherhood of Man;" "Jesus Christ leads and inspires us." What were
these men, Christians or socialists? They could not be both. The Frenchmen
lost all their bearings when they heard Keir Hardie, the veteran English labor leader and socialist, repudiating clericalism, but glorifying the Gospel

and the spirit of Christ, and declaring that it was Christianity which had made a socialist of him.

The antireligious attitude of continental socialism is comprehensible enough if we study its historical causes dispassionately. Its most active ingredient is anticlericalism. I surmise that if some of us Americans had been in the shoes of these foreign workingmen and had seen the priest from their angle of vision, we should be anticlerical too. But in the old churches religion, the Church, and the priest mean the same thing; you must accept all or reject all. Men do not discriminate when they are hot with ancient wrongs.

Another ingredient in socialist unbelief is modern science and skepticism. Socialists share their irreligion with other radicals. They are unbelievers, not simply because they are socialists, but because they are children for their time. Great masses of upper-class and middle-class people in Europe are just as skeptical and materialistic, though they show no touch of red. Socialists have no monopoly of unbelief.

But in addition to this, materialistic philosophy does come to socialists embodied in their own literature as part of socialist "science." The socialist faith was formulated by its intellectual leaders at a time when naturalism and materialism was the popular philosophy of the intellectuals, and these elements were woven into the dogma of the new movement. Great movements always perpetuate the ideas current at the time when they are in their fluid and formative stage. For instance, some of the dogmas of the Christian Church as still formulated in the terminology of a philosophy that was current in the third and fourth centuries. Calvin worked out a system of thought that is stamped and with his powerful personality and with peculiarities of his age. But after it had once become the dogmatic fighting faith of great organized bodies, it was all handed on as God's own truth. Socialism is the most solid and militant organization since Calvinism, and it is just as dogmatic. Thus we have a tragic fact that the most idealist mass movement of modern times was committed at the outset to a materialistic philosophy with which it had no essential connection, and every individual who comes under its influence and control is liable to be assimilated to its type of thought in religion as well as in economics.

Those who fear the influence of the social interest on personal religion are not, therefore, wholly wrong. In any powerful spiritual movement, even the best, there are yeasty, unsettling forces which may do good in the long run, but harm in the short run. Atheistic socialism may influence the religious life of great classes as deforestation affects a mountain side.

On the other hand, where the new social spirit combines harmoniously with the inherited Christian life, a new type of personal religion is produced which has at least as good a right to existence as any other type. Jesus was not a theological Christian, not a churchman, nor an emotionalist, not an ascetic, nor a contemplative mystic. A mature social Christian comes closer to the likeness of Jesus Christ than any other type.

In religious individualism, even in its sweetest forms, there was a subtle twist of self-seeking which vitiated it Christlikeness. Thomas a Kempis' "Imitation of Christ" and Bunyan's "Pilgrim's Progress" are classical expressions of personal religion, the one Roman Catholic and monastic, the other Protestant and Puritan. In both piety is self-centered. In both we are taught to seek the highest good of the soul by turning away from the world of men. Doubtless the religion of the monastery and of the Puritan community was far more social and human than the theory might indicate. Bunyan seems to have felt by instinct that it was not quite right to have Christian leave his wife and children and neighbors behind to get rid of his burden and reach the heavenly city. So he wrote a sequel to his immortal story in which the rest of the family with several friends set out on the same pilgrimage. This second part is less thrilling, but more wholesomely Christian. There is family life, love-making, and marriage on the way. A social group coöperate in salvation. Bunyan was feeling his way toward social Christianity.

Evangelicalism prides itself on its emphasis on sin and the need of conversion, yet some of the men trained in its teachings do not seem to know the devil when they meet him on the street. The most devastating sins of our age do not look like sins to them. They may have been converted from the world, but they contentedly make their money in the common ways of the world. Social Christianity involves a more trenchant kind of conversion and more effective means of grace. It may teach a more lenient theory of sin, but it gives a far keener eye for the lurking places of concrete and profitable sins. A man who gets the spiritual ideals of social Christianity is really set at odds with "the world" and enlisted in a lifelong fight with organized evil. But no man who casts out devils is against Christ. To fight evil involves a constant affirmation of holiness and hardens the muscles of Christian character better than any religious gymnasium work. To very many Christians of the old type the cross of Christ meant only an expedient in the scheme of redemption, not a law of life for themselves. A man can be an exponent of "the higher life" and never suffer any persecution whatever from the powers that control our sin-ridden social life. On the other hand, if any man takes social Christianity at all seriously, he will certainly encounter opposition and be bruised somehow. Such an experience will throw him back on the comforts of God and make his prayers more than words. When he bears on his own body and soul the marks of the Lord Jesus, the cross will be more than a doctrine to him. It will be a bond uniting him with Christ in a fellowship of redemptive love.

The personal religion created by social Christianity will stand one practical test of true religion which exceeds in value most of the proofs offered by theology: it creates a larger life and the power of growth. Dead religion narrows our freedom, contracts our horizon, limits our sympathies, and dwarfs our stature. Live religion brings a sense of emancipation, the exhilaration of spiritual health, a tenderer affection for all living things, widening thoughts and aims, and a sure conviction of the reality and righteousness of God. Devotion to the Reign of God on earth will do that for a man, and will do it continuously. A self-centered religion reaches the dead line soon. Men get to know the whole scheme of salvation, and henceforth they march up the hill only to march down again. On the contrary, when a man's prime object is not his soul, but the Kingdom of God, he has set his hands to a task that will never end and will always expand. It will make ever larger demands on his intellect, his sympathy, and his practical efficiency. It will work him to the last ounce of his strength. But it will keep him growing.

. . .

Every individual reconstructs his comprehension of life and duty, of the world and of God, as he passes from one period of his development to the next. If he fails to do so, his religion will lose its grasp and control. In the same way humanity must reconstruct its moral and religious synthesis whenever it passes from one era to another. When all other departments of life and thought are silently changing, it is impossible for religion to remain unaffected. Other-worldly religion was the full expression of the highest aspirations of ancient and medieval life. Contemporary philosophy supported it. The Ptolemaic astronomy made it easy to conceive of a heaven localized about the starry firmament, which was only a few miles up. But to-day the whole *Weltanschauung* which supported those religious conceptions has melted away irretrievably. Copernican astronomy, the conviction of the universal and majestic reign of law, the evolutionary conception of the history of this earth and of the race, have made the religious ideas that were the natural denizens of the old world of thought seem like antique survivals to-day, as if a company of Athenians should walk down Broadway in their ancient dress. When Christianity invaded the ancient world, it was a modernist religion contemptuously elbowing aside the worn-out superstitions of heathenism, and the live intellects seized it as an adequate expression of their religious consciousness. To-day the livest intellects have the greatest difficulty in maintaining their connection with it. Many of its defenders are querulously lamenting the growth of unbelief. They stand on a narrowing island amid a growing flood, saving what they can of the wreckage of faith. Is religion dying? Is the giant faith of Christianity tottering to its grave?

Religion is not dying. It is only molting its feathers, as every winged thing must at times. A new springtide is coming. Even now the air is full of mating calls and love songs. Soon there will be a nest in every tree.

As the modern world is finding itself, religion is returning to it in new ways. Philosophy in its most modern forms is tending toward an idealistic conception of the universe, even when it calls itself materialistic. It realizes spirit behind all reality. The new psychology is full of the powers of mysteries of the soul. It is no slight achievement of faith to think of God immanent in the whole vast universe, but those who accomplish that act of faith feel him very near and mysteriously present, pulsating in their own souls in every yearning for truth and love and right. Life once more becomes miraculous; for every event in which we realize God and our soul is a miracle. All history becomes the unfolding of the purpose of the immanent God who is working in the race toward the commonwealth of spiritual liberty and righteousness. History is the sacred workshop of God. There is a presentiment abroad in modern thought that humanity is on the verge of a profound change, and that feeling heralds the fact. We feel that all this wonderful liberation of redemptive energy is working out a truer and divine order in which our race will rise to a new level of existence. But such a higher order can rise out of the present only if superior spiritual forces build and weave it. Thousands of young minds who thought a few years ago that they had turned their back on religion forever are full of awe and a sense of mystery as they watch the actualities of life in this process of upbuilding. By coöperating with God in his work they are realizing God. Religion is insuppressible.

It is true that the social enthusiasm is an unsettling force which may unbalance for a time, break old religious habits and connections, and establish new contacts that are a permanent danger to personal religion. But the way to meet this danger is not to fence out the new social spirit, but to let it fuse with the old religious faith and create a new total that will be completer and more Christian than the old religious individualism at its best. Such a combination brings a triumphant enlargement of life which proves its own value and which none would give up again who has once experienced it. There is so much religion even in nonreligious social work that some who had lost their conscious religion irretrievably have found it again by this new avenue. God has met them while they were at work with him in social redemption, and they have a religion again and a call to a divine ministry. Faith in a new social order is so powerful a breeder of religion that great bodies of men who in theory scorn and repudiate the name of religion, in practice show evidence of possessing some of the most powerful instances and motives of religion. One of the most valuable achievements in the domain of personal religion which is now open to any man is to build up a rounded and harmonious Christian personality in which all the sweetness and intensity of the old religious life shall combine with the breadth, intelligence, and fighting vigor of the social spirit. Every such individuality will reproduce itself in others who are less mature, and so multiply this new species of the genus "Christian."

9

The Socializing of Property*

From *Christianizing the Social Order,*
Part VI, Chapter 3

Walter Rauschenbusch

Walter Rauschenbusch's social salvation required the dismantling of the capitalist system and the individualism in which it was grounded. As he indicates in the following selection, this meant the negation of private rights of property so that property could be directed toward social use.

In the preceding chapter we have called for compensation in case of disablement or death through industrial accident or occupational disease, for pensions in old age, and for the care of working women during the period of maternity. But where is the money to come from for all these new expenditures? Will not taxes become excessive and discourage thrift? Manifestly we cannot increase the public expenditures without increasing the public income. Our American communities are all poor, all in debt, and many are perpetually near the debt limit. They usually have plenty of wealthy people among their citizens, but as communities they have often been threadbare, out at the elbows, and apparently without soap to clean up. There is plenty of property, but it is not available for social purposes. If we want to conserve life, we shall have to resocialize property.

What do we mean by socializing property? If a farmer who has a spring on his land near the road should set up a trough on the road and allow the public the use of the water, he would socialize the spring and be a public benefactor. If a man closed up a vacant lot and refused the boys permission to play

* Editors' Note: Walter Rauschenbusch, *Christianizing the Social Order* (New York: The Macmillan Company, 1912), 419–29. The author's footnotes have been omitted.

ball on it, he would desocialize it. If a Scotch laird forced crofters from the
land and converted it into a game preserve, he would desocialize it. When the
London County Council opened the many small parks to the public, to which
hitherto only a few adjoining property owners had had access, it socialized
their use. When the robber barons along the Rhine levied tribute on the merchants teaming along the road, they partly desocialized the great trade route
of the river valley. When the burghers of the commercial towns bought them
off for a lump sum, they partly resocialized the public highway, and when
they finally razed the barons' castles as nests of social vermin, they socialized
the road more fully. When the Interstate Commerce Commission in 1912
compelled the Express Companies to improve their antiquated service and to
lower their extortionate charges, it partly socialized a great branch of transportation, and when Congress at last established the parcels post, it socialized
the same branch more fully.

By "socializing property" we mean, then, that it is made to serve the public good, either by the service its uses render to the public welfare, or by the
income it brings to the public treasury. In point of fact, however, no important form of property can be entirely withdrawn from public service; human
life is too social in its nature to allow it. If a rich man builds a ten-foot wall
around his estate and admits nobody, the birds will still nest and sing there to
the poorest passer-by, and his trees will produce oxygen that is wafted to the
slum. Socializing property will mean, therefore, that instead of serving the
welfare of a small group directly, and the public welfare only indirectly, it will
be made more directly available for the service of all.

The socializing of property at times becomes of life and death importance
to society when the slow accumulation of great social changes has turned old
rights into present wrongs. That is the present situation in our country. When
our great territory was being settled men took possession of the land, hunted
and fished, cut down the forest, and encroached on no right of society in doing so. In fact, they were effectively socializing the land by using it as their
private property. If they were enterprising enough to use water power for a
dam and mill also, or opened a mine, they were serving the common good.
But as the country fills up and its resources are needed for the use of thousands, the old rights change. Cutting or burning the forest becomes a menace
to far-off farming tracts which are deprived of their rainfall and to cities in the
valleys which are threatened by flood. Defiling the watershed from which
cities draw their water may become more deadly than murder. The modern
wholesale methods of utilizing the natural resources make inroads on the
common wealth of the nation of a wholly different character from formerly.
Fishing with a rod or hand-net is one thing; scooping the whitefish out of the
great lakes by steam power is a very different thing. No one feared the settler

with his axe; a lumber company slashing square miles of timber and replanting none may be a public menace.

Thus the mere expansion of society has caused a shifting of right and wrong in all property questions. Our moral and legal theories about the rights of the individual in using the resources of nature and in operating his tools to get wealth, are based on the assumption of a sparse population and of simple methods of production which we have largely outgrown. What was once legitimate and useful is now becoming a dangerous encroachment on the rights of society. Property rights will have to be resocialized to bring them into accordance with our actual moral relations. If all memory of past property rights were miraculously blotted from our minds overnight, no sane man would think of allotting property as it is now allotted. All would realize that the great necessities of society, our coal and iron mines, our forests, our watersheds and harbor fronts must be owned by society and operated for the common good. But the plain path of justice and good sense is blocked by the property rights brought down from a different past. We can blame no one for holding and defending what he has bought or inherited. But what is society to do? The same question confronted the world when it was emerging from the feudal into the industrial age at the end of the eighteenth century. The rising business class found the world divided up between the Church, the feudal nobles, and the city guilds. It cleared the deck to suit its needs by abrogating old property rights wholesale. Whenever it suited its needs, Capitalism has been the great expropriator *par excellence*. May it not be done by as it did, for it rode into power roughshod, reckless of the suffering it inflicted.

One universal problem of civilization is how to resocialize the land on which our cities stand. Public health and public wealth alike demand its social ownership. The time was when the land on which lower New York now stands was worth a trifle. If it had then been acquired by the community and leased to the citizens at moderate rentals, increasing as the value of the land increased, New York would always have had ample funds for all public needs without raising a dollar of taxes, and it would be incomparably the richest and most sumptuous city in the world. All the graft inevitably fastening on such wealth could not, in the nature of things, have made away with quite so much public property as the private appropriation of the unearned increment has actually sequestered. That the city lands would have been built up under a system of leaseholds is proved by the fact that the lands of the Astors, the Goelets, the Rhinelanders, and of Snug Harbor are well built up. If the land could be Astorized, why could it not have been socialized? England has been owned by a few people; the people had to pay the State taxes and the landlords rent; yet the English nation has grown rich. Would it not have grown richer if the nation had owned the land, and the people had paid their rent to the State and no taxes to anybody?

The question is how to socialize the land now that the enormous social values are in private hands, and to wrong nobody in the doing of it. There would be no wrong if the community decided by law to take any unearned increase of value accruing after a given date; that would leave all past values intact for the present owners. There would be a minimum of suffering if the taxation of land values were gradually increased through a term of ten or twenty years until it came near absorbing the whole annual rental value. If buildings were simultaneously relieved of taxation, the earnings of private thrift would go into private hands, and the results of social growth would go to society. The man that can get no wisdom from the Singletaxers has padlocked his intellect.

The Single Tax would leave the title to the land with the present owners and merely socialize the unearned rental values. But it would be highly desirable for every community to own outright far more land than our communities now own, as a basis for a larger and finer community life, for more spacious public buildings, and for the housing of the poorer classes. Some English cities have bought up their slum districts, torn down the old tenements, and laid out new and splendid streets, at great profit to the public treasury and great detriment to the death rate. When New York laid out Central Park, it seemed like riotous finance, but the park has long ago paid for itself by the increase of taxable values around it. When city planning is going on, why should not the cities themselves get the increased values they create by buying land affected and leasing it under restrictions as to architectural excellence? German cities buy large suburban tracts, lay them out in lots of assorted sizes, fence them, and rent them out as gardens to people who enjoy spending their evenings and Sundays in open-air life, raising flowers and vegetables. As the city grows, the entire tract is laid out for building lots in accordance with plans made long ahead. In several countries taxpayers are allowed to fix their own assessments, but the community has the right to buy the property at the figure they name. There is material for a delicious comedy in the agonies of a clever taxpayer who tries to beat the devil around the stump under these conditions.

The time is coming now when large capital will invest in agricultural lands. Would it be for the public good for a corporation to own a half or a quarter of a State and control the tenant farmers on it? All history answers that any approximation to such a condition would be a peril. If so, this is the time to make it impossible. New Zealand levies a progressive tax on large holdings. Our States and the federal government should keep all the land they still have and henceforth lease it instead of selling. And if the conditions of any land grants have not been fulfilled, they should be revoked. The Conservation

Movement has come too late for the good of our nation, but we still have a remnant of our heritage to hold for our children.

Mines, oil wells, and natural gas wells are specialized forms of land, of the highest importance to an industrialized nation. While mines were small and operated competitively, private ownership was the best way to socialize their products. Now that mines are great social undertakings, and their products are sold at monopoly prices, has private ownership any basis in reason or ethics? The idea that there can be any absolute ownership in a mine, as in a coat, is preposterous. Did the Almighty stock the rocks of Pennsylvania with anthracite for the benefit of a few thousand stockholders, or did he provide for the use of a great nation? God made the coal; the mining companies made the holes in the coal; they have a right to what they made. Mining rights are essentially like franchises; the obligation to render public service is an expressed or implied condition of the grant and the sole moral basis of it. If a corporation uses the gift of the people to charge the same people extortionate prices for the necessaries of life, the action is morally base and forfeits most of the claim to consideration that property owners otherwise have.

Water power, too, a joint product of the sun and the strata of the rocks, is a social possession and should never be alienated outright by the community. The laws governing riparian rights need overhauling. The absurd legal assumption that the beds of rivers, and even lakes, is owned by the abutting property owners, was imported from England, a land of tiny rivers and huge landlords with lawmaking powers. My city of Rochester is cut in two by the Genesee, a river of dangerous floods, with three great falls and a deep gorge within the city limits. The city bears the expense of costly bridges and liability for damages by flood, but it gets no compensating income from the river. The water rights were alienated long ago, and are now mostly held by a single corporation. Even under private ownership the river has helped to make Rochester. If all its possibilities were socialized, the city would become splendid.

The problem of socializing property becomes most acute wherever private ownership has established a virtual monopoly and charges monopoly prices. In that case private ownership has become positively unsocial. "The very purpose of monopoly is to secure unearned income,"[1] and how can such a purpose be either social or moral? The problem with which our nation is now wrestling is how to resocialize monopolistic corporations that refuse to bow their mighty necks under the yoke of public service. We are proceeding at present under the assumption that government inspection and control, publicity and the pressure

---

1. Editors' Note: Rauschenbusch refers here to Richard T. Ely's *Socialism and Social Reform*.

of public opinion, can socialize them. But can it? Is not the form of their organization too exclusive, and the purpose of their profit-making too unsocial,
ever to make them more than forced servants of the common good?

Private property is an indispensable basis of civilization and morality. The
per capita amount of it ought not to lessen; it ought to increase. But for the
present the great ethical need is to reëmphasize and reclaim social property
rights which are forgotten or denied. Society has rights even in the most
purely private property. Neither religion, nor ethics, nor law recognizes such
a thing as an absolute private property right. Religion teaches that all property is a trust and the owner but a steward. Ethics makes the moral title to
property depend on the service the owner renders by means of it. The law can
dispossess me under the right of eminent domain if the community needs my
property. In war the State can commandeer anything I have, even my body.
Private property is historically an offshoot of communal property and exists
by concession and sufferance. The whole institution of private property exists
because it is for the public good that it shall exist. If in any particular it becomes dangerous to the public welfare, it must cease. *Salus reipublicae
summa lex*. Religious teaching can do much to make the partnership of the
community in private property a conscious force in public thought. The doctrine of stewardship must be backed by knowledge of law and history, and become more than an amiable generality.

The right of a man to his home, his clothing, and any simple savings of his
labor is not practically questioned by anybody. The social use of that can easily be controlled by law. It is different with great fortunes. Even if their accumulation is just, their perpetuation is dangerous. The community may allow the man who has collected a great fortune its undisturbed possession
during his lifetime, but the moral claim to it weakens when he tries to govern
it by his will after he is dead and gone. The right to make a will and to have
the community enforce it is historically a recent right, and all governments
limit it. A man cannot do what he will with his own; in America he cannot
completely disinherit his wife, and in Germany his child. The law recognizes
the right of the State to take a share, and a large share, of an estate at death.
A progressive inheritance tax is one of the most approved ways of resocializing large fortunes, and it should be applied far more thoroughly than hitherto,
not only to add to the public income, but to protect the social order.

Every successful effort to better the pay in depressed industries, to shorten
the hours, to increase the comforts and safety of the workers, to provide for
them in case of disablement, and to put a larger proportion of the profits of
business at the service of the working class is a partial socialization of business. The social dividend, which arises through the coöperation of all social
factors in production, is to-day appropriated by limited private groups, and di-

vided among them according to their ability to seize it. The people have lost control of it. How far society will go in coming days in resuming control, no one can now foretell. But it is plain that it must get a far different grip on the social property and social rights involved in so-called private business. A private business that employs thousands of people, uses the natural resources of the nation, enjoys exemptions and privileges at law, and is essential to the welfare of great communities is not a private business. It is public, and the sooner we abandon the fiction that it is private, the better for our good sense.

Finally I want to mention, what logically ought to go first,—the socialization of public money. Taxes are a beneficent social institution; they buy more for us than any other money we spend. But they have been put to very unsocial uses. Conquerors and despots have taxed nations, not in order to have funds for public improvements, but to carry off the swag and consume it in riotous living, which they called regal magnificence. We still have duodecimo kinglets, who use some of our taxes for giving themselves or their courtiers easy jobs or junketing trips. They desocialize the public income. The best way to put a stop to them is to socialize the machinery of government still further by direct nominations, direct legislation, and the recall.

The method of collecting taxes has also been made to accomplish side purposes profitable to private interests. Rome used to farm out the taxes of provinces as we farm out street railway franchises, and the Roman business men who bought the right to collect the taxes used them to collect a great deal more for themselves beside. These were the "publicans" whose underlings appear in the New Testament as persons so detested that it took the religious insight of Jesus to discover any good in them. We have similarly tried to make our system for collecting taxes on imports serve the additional purpose of exempting our business men from the stress of foreign competition, in the hope that they would, of their own free will, socialize the benefits of their "protection" for their workingmen and the public. We are not at present enthusiastic about the results of our generosity, and find it urgently necessary to resocialize our revenue system. The surest way to make our taxation serve public uses only is to collect direct taxes only. Indirect taxes are supposed to be easy to collect because the people do not feel them. In other words, they are a device to hoodwink the people. They are, in fact, an invention of unsocial governments, of an age when Government and the People were not identical, but hostile interests. Indirect taxes are a cover for all kinds of deceptions, and in the end the most costly of all taxes.

The resocializing of property is an essential part of the christianizing of the social order. If we can give back to the community which creates them the unearned ingredients in rent and profit, we shall make commerce and industry honest, and at the same time increase the public wealth available for the protection of life, for the education of the young, and for the enrichment of culture and civilization. If we can resocialize the public property which is now in private possession, we shall democratize industry, secure far greater attention to the problems of public welfare, and win more genuine respect for what is truly private property.

The problem is how to accomplish these very righteous ends without inflicting too much incidental suffering. Some suffering there is bound to be. It is humanly impossible to straighten a crippled limb without pain. We shall have to set over against the possible cost of suffering inflicted by a Christian reorganization of property the far greater suffering that is now inflicted every day and hour by the continuance of ancient wrongs, and the still vaster suffering that will grow out of our sins if we fail now to right them. For "the wages of sin is death," and humanity is so closely bound together that the innocent must weep and die for the sins the dead have done. In his second inaugural Abraham Lincoln said:—

> "Fondly do we hope, devoutly do we pray, that this mighty scourge of war may pass away. Yet if it is God's will that it continue until the wealth piled by bondsmen by two hundred and fifty years of unrequited toil shall be sunk, and until every drop of blood drawn with the lash shall be paid with another drawn with the sword, as was said three thousand years ago, so it must still be said, that 'the judgments of the Lord are true and righteous altogether.'"

10

My Pedagogic Creed*

John Dewey

A professor of philosophy at Columbia University and prolific author of philosophical, educational, and reform treatises, John Dewey (1859–1952) made his greatest contribution to the Progressive Movement through his works on educational theory and reform. Among these, his best-known works are *The School and Society* (1899) and *Democracy and Education* (1916), the latter of which gives the most comprehensive statement of his radical reconstruction of the theory and purposes of education as traditionally understood. Dewey eliminated religious conceptions of reality and substituted complete faith in the democratic ideal realized through state control of education. The following selection is a succinct statement of his philosophy of education.

ARTICLE ONE. WHAT EDUCATION IS

I believe that all education proceeds by the participation of the individual in the social consciousness of the race. This process begins unconsciously almost at birth, and is continually shaping the individual's powers, saturating his consciousness, forming his habits, training his ideas, and arousing his feelings and emotions. Through this unconscious education the individual gradually comes to share in the intellectual and moral resources which humanity has succeeded in getting together. He becomes an inheritor of the funded capital of civilization. The most formal and technical education in the world cannot safely depart from this general process. It can only organize it; or differentiate it in some particular direction.

---

* Editors' Note: John Dewey, "My Pedagogic Creed," *School Journal* 54 (January 1897): 77–80.

I believe that the only true education comes through the stimulation of the child's powers by the demands of the social situations in which he finds himself. Through these demands he is stimulated to act as a member of a unity, to emerge from his original narrowness of action and feeling and to conceive of himself from the standpoint of the welfare of the group to which he belongs. Through the responses which others make to his own activities he comes to know what these mean in social terms. The value which they have is reflected back into them. For instance, through the response which is made to the child's instinctive babblings the child comes to know what those babblings mean; they are transformed into articulate language and thus the child is introduced into the consolidated wealth of ideas and emotions which are now summed up in language.

I believe that this educational process has two sides—one psychological and one sociological; and that neither can be subordinated to the other or neglected without evil results following. Of these two sides, the psychological is the basis. The child's own instincts and powers furnish the material and give the starting point for all education. Save as the efforts of the educator connect with some activity which the child is carrying on of his own initiative independent of the educator, education becomes reduced to a pressure from without. It may, indeed, give certain external results but cannot truly be called educative. Without insight into the psychological structure and activities of the individual, the educative process will, therefore, be haphazard and arbitrary. If it chances to coincide with the child's activity it will get a leverage; if it does not, it will result in friction, or disintegration, or arrest of the child nature.

I believe that knowledge of social conditions, of the present state of civilization, is necessary in order properly to interpret the child's powers. The child has his own instincts and tendencies, but we do not know what these mean until we can translate them into their social equivalents. We must be able to carry them back into a social past and see them as the inheritance of previous race activities. We must also be able to project them into the future to see what their outcome and end will be. In the illustration just used, it is the ability to see in the child's babblings the promise and potency of a future social intercourse and conversation which enables one to deal in the proper way with that instinct.

I believe that the psychological and social sides are organically related and that education cannot be regarded as a compromise between the two, or a superimposition of one upon the other. We are told that the psychological definition of education is barren and formal—that it gives us only the idea of a development of all the mental powers without giving us any idea of the use to which these powers are put. On the other hand, it is urged that the social definition of education, as getting adjusted to civilization, makes of it a forced and external process, and results in subordinating the freedom of the individual to a preconceived social and political status.

I believe each of these objections is true when urged against one side isolated from the other. In order to know what a power really is we must know what its end, use, or function is; and this we cannot know save as we conceive of the individual as active in social relationships. But, on the other hand, the only possible adjustment which we can give to the child under existing conditions, is that which arises through putting him in complete possession of all his powers. With the advent of democracy and modern industrial conditions, it is impossible to foretell definitely just what civilization will be twenty years from now. Hence it is impossible to prepare the child for any precise set of conditions. To prepare him for the future life means to give him command of himself; it means so to train him that he will have the full and ready use of all his capacities; that his eye and ear and hand may be tools ready to command, that his judgment may be capable of grasping the conditions under which it has to work, and the executive forces be trained to act economically and efficiently. It is impossible to reach this sort of adjustment save as constant regard is had to the individual's own powers, tastes, and interests—say, that is, as education is continually converted into psychological terms. In sum, I believe that the individual who is to be educated is a social individual and that society is an organic union of individuals. If we eliminate the social factor from the child we are left only with an abstraction; if we eliminate the individual factor from society, we are left only with an inert and lifeless mass. Education, therefore, must begin with a psychological insight into the child's capacities, interests, and habits. It must be controlled at every point by reference to these same considerations. These powers, interests, and habits must be continually interpreted—we must know what they mean. They must be translated into terms of their social equivalents—into terms of what they are capable of in the way of social service.

ARTICLE TWO. WHAT THE SCHOOL IS

I believe that the school is primarily a social institution. Education being a social process, the school is simply that form of community life in which all those agencies are concentrated that will be most effective in bringing the child to share in the inherited resources of the race, and to use his own powers for social ends.

I believe that education, therefore, is a process of living and not a preparation for future living.

I believe that the school must represent present life—life as real and vital to the child as that which he carries on in the home, in the neighborhood, or on the play-ground.

I believe that education which does not occur through forms of life, forms that are worth living for their own sake, is always a poor substitute for the genuine reality and tends to cramp and to deaden.

I believe that the school, as an institution, should simplify existing social life; should reduce it, as it were, to an embryonic form. Existing life is so complex that the child cannot be brought into contact with it without either confusion or distraction; he is either overwhelmed by multiplicity of activities which are going on, so that he loses his own power of orderly reaction, or he is so stimulated by these various activities that his powers are prematurely called into play and he becomes either unduly specialized or else disintegrated.

I believe that, as such simplified social life, the school life should grow gradually out of the home life; that it should take up and continue the activities with which the child is already familiar in the home.

I believe that it should exhibit these activities to the child, and reproduce them in such ways that the child will gradually learn the meaning of them, and be capable of playing his own part in relation to them.

I believe that this is a psychological necessity, because it is the only way of securing continuity in the child's growth, the only way of giving a background of past experience to the new ideas given in school.

I believe it is also a social necessity because the home is the form of social life in which the child has been nurtured and in connection with which he has had his moral training. It is the business of the school to deepen and extend his sense of the values bound up in his home life.

I believe that much of present education fails because it neglects this fundamental principle of the school as a form of community life. It conceives the school as a place where certain information is to be given, where certain lessons are to be learned, or where certain habits are to be formed. The value of these is conceived as lying largely in the remote future; the child must do these things for the sake of something else he is to do; they are mere preparation. As a result they do not become a part of the life experience of the child and so are not truly educative.

I believe that moral education centres about this conception of the school as a mode of social life, that the best and deepest moral training is precisely that which one gets through having to enter into proper relations with others in a unity of work and thought. The present educational systems, so far as they destroy or neglect this unity, render it difficult or impossible to get any genuine, regular moral training.

I believe that the child should be stimulated and controlled in his work through the life of the community.

I believe that under existing conditions far too much of the stimulus and control proceeds from the teacher, because of neglect of the idea of the school as a form of social life.

I believe that the teacher's place and work in the school is to be interpreted from this same basis. The teacher is not in the school to impose certain ideas or to form certain habits in the child, but is there as a member of the community to select the influences which shall affect the child and to assist him in properly responding to these influences.

I believe that the discipline of the school should proceed from the life of the school as a whole and not directly from the teacher.

I believe that the teacher's business is simply to determine on the basis of larger experience and riper wisdom, how the discipline of life shall come to the child.

I believe that all questions of the grading of the child and his promotion should be determined by reference to the same standard. Examinations are of use only so far as they test the child's fitness for social life and reveal the place in which he can be of most service and where he can receive the most help.

ARTICLE THREE. THE SUBJECT MATTER OF EDUCATION

I believe that the social life of the child is the basis of concentration, or correlation, in all his training or growth. The social life gives the unconscious unity and the background of all his efforts and of all his attainments.

I believe that the subject-matter of the school curriculum should mark a gradual differentiation out of the primitive unconscious unity of social life.

I believe that we violate the child's nature and render difficult the best ethical results, by introducing the child too abruptly to a number of special studies, of reading, writing, geography, etc., out of relation to this social life.

I believe, therefore, that the true centre of correlation of the school subjects is not science, nor literature, nor history, nor geography, but the child's own social activities.

I believe that education cannot be unified in the study of science, or so-called nature study, because apart from human activity, nature itself is not a unity; nature in itself is a number of diverse objects in space and time, and to attempt to make it the centre of work by itself, is to introduce a principle of radiation rather than one of concentration.

I believe that literature is the reflex expression and interpretation of social experience; that hence it must follow upon and not precede such experience.

It, therefore, cannot be made the basis, although it may be made the summary of unification.

I believe once more that history is of educative value in so far as it presents phases of social life and growth. It must be controlled by reference to social life. When taken simply as history it is thrown into the distant past and becomes dead and inert. Taken as the record of man's social life and progress it becomes full of meaning. I believe, however, that it cannot be so taken excepting as the child is also introduced directly into social life.

I believe accordingly that the primary basis of education is in the child's powers at work along the same general constructive lines as those which have brought civilization into being.

I believe that the only way to make the child conscious of his social heritage is to enable him to perform those fundamental types of activity which makes civilization what it is.

I believe, therefore, in the so-called expressive or constructive activities as the centre of correlation.

I believe that this gives the standard for the place of cooking, sewing, manual training, etc., in the school.

I believe that they are not special studies which are to be introduced over and above a lot of others in the way of relaxation or relief, or as additional accomplishments. I believe rather that they represent, as types, fundamental forms of social activity; and that it is possible and desirable that the child's introduction into the more formal subjects of the curriculum be through the medium of these activities.

I believe that the study of science is educational in so far as it brings out the materials and processes which make social life what it is.

I believe that one of the greatest difficulties in the present teaching of science is that the material is presented in purely objective form, or is treated as a new peculiar kind of experience which the child can add to that which he has already had. In reality, science is of value because it gives the ability to interpret and control the experience already had. It should be introduced, not as so much new subject-matter, but as showing the factors already involved in previous experience and as furnishing tools by which that experience can be more easily and effectively regulated.

I believe that at present we lose much of the value of literature and language studies because of our elimination of the social element. Language is almost always treated in the books of pedagogy simply as the expression of thought. It is true that language is a logical instrument, but it is fundamentally and primarily a social instrument. Language is the device for communication; it is the tool through which one individual comes to share the ideas and feelings of others. When treated simply as a way of getting individual information, or as a means of showing off what one has learned, it loses its social motive and end.

I believe that there is, therefore, no succession of studies in the ideal school curriculum. If education is life, all life has, from the outset, a scientific aspect; an aspect of art and culture and an aspect of communication. It cannot, therefore, be true that the proper studies for one grade are mere reading and writing, and that at a later grade, reading, or literature, or science, may be introduced. The progress is not in the succession of studies but in the development of new attitudes towards, and new interests in, experience.

I believe finally, that education must be conceived as a continuing reconstruction of experience; that the process and the goal of education are one and the same thing.

I believe that to set up any end outside of education, as furnishing its goal and standard, is to deprive the educational process of much of its meaning and tends to make us rely upon false and external stimuli in dealing with the child.

ARTICLE FOUR. THE NATURE OF METHOD

I believe that the question of method is ultimately reducible to the question of the order of development of the child's powers and interests. The law for presenting and treating material is the law implicit within the child's own nature. Because this is so I believe the following statements are of supreme importance as determining the spirit in which education is carried on:

1. I believe that the active side precedes the passive in the development of the child nature; that expression comes before conscious impression; that the muscular development precedes the sensory; that movements come before conscious sensations; I believe that consciousness is essentially motor or impulsive; that conscious states tend to project themselves in action.

I believe that the neglect of this principle is the cause of a large part of the waste of time and strength in school work. The child is thrown into a passive, receptive or absorbing attitude. The conditions are such that he is not permitted to follow the law of his nature; the result is friction and waste.

I believe that ideas (intellectual and rational processes) also result from action and devolve for the sake of the better control of action. What we term reason is primarily the law of orderly or effective action. To attempt to develop the reasoning powers, the powers of judgment, without reference to the selection and arrangement of means in action, is the fundamental fallacy in our present methods of dealing with this matter. As a result we present the child with arbitrary symbols. Symbols are a necessity in mental development, but they have their place as tools for economizing effort; presented by themselves they are a mass of meaningless and arbitrary ideas imposed from without.

2. I believe that the image is the great instrument of instruction. What a child gets out of any subject presented to him is simply the images which he himself forms with regard to it.

I believe that if nine-tenths of the energy at present directed towards making the child learn certain things, were spent in seeing to it that the child was forming proper images, the work of instruction would be indefinitely facilitated.

I believe that much of the time and attention now given to the preparation and presentation of lessons might be more wisely and profitably expended in training the child's power of imagery and in seeing to it that he was continually forming definite, vivid, and growing images of the various subjects with which he comes in contact in his experience.

3. I believe that interests are the signs and symptoms of growing power. I believe that they represent dawning capacities. Accordingly the constant and careful observation of interests is of the utmost importance for the educator.

I believe that these interests are to be observed as showing the state of development which the child has reached.

I believe that they prophesy the stage upon which he is about to enter.

I believe that only through the continual and sympathetic observation of childhood's interests can the adult enter into the child's life and see what it is ready for, and upon what material it could work most readily and fruitfully.

I believe that these interests are neither to be humored nor repressed. To repress interest is to substitute the adult for the child, and so to weaken intellectual curiosity and alertness, to suppress initiative, and to deaden interest. To humor the interests is to substitute the transient for the permanent. The interest is always the sign of some power below; the important thing is to discover this power. To humor the interest is to fail to penetrate below the surface and its sure result is to substitute caprice and whim for genuine interest.

4. I believe that the emotions are the reflex of actions.

I believe that to endeavor to stimulate or arouse the emotions apart from their corresponding activities, is to introduce an unhealthy and morbid state of mind.

I believe that if we can only secure right habits of action and thought, with reference to the good, the true, and the beautiful, the emotions will for the most part take care of themselves.

I believe that next to deadness and dullness, formalism and routine, our education is threatened with no greater evil than sentimentalism.

I believe that this sentimentalism is the necessary result of the attempt to divorce feeling from action.

ARTICLE FIVE. THE SCHOOL AND SOCIAL PROGRESS

I believe that education is the fundamental method of social progress and reform.

I believe that all reforms which rest simply upon the enactment of law, or the threatening of certain penalties, or upon changes in mechanical or outward arrangements, are transitory and futile.

I believe that education is a regulation of the process of coming to share in the social consciousness; and that the adjustment of individual activity on the basis of this social consciousness is the only sure method of social reconstruction.

I believe that this conception has due regard for both the individualistic and socialistic ideals. It is duly individual because it recognizes the formation of a certain character as the only genuine basis of right living. It is socialistic because it recognizes that this right character is not to be formed by merely individual precept, example, or exhortation, but rather by the influence of a certain form of institutional or community life upon the individual, and that the social organism through the school, as its organ, may determine ethical results.

I believe that in the ideal school we have the reconciliation of the individualistic and the institutional ideals.

I believe that the community's duty to education is, therefore, its paramount moral duty. By law and punishment, by social agitation and discussion, society can regulate and form itself in a more or less haphazard and chance way. But through education society can formulate its own purposes, can organize its own means and resources, and thus shape itself with definiteness and economy in the direction in which it wishes to move.

I believe that when society once recognizes the possibilities in this direction, and the obligations which these possibilities impose, it is impossible to conceive of the resources of time, attention, and money which will be put at the disposal of the educator.

I believe it is the business of everyone interested in education to insist upon the school as the primary and most effective instrument of social progress and reform in order that society may be awakened to realize what the school stands for, and aroused to the necessity of endowing the educator with sufficient equipment properly to perform his task.

I believe that education thus conceived marks the most perfect and intimate union of science and art conceivable in human experience.

I believe that the art of thus giving shape to human powers and adapting them to social service, is the supreme art; one calling into its service the best of artists; that no insight, sympathy, tact, executive power is too great for such service.

John Dewey

I believe that with the growth of psychological science, giving added insight into individual structure and laws of growth; and with growth of social science, adding to our knowledge of the right organization of individuals, all scientific resources can be utilized for the purposes of education.

I believe that when science and art thus join hands the most commanding motive for human action will be reached; the most genuine springs of human conduct aroused and the best service that human nature is capable of guaranteed.

I believe, finally, that the teacher is engaged, not simply in the training of individuals, but in the formation of the proper social life.

I believe that every teacher should realize the dignity of his calling; that he is a social servant set apart for the maintenance of proper social order and the securing of the right social growth.

I believe that in this way the teacher always is the prophet of the true God and the usherer in of the true kingdom of God.

Father Blakely States the Issue*

Unsigned Editorial in *The New Republic*

Anonymous

Founded in 1914 by Herbert Croly and Walter Lippmann, *The New Republic*
quickly became an important organ of progressive opinion. Like this one, many
of its editorials were unsigned, although most at this time were either written by
Croly himself or, at least, edited and approved by him. The editorialist(s) in this
case take up the cause of greater public intervention in religious education, and
respond, in particular, to the defense of parochial schools in New York made by
a Father Paul Blakely. The editorial provides a concise and strikingly clear example of the way some progressives conceived of church-state relations, of the
role of the state in child rearing and education, and of the new meaning of tol-
eration.

· · ·

The old warfare between church and state, between theology and science,
underlies the struggle in New York. It is the struggle which France fought recently and won, leaving the Papacy anti-French in the war. It is the struggle
so poignant in Massachusetts. It is a struggle which distracts the world of education, a struggle which most people observe, and few discuss. Father
Blakely gives the real reason why the hierarchy resents public criticism. He
has put his finger on the reason why Catholics have resented bitterly what
non-Catholics took as a matter of course. The reason is that lay control of education and philanthropy is opposed by the political tradition of the Church,

---

* Editors' Note: Unsigned editorial, "Father Blakely States the Issue," *The New Republic*, July 29,
1916, 319–20. Excerpt.

and Mayor Mitchel's attempt to regulate private institutions taking public money was treated at once by Catholic leaders as a war of church and state. The enemy, as Father Blakely so plainly says, is the secularizing tendency of modern life. The church has never accepted the American public school. It has fought it with the parochial school, it has never acquiesced in the taxation of Catholics for lay education, and it has persistently tried to secure a political control of school boards. From a like motive it now resists Mayor Mitchel as one who would take God out of the hearts of little children. From its own point of view the church is perfectly right in its antagonism, however unwise the tactics it pursues. The secularization of philanthropy is one of the clear intentions of modern liberals, and though liberals wish to proceed moderately and with all possible fairness they do intend to proceed.

They have begun merely with an attempt to enforce the law and to secure minimum standards of sanitation and treatment. Catholics like Father Blakely know, however, that this is merely the entering wedge in a greater movement to extend public control over education and philanthropy. They know that modern science does not look favorably upon institutional life for normal children. They know that reformers plan to withdraw dependent children who are not defective from institutions and put them into homes where the child can have the advantage of family life and a less mechanical care. Knowing all this, they fight at the drop of the hat, fight even inspection to do away with vermin and bad ventilation and darkness. They fight for the right of the church to mould the child to its own ideals and for the perpetuation of the great vested interest of private institutions.

What Father Blakely calls "modern sociology" is really the beginning of an effort to formulate democracy as a positive ideal. The older theories of democracy were negative, built up to protest against kings, aristocracies, and oppression. Those theories were concerned chiefly in saying what government must not do. But during the nineteenth century popular rule became increasingly a reality, and people came to feel that government is not an alien thing to be limited, but a social instrument to be used. Democracy has been evolving from a protest into a purpose. It is becoming a philosophy of life, no longer protestant but in its own way catholic. To be a democrat to-day is to be something more than a voter. It is to believe in a scale of human values, to have a morality and to think with certain assumptions. "Modern sociologists" are simply men engaged in stating the affirmative faith of democracy.

This has brought about a change in the meaning of tolerance. The older view of eighteenth-century liberalism was that the democratic state must allow every one freedom to practise almost any creed, even though the creed was opposed to freedom. It thought of democracy as a vacuum in which all might compete for place. But twentieth-century democracy believes that the community has certain positive ends to achieve, and if they are to be achieved the community must control the education of the young. It believes that training in scientific habits of mind is fundamental to the progress of democracy. It believes that freedom and tolerance mean the development of independent powers of judgment in the young, not the freedom of older people to impose their dogmas on the young. Democracy claims no right to interfere with worship or opinion, but it does claim the right to develop in every child the capacity for testing its own convictions. It insists that the plasticity of the child shall not be artificially and prematurely hardened into a philosophy of life, but that experimental naturalistic aptitudes shall constitute the true education.

It is this demand of democracy which Father Blakely has in mind when he says that more money should be given to Catholic institutions because "the destiny of immortal souls" may hang upon the endowment. The candid democrat must reply to him that no one has a monopoly on salvation, that there may be other destinies besides those conceived by Father Blakely, and that the power to choose and control destiny is the ambition of democrats educated in an age of science.

IV

LEADERSHIP AND THE AMERICAN PRESIDENCY

12

Leaders of Men*

Woodrow Wilson

In this speech that he delivered on several occasions in 1889 and 1890, Woodrow Wilson lays out what would become the essential principles of modern, democratic leadership: the direct connection of the leader to the people, the leader's use of rhetoric to move men in the mass, and the leader's embodiment of the people's spirit. It was these very qualities that led the American founders to fear the problem of demagoguery, and even Wilson seems to concede such a concern by making a great effort here to distinguish between demagoguery and his conception of leadership.

. . .

That the leader of men must have such sympathetic insight as shall enable him to know quite unerringly the motives which move other men in the mass is of course self-evident; but this insight which he must have is not the Shakespearean insight. It need not pierce the particular secrets of individual men: it need only know what it is that lies waiting to be stirred in the minds and purposes of groups and masses of men. Besides it is not a sympathy that serves, but is a sympathy whose power is to command, to command by knowing its instrument. The seer, whose function is imaginative interpretation, is the man of science; the leader is the mechanic. The chemist knows his materials interpretatively: he can make subtlest analysis of all their affinities, of all their antipathies; can give you the point of view of every gas or metal or liquid with

* Editors' Note: Woodrow Wilson, "Leaders of Men," in *Leaders of Men*, edited by T. H. Vail Motter (Princeton, N.J.: Princeton University Press, 1952), 23–46. Excerpt.

regard to every other liquid or gas or metal; he can marry, he can divorce, he can destroy them. He could suppose fictitious cases with regard to the conduct of the elements which would appear most clever and probable to other chemists: would appear witty and credible, doubtless, to the elements themselves, could they know. But the mining-engineer's point of view is very different. He, too, must know chemical properties, but only in order that he may use them—only in order to have the right sort of explosion at the right place. So, too, the mechanic's point of view must be quite different from that of the physicist. He must know what his tools can do and what they will stand; but he must be something more than interpreter of their qualities—and something quite different. "It is the general opinion of locomotive superintendents that it is not essential that the men who run locomotives should be good mechanics. Brunel, the distinguished civil engineer, said that he never would trust himself to run a locomotive because he was sure to think of some problem relating to his profession which would distract his attention from the engine. It is probably a similar reason which unfits good mechanics for being good locomotive runners."[1]

Imagine Thackeray leading the House of Commons, or Mr. Lowell on the stump! How comically would their very genius defeat them! The special gift of these two men is a critical understanding of other men, their fallible fellow-creatures. How could their keen humorous sense of what was transpiring in the breasts of their followers and fellow-partisans be held back from banter? How could they take the mass seriously—themselves refrain from laughter and also from the temptation of provoking it? Thackeray argue patiently and respectfully with a dense country member, equipped with nothing but diverting scruples and laughable prejudices? Impossible. As well ask a biologist to treat a cat or a rabbit as if it were a pet with no admirable machinery inside to tempt the dissecting knife.

The competent leader of men cares little for the interior niceties of other people's characters: he cares much—everything for the external uses to which they may be put. His will seeks the lines of least resistance; but the whole question with him is a question as to the application of force. There are men to be moved: how shall he move them? He supplies the power; others supply only the materials upon which that power operates. The power will fail if it be misapplied; it will be misapplied if it be not suitable both in its character and in its method to the nature of the materials upon which it is spent; but that nature is, after all, only its means. It is the power which dictates, dominates; the materials yield. Men are as clay in the hands of the consummate leader.

---

1. "American Locomotives and Cars," *Scribner's Magazine* 4: 192.

It often happens that the leader displays a sagacity and an insight in the handling of men in the mass which quite baffle the wits of the shrewdest analyst of individual character. Men in the mass differ from men as individuals. A man who knows, and keenly knows, every man in town may yet fail to understand a mob or a mass-meeting of his fellow-townsmen. Just as the whole tone and method suitable for a public speech are foreign to the tone and method proper in individual, face to face dealings with separate men, so is the art of leading different from the art of writing novels.

Some of the gifts and qualities which most commend the literary man to success would inevitably doom the would-be leader to failure. One could wish no better proof and example of this than is furnished by the career of that most notable of great Irishmen, Edmund Burke. Everyone knows that Burke's life was spent in Parliament, and everyone knows that the eloquence he poured forth there is as deathless as our literature; and yet everyone is left to wonder that he was of so little consequence in the actual direction of affairs. How noble a figure in the history of English politics: how large a man, how commanding a mind; and yet how ineffectual in the work of bringing men to turn their faces as he would have them, toward the high purposes he had ever in view. We hear with astonishment that after the delivery of that consummate speech on the Nabob of Arcot's debts, which everybody has read, Pitt and Grenville easily agree that they need not trouble themselves to make any reply. His speech on conciliation with America is not only wise beyond precedent in the annals of debate but marches with a force of phrase which, it would seem must have been irresistible—and yet we know that it emptied the House of all audience. You remember what Goldsmith playfully suggested for Burke's epitaph:

> "Here lies our good Edmund, whose genius was such,
> We scarcely can praise it, or blame it, too much;
> Who, too deep for his hearers, still went on refining,
> And thought of convincing while they thought of dining:
> Though equal to all things, for all things unfit,
> Too nice for a statesman, too proud for a wit;
> For a patriot too cool; for a drudge disobedient,
> And too fond of the *right* to pursue the *expedient*.
> In short, 'twas his fate, unemploy'd, or in place, sir,
> To eat mutton cold, and cut blocks with a razor."

Certainly this is too small a measure for so big a man, as Goldsmith himself would have been the first to admit; but the description is almost as true as it is clever. It is better to read Burke than to have heard him; and the thoughts which miscarried in the parliaments of George III have had their triumphs in parliaments of a later day—have established themselves at the heart of such policies as are liberalizing the world. His power was literary, not forensic; he was no leader of men; he was an organizer of thought, but not of party victories. "Burke is a wise man," said Fox, "but he is wise too soon." He was wise also too much. He went on from the wisdom of to-day to the wisdom of to-morrow, to the wisdom which is for all time: and it was impossible he should be followed so far. Men want the wisdom which they are expected to apply to be obvious and conveniently limited in amount. They want a thoroughly reliable article, with very simple adjustments and manifest present uses. Elaborate it—increase the expenditure of thought necessary to obtain it—and they will decline to listen to any propositions concerning it. You must keep it in stock for the use of the next generation.

Men are not led by being told what they don't know. Persuasion is a force, but not information; and persuasion is accomplished by creeping into the confidence of those you would lead. Their confidence is gained by qualities which they can recognize, by arguments which they can assimilate: by the things which find easy entrance into their minds and are easily transmitted to the palms of their hands or the ends of their walking-sticks in the shape of applause. Burke's thoughts penetrate the mind and possess the heart of the quiet student; his style of saying things fills the attention as if it were finest music; but they are not thoughts to be shouted over; it is not a style to ravish the ear of the voter at the hustings. If you would be a leader of men, you must lead your own generation, not the next. Your playing must be good now, while the play is on the boards and the audience in the seats: it will not get you the repute of a great actor to have excellences discovered in you afterwards. Burke's genius made conservative men uneasy. How could a man be safe who had so many ideas?

Englishmen of the present generation wonder that England should have been ruled once by John Addington, a man about whom nothing was accentuated but his dullness; by Mr. Perceval, a sort of Tory squire without blood or any irregularity; by Lord Castlereagh, whose speaking was so bad as to drive his hearers to assume that there must be some great purpose lurking behind its amorphous masses somewhere simply because it was inconceivable that there should be in it so little purpose as it revealed. Accustomed to the persistent power of Gladstone, the epigrammatic variety of Disraeli, the piquant indiscretions of Salisbury, they naturally marvel that they could have been interested enough in such men to heed or follow them. But after all the Englishman has not changed. He still prefers Northcote to more exciting financiers; still listens to a mild young Scotchman acquiescently touching weighty Irish affairs; still thinks Lord Hartington, who cannot speak with point safer than Sir Vernon Harcourt who can; still has a sneaking liking for prosy Mr. W. H. Smith, the successful newsvender, and a sneaking distrust of successful men of thought like Mr. John Morley. He is made as uncomfortable and as indignant by the vagaries of Lord Randolph Churchill as he once was, in times he has forgotten, by the equally bumptious young Disraeli. The story is told of a thoroughgoing old country Tory of the time when Pitt was displaced by Addington that, going to tell a friend of the formation of a new ministry by that excellent mediocrity, he repeated with unction the whole list of commonplace men who were to constitute the new Government, and then, rubbing his hands in demonstrative satisfaction, exclaimed, "Well, thank God, we have at last got a ministry without one of those confounded men of genius in it!" Cobden was doubtless right when he said that "the only way in which the soul of a great nation can be stirred, is by appealing to its sympathies with a true principle in its unalloyed simplicity," and that it was "necessary for the concentration of a people's mind that an individual should become the incarnation of a principle"; but the emphasis must be laid on the "unalloyed simplicity" of the principle. It will not do to incarnate too many ideas at a time if you are to be universally understood and numerously followed.

Cobden himself is an excellent case in point. Embodying the true principle of unhampered commerce "in its unalloyed simplicity," he became a power in England second to none. Never before he mounted the platform had England so steadily yielded to argument, so completely thawed under persuasion. Cobden was singularly equipped for leadership—especially for leadership of this practical, business-like kind. He had nothing in him of the literary mind, which conceives images and is dominated by associations: he conceived only facts, and was dominated by programs of reform. Going to Greece, he found Ilissus and Cephissus, the famed streams of Attica, ridiculous rivulets and wondered that the world should pause so often to study such Lilliputian states as classical Hellas contained when there were the politics of the United States and the vast rivers and mountains of the new continents to think about. "What famous puffers those old Greeks were!" he exclaims.

He journeyed to Egypt and sat beside Mehemet Ali, one of the fiercest warriors and most accomplished tyrants of our century, with an eye open to the fact that the royal viceroy was a somewhat fat personage who fell into blunders when he boasted of the cotton crops of the land he had under his heel; seeing also that his conductor and introducer, Col. C., had hit upon the wrong resource in beginning the conversation by a reference to the excellent weather in a latitude "where uninterrupted sunshine prevails for seven years together." Nothing in means of travel, in the manners and resources of the countries he visited, or in the remarks of the people he met upon practical matters escaped him. He is in Constantinople, and notes that Mr. Perkins, whoever he may have been, "is opposed to the belief in the regeneration of the Turk." His diary chronicles, under date at Malta, that Waghorn said that the English admirals were all too old and that that accounted for the service being less efficient than formerly. He keeps the world of practical details under constant cross-examination. And when, in later days, the great anti-corn-law League is in the heat of its task of reforming the English tariff, how seriously this earnest man takes the vast fairs, the colossal bazaars and all the other homely, bourgeois machinery by means of which the League keeps itself supplied at once with funds for its work and with that large measure of popular attention necessary to its success. This is the organizer! who is incapable of being fatigued by the commonplace—or amused by it—and who is thoroughly in love with working at a single idea.

Mark the simplicity and directness of the arguments and ideas of such men. The motives which they urge are elemental; the morality which they seek to enforce is large and obvious; the policy they emphasize, purged of all subtlety. They give you the fine gold of truth in the nugget, not cunningly beaten into elaborate shapes and chased with intricate patterns. "If oratory were a business and not an art," says Mr. Justin McCarthy, "then it might be contended reasonably enough that Mr. Cobden was one of the greatest orators England has ever known. Nothing could exceed the persuasiveness of his style. His manner was simple, sweet and earnest. It persuaded by convincing. It was transparently sincere." In a word, its simplicity and clearness gave it entrance into the minds of his auditors, its sincerity into their hearts.

But we see the same things in the oratory of Bright, with whom oratory was not a business but an art. Hear him appeal to his constituents in Birmingham, that capital of the spirit of gain, touching what he deemed an iniquitous foreign policy:

"I believe," he exclaims, "there is no permanent greatness in a nation except it be based upon morality. I do not care for military greatness or military renown. I care for the condition of the people among whom I live. There is no man in England who is less likely to speak irreverently of the Crown and Monarchy of England than I am; but crowns, coronets, mitres, military display, the pomp of war, wide colonies, and a huge empire, are, in my view, all trifles light as air, and not worth considering, unless with them you can have a fair share of comfort, contentment, and happiness among the great body of the people. Palaces, baronial castles, great halls, stately mansions, do not make a nation. The nation in every country dwells in the cottage; and unless the light of your constitution can shine there, unless the beauty of your legislation and the excellence of your statesmanship are impressed there on the feelings and conditions of the people, rely upon it you have yet to learn the duties of government. . . .

"You can mould opinion, you can create political power—you cannot think a good thought on this subject and communicate it to your neighbours—you cannot make these points topics of discussion in your social circles and more general meetings, without affecting sensibly and speedily the course which the Government of your country will pursue. May I ask you, then, to believe, as I do most devoutly believe, that the moral law was not written for men alone in their individual character, but that it was written as well for nations, and for nations great as this of which we are citizens. If nations reject and deride that moral law, there is a penalty which will inevitably follow. It may not come at once, it may not come in our lifetime; but, rely upon it, the great Italian poet is not a poet only, but a prophet, when he says—

> 'The sword of heaven is not in haste to smite,
> Nor yet doth linger.'

We have experience, we have beacons, we have landmarks enough. We know what the past has cost us, we know how much and how far we have wandered, but we are not left without a guide. It is true we have not, as an ancient people had, Urim and Thummim—those oraculous gems on Aaron's breast—from which to take counsel, but we have the unchangeable and eternal principles of the moral law to guide us, and only so far as we walk by that guidance can we be permanently a great nation, or our people a happy people."

How simple, how evident it all is—how commonplace the motives appealed to—how old the moral maxim—how obvious every consideration urged! And yet how effective such a passage is—how it carries!—what a thrill of life and of power there is in it. As simple as the quiet argument of Cobden, though more alight with passionate feeling. As direct and unpretentious as a bit of conversation, though elevated above the level of conversation by a sweep of accumulating phrase such as may be made effectual for the throwing down of strongholds.

Style has of course a great deal to do with such effects in popular oratory. Armies do not win battles by sword-fencing, but by the fierce cut of the sabre, the direct volley of musketry, the straightforward argument of artillery, the impetuous dash of cavalry. And it is in the same way that oratorical battles are won: not by the nice refinements of statement, the deft sword-play of dialectic fence, but by the straight and speedy thrusts of speech sent through and through the gross and obvious frame of a subject. It must be clear and always clear what the sentences would be about. They must be advanced with the firm tread of disciplined march. Their meaning must be clear and loud.

There is much also in physical gifts, as everybody knows. The popular orator should be satisfying to the eye and to the ear: broad, sturdy, clear-eyed, musically voiced, like John Bright; built with the stature and mien of a Norse god, like Webster; towering, imperious, persuading by voice and carriage, like Clay; or vast, rugged, fulminating, like O'Connell, fit for a Celtic Olympus.

It is easy to call a man like Daniel O'Connell a demagogue, but it is juster
to see in him a born leader of men. We remember him as the agitator, simple,
loud, incessant, a bit turbulent, not a little coarse also, full of flouts and jibes,
bitter and abusive, in headlong pursuit of the aims of Irish liberty. We ought
to remember him as the ardent supporter of every policy that made for English and for human liberty also, a friend of reform when reform was unpopu-
lar, a champion of oppressed classes who had almost no one else to speak for
them, a battler for what was liberal and enlightened and against what was unfair and prejudiced, all along the line. He was no courter of popularity: but his
heart was the heart of his people: their cause and their hopes were his. He was
not their slave, nor were they his dupes. He was their mouth-piece. And what
a mouth-piece! Nature seems to have planned him for utterance. His figure
and influence loom truly grand as we look back to him standing, as he so often did, before concourses mustered, scores of thousands strong, upon the
open heath to hear and to protest of Ireland's wrongs.

> "His Titan strength must touch what gave it birth;
> Hear him to mobs, and on his mother earth!"

Here is the testimony of one who saw one of those immeasurable assemblies stand round about the giant Celt and saw the Master wield his spell:

> "Methought no clarion could have sent its sound
> Even to the centre of the hosts around;
> And as I thought rose the sonorous swell,
> As from some church-tower swings the silvery bell.
> Aloft and clear, from airy tide to tide,
> It glided, easy as a bird may glide;
> To the last verge of that vast audience sent,
> It play'd with each wild passion as it went;
> Now stirred the uproar, now the murmur still'd,
> And sobs or laughter answer'd as it will'd.
> Then did I know what spells of infinite choice,
> To rouse or lull, has the sweet human voice;
> Then did I seem to seize the sudden clue
> To the grand troublous Life Antique—to view
> Under the rock-stand of Demosthenes,
> Mutable Athens heave her noisy seas."

This huge organization, this thrilling voice, ringing out clear and effectual
over vast multitudes were, it would seem, too big, too voluminous for Parliament. There no channels offered which were broad and free enough to give
effective course to the crude force of the man. The gross and obvious force of

him shocked sensitive, slow, and decorous men, not accustomed to having sense served up to them with a shout. The open heath was needed to contain O'Connell. But even in Parliament where the decorum and reserve of debate offered him no effective play, his honesty, his ardor for liberty, his good humour, his transparent genuineness won for O'Connell at last almost his due meed of respect. The qualities that made him irresistible with the people won him regard, if not influence, with the people's representatives.

The whole question of leadership receives a sharp practical test in a popular legislative assembly. The revolutions which have changed the whole principle and method of government within the last hundred years have created a new kind of leadership in legislation: a leadership which is not yet, perhaps, fully understood. It used to be thought that legislation was an affair proper to be conducted only by the few who were instructed for the benefit of the many who were uninstructed: that statesmanship was a function of origination for which only trained and instructed men were fit. Those who actually conducted legislation and undertook affairs were rather whimsically chosen by Fortune to illustrate this theory, but such was the ruling thought in politics. The Sovereignty of the People, however, that great modern principle of politics, has erected a different conception — or, if so be that, in the slowness of our thought, we hang on to the old conception, has created a very different practice. When we are angry with public men nowadays we charge them with subserving instead of forming and directing public opinion. It is to be suspected that when we make such charges we are suffering our standards of judgment to lag behind our politics. When an Englishman declares that Mr. Gladstone is truckling to public opinion in his Irish policy, he surely cannot expect us to despise Mr. Gladstone on that account, even if the declaration be true, inasmuch as it is now quite indisputably the last part of the Nineteenth Century, and the nineteenth is a century, we know, which has established the principle that public opinion must be truckled to (if you will use a disagreeable word) in the conduct of government. A man, surely, would not fish for votes (if that be what Mr. Gladstone is doing) among the minority — particularly if he be in his eightieth year and in need of getting the votes at once if he is to get them at all. He must believe, at any rate, that he is throwing his bait among the majority. And it is a dignified proposition with us — is it not? — that as is the majority, so ought the government to be.

Pray do not misunderstand me. I am not radical. I would not for the world be instrumental in discrediting the ancient and honorable pastime of abusing demagogues. Demagogues were quite evidently, it seems to me, meant for abuse, if we are to argue by exclusion: for assuredly they were never known to serve any other useful purpose. I will follow the hounds any day in pursuit of one of the wily, doubling rascals, however rough the country to be ridden over! But you must allow me to make my condemnations tally with my theory of government. Is Irish opinion ripe for Home Rule, as the Liberals claim? Very well then: let them have Home Rule. Every community, says my political philosophy, should be governed for its own interests, not for the satisfaction of any other community.

Still I seem radical, without in reality being so. I advance my explanation, therefore, another step. Society is not a crowd, but an organism; and, like every organism, it must grow as a whole or else be deformed. The world is agreed, too, that it is an organism also in this, that it will die unless it be vital in every part. That is the only line of reasoning by which we can really establish the majority in legitimate authority. This organic whole, Society, is made up, obviously, for the most part, of the majority. It grows by the development of its aptitudes and desires, and under their guidance. The evolution of its institutions must take place by slow modification and nice all-round adjustment. And all this is but a careful and abstract way of saying that no reform may succeed for which the major thought of the nation is not prepared: that the instructed few may not be safe leaders, except in so far as they have communicated their instruction to the many, except in so far as they have transmuted their thought into a common, a popular thought.

Let us fairly distinguish, therefore, the peculiar and delicate duties of the popular leader from the not very peculiar or delicate crimes of the demagogue. Leadership, for the statesman, is interpretation. He must read the common thought: he must test and calculate very circumspectly the preparation of the nation for the next move in the progress of politics. If he fairly hit the popular thought, when we have missed it, are we to say that he is a demagogue? The nice point is to distinguish the firm and progressive popular thought from the momentary and whimsical popular mood, the transitory or mistaken popular passion. But it is fatally easy to blame or misunderstand the statesman. Our temperament is one of logic, let us say. We hold that one and one make two and we see no salvation for the people except they receive the truth. The statesman is of another opinion. One and one doubtless make two, he is ready to admit, but the people think that one and one make more than two and until they see otherwise we shall have to legislate on that supposition. This is not to talk nonsense. The Roman augurs very soon discovered that sacred fowls drank water and pecked grain with no sage intent of prophecy, but from motives quite mundane and simple. But it would have been a revolution to say so and act so in the face of a people who believed otherwise, and executive policy had to proceed on the theory of a divine method of fowl digestion. The divinity that once did hedge a king, grows—not now very high about the latest Hohenzollern—not so high but that one may see that he is a bumptious young gentleman slenderly equipped with wisdom or discretion. But who that prefers growth to revolution would propose that legislation in Germany proceed independently of this hereditary accident?

In no case may we safely hurry the organism away from its habit: for it is held together by that habit, and by it is enabled to perform its functions completely. The constituent habit of a people inheres in its thought, and to that thought legislation—even the legislation that advances and modifies habit—must keep very near. The ear of the leader must ring with the voices of the people. He cannot be of the school of the prophets; he must be of the number of those who studiously serve the slow-paced daily need.

In what, then, does political leadership consist? It is leadership in conduct, and leadership in conduct must discern and strengthen the tendencies that make for development. The legislative leader must perceive the direction of the nation's permanent forces and must feel the speed of their operation. There is initiative here, but not novelty; there are old thoughts, but a progressive application of them. There is such initiative as we may conceive the man part of the mythical centaur to have exercised. Doubtless the centaur acted not as a man, but as a horse would act, the head conceiving only such things as were possible for the performance of its lower and nether, equine, parts. He never dared to climb where hoofs could gain no sure foothold: and he knew that there were four feet, not two, to be provided with standing-room. There must have been the caper of the beast in all his schemes. He would have had as much respect for a blacksmith as for a haberdasher. He must have had the standards of the stable rather than the standards of the drawing-room. The headship of the mind over the body is a like headship for all of us; it is observant of possibility and of physical environment.

The inventing mind is impatient of such restraints: the aspiring soul has at all times longed to be loosed from the body. But such are the conditions of organic life. If the body is to be put off, dissolution must be endured. As the conceiving mind is tenant of the body, so is the conceiving legislator tenant of that greater body, Society. Practical leadership may not beckon to the slow masses of men from beyond some dim, unexplored space or some intervening chasm: it must daily feel the road that leads to the goal proposed, knowing that it is a slow, a very slow, evolution to wings, and that for the present, and for a very long future also, Society must walk, dependent upon practicable paths, incapable of scaling sudden, precipitous heights, a road-breaker, not a fowl of the air. In the words of the Master, Burke, "to follow, not to force, the public inclination—to give a direction, a form, a technical dress, and a specific sanction, to the general sense of the community, is the true end of legislation." That general sense of the community may wait to be aroused, and the statesman must arouse it; may be inchoate and vague, and the statesman must formulate and make it explicit. But he cannot, and should not, do more. The forces of the public thought may be blind: he must lend them sight; they may blunder: he must set them right. He can do something to create such forces of opinion; but it is a creation of forms, not of substance, and without such forces at his back he can do nothing effective.

This function of interpretation, this careful exclusion of individual origination it is that makes it difficult for the impatient original mind to distinguish the popular statesman from the demagogue. The demagogue sees and seeks self-interest in an acquiescent reading of that part of the public thought upon which he depends for votes; the statesman, also reading the common inclination, also, when he reads aright, obtains the votes that keep him in power. But if you will justly observe the two, you will find the one trimming to the inclinations of the moment, the other obedient to the permanent purposes of the public mind. The one adjusts his sails to the breeze of the day; the other makes his plans to ripen with the slow progress of the years. While the one solicitously watches the capricious changes of the weather, the other diligently sows the grains in their seasons. The one ministers to himself, the other to the race.

. . .

13

The President of the United States*

From *Constitutional Government in the United States*, Chapter 3

Woodrow Wilson

This chapter on the presidency comes from a series of lectures Woodrow Wilson gave at Columbia in 1907, subsequently published as *Constitutional Government in the United States*. While his earlier writings had not regarded the president so highly, this work marks Wilson's new vision of the presidency as the primary means of transcending the separation-of-powers system he despised. This was not a change in principles but was, instead, a discovery of a new institutional mode of effecting his long-held commitment to progressive government. Wilson lays out here a teaching on presidential leadership that helps to shape the modern presidency.

It is difficult to describe any single part of a great governmental system without describing the whole of it. Governments are living things and operate as organic wholes. Moreover, governments have their natural evolution and are one thing in one age, another in another. The makers of the Constitution constructed the federal government upon a theory of checks and balances which was meant to limit the operation of each part and allow to no single part or organ of it a dominating force; but no government can be successfully conducted upon so mechanical a theory. Leadership and control must be lodged somewhere; the whole art of statesmanship is the art of bringing the several parts of government into effective cooperation for the accomplishment of particular common objects,—and party objects at that. Our study of each part of our federal system, if we are to discover our real government as it lives, must

---

* Editors' Note: Woodrow Wilson, "The President of the United States," in *Constitutional Government in the United States* (New York: Columbia University Press, 1908), 54–81.

be made to disclose to us its operative coördination as a whole: its places of
leadership, its method of action, how it operates, what checks it, what gives
it energy and effect. Governments are what politicians make them, and it is
easier to write of the President than of the presidency.

The government of the United States was constructed upon the Whig theory
of political dynamics, which was a sort of unconscious copy of the Newtonian
theory of the universe. In our own day, whenever we discuss the structure or
development of anything, whether in nature or in society, we consciously or
unconsciously follow Mr. Darwin; but before Mr. Darwin, they followed Newton. Some single law, like the law of gravitation, swung each system of
thought and gave it its principle of unity. Every sun, every planet, every free
body in the spaces of the heavens, the world itself, is kept in its place and
reined to its course by the attraction of bodies that swing with equal order and
precision about it, themselves governed by the nice poise and balance of forces
which give the whole system of the universe its symmetry and perfect adjustment. The Whigs had tried to give England a similar constitution. They had
had no wish to destroy the throne, no conscious desire to reduce the king to a
mere figurehead, but had intended only to surround and offset him with a system of constitutional checks and balances which should regulate his otherwise
arbitrary course and make it at least always calculable.

They had made no clear analysis of the matter in their own thoughts; it has
not been the habit of English politicians, or indeed of English-speaking politicians on either side of the water, to be clear theorists. It was left to a Frenchman to point out to the Whigs what they had done. They had striven to make
Parliament so influential in the making of laws and so authoritative in the criticism of the king's policy that the king could in no matter have his own way
without their coöperation and assent, though they left him free, the while, if
he chose, to interpose an absolute veto upon the acts of Parliament. They had
striven to secure for the courts of law as great an independence as possible,
so that they might be neither over-awed by parliament nor coerced by the
king. In brief, as Montesquieu pointed out to them in his lucid way, they had
sought to balance executive, legislature, and judiciary off against one another
by a series of checks and counterpoises, which Newton might readily have
recognized as suggestive of the mechanism of the heavens.

The makers of our federal Constitution followed the scheme as they found
it expounded in Montesquieu, followed it with genuine scientific enthusiasm.
The admirable expositions of the *Federalist* read like thoughtful applications
of Montesquieu to the political needs and circumstances of America. They are
full of the theory of checks and balances. The President is balanced off
against Congress, Congress against the President, and each against the courts.
Our statesmen of the earlier generations quoted no one so often as Mon-

tesquieu, and they quoted him always as a scientific standard in the field of politics. Politics is turned into mechanics under his touch. The theory of gravitation is supreme.

The trouble with the theory is that government is not a machine, but a living thing. It falls, not under the theory of the universe, but under the theory of organic life. It is accountable to Darwin, not to Newton. It is modified by its environment, necessitated by its tasks, shaped to its functions by the sheer pressure of life. No living thing can have its organs offset against each other as checks, and live. On the contrary, its life is dependent upon their quick coöperation, their ready response to the commands of instinct or intelligence, their amicable community of purpose. Government is not a body of blind forces; it is a body of men, with highly differentiated functions, no doubt, in our modern day of specialization, but with a common task and purpose. Their coöperation is indispensable, their warfare fatal. There can be no successful government without leadership or without the intimate, almost instinctive, coördination of the organs of life and action. This is not theory, but fact, and displays its force as fact, whatever theories may be thrown across its track. Living political constitutions must be Darwinian in structure and in practice.

Fortunately, the definitions and prescriptions of our constitutional law, though conceived in the Newtonian spirit and upon the Newtonian principle, are sufficiently broad and elastic to allow for the play of life and circumstance. Though they were Whig theorists, the men who framed the federal Constitution were also practical statesmen with an experienced eye for affairs and a quick practical sagacity in respect of the actual structure of government, and they have given us a thoroughly workable model. If it had in fact been a machine governed by mechanically automatic balances, it would have had no history; but it was not, and its history has been rich with the influences and personalities of the men who have conducted it and made it a living reality. The government of the United States has had a vital, and normal organic growth and has proved itself eminently adapted to express the changing temper and purposes of the American people from age to age.

That is the reason why it is easier to write of the President than of the presidency. The presidency has been one thing at one time, another at another, varying with the man who occupied the office and with the circumstances that surrounded him. One account must be given of the office during the period 1789 to 1825, when the government was getting its footing both at home and abroad, struggling for its place among the nations and its full credit among its own people; when English precedents and traditions were strongest; and when the men chosen for the office were men bred to leadership in a way that attracted to them the attention and confidence of the whole country. Another account must be given of it during Jackson's time, when an imperious man, bred not in deliberative assemblies or quiet councils, but in the field and upon a rough frontier, worked his own will upon affairs, with or without formal sanction of law, sustained by a clear undoubting conscience and the love of a people who had grown deeply impatient of the régime he had supplanted. Still another account must be given of it during the years 1836 to 1861, when domestic affairs of many debatable kinds absorbed the country, when Congress necessarily exercised the chief choices of policy, and when the Presidents who followed one another in office lacked the personal force and initiative to make for themselves a leading place in counsel. After that came the Civil War and Mr. Lincoln's unique task and achievement, when the executive seemed for a little while to become by sheer stress of circumstances the whole government, Congress merely voting supplies and assenting to necessary laws, as Parliament did in the time of the Tudors. From 1865 to 1898 domestic questions, legislative matters in respect of which Congress had naturally to make the initial choice, legislative leaders the chief decisions of policy, came once more to the front, and no President except Mr. Cleveland played a leading and decisive part in the quiet drama of our national life. Even Mr. Cleveland may be said to have owed his great role in affairs rather to his own native force and the confused politics of the time, than to any opportunity of leadership naturally afforded him by a system which had subordinated so many Presidents before him to Congress. The war with Spain again changed the balance of parts. Foreign questions became leading questions again, as they had been in the first days of the government, and in them the President was of necessity leader. Our new place in the affairs of the world has since that year of transformation kept him at the front of our government, where our own thoughts and the attention of men everywhere is centred upon him.

Both men and circumstances have created these contrasts in the administration and influence of the office of President. We have all been disciples of Montesquieu, but we have also been practical politicians. Mr. Bagehot once remarked that it was no proof of the excellence of the Constitution of the United States that the Americans had operated it with conspicuous success because the Americans could run any constitution successfully; and, while the compliment is altogether acceptable, it is certainly true that our practical sense is more noticeable than our theoretical consistency, and that, while we were once all constitutional lawyers, we are in these latter days apt to be very impatient of literal and dogmatic interpretations of constitutional principle.

The makers of the Constitution seem to have thought of the President as what the stricter Whig theorists wished the king to be: only the legal executive, the presiding and guiding authority in the application of law and the execution of policy. His veto upon legislation was only his 'check' on Congress,—was a power of restraint, not of guidance. He was empowered to prevent bad laws, but he was not to be given an opportunity to make good ones. As a matter of fact he has become very much more. He has become the leader of his party and the guide of the nation in political purpose, and therefore in legal action. The constitutional structure of the government has hampered and limited his action in these significant rôles, but it has not prevented it. The influence of the President has varied with the men who have been Presidents and with the circumstances of their times, but the tendency has been unmistakably disclosed, and springs out of the very nature of government itself. It is merely the proof that our government is a living, organic thing, and must, like every other government, work out the close synthesis of active parts which can exist only when leadership is lodged in some one man or group of men. You cannot compound a successful government out of antagonisms. Greatly as the practice and influence of Presidents has varied, there can be no mistaking the fact that we have grown more and more inclined from generation to generation to look to the President as the unifying force in our complex system, the leader both of his party and of the nation. To do so is not inconsistent with the actual provisions of the Constitution; it is only inconsistent with a very mechanical theory of its meaning and intention. The Constitution contains no theories. It is as practical a document as Magna Carta.

The rôle of party leader is forced upon the President by the method of his selection. The theory of the makers of the Constitution may have been that the presidential electors would exercise a real choice, but it is hard to understand how, as experienced politicians, they can have expected anything of the kind. They did not provide that the electors should meet as one body for consultation and make deliberate choice of a President and Vice-President, but that they should meet "in their respective states" and cast their ballots in separate groups, without the possibility of consulting and without the least likelihood of agreeing, unless some such means as have actually been used were employed to suggest and determine their choice beforehand. It was the practice at first to make party nominations for the presidency by congressional caucus. Since the Democratic upheaval of General Jackson's time nominating conventions have taken the place of congressional caucuses; and the choice of Presidents by party conventions has had some very interesting results.

We are apt to think of the choice of nominating conventions as somewhat haphazard. We know, or think that we know, how their action is sometimes determined, and the knowledge makes us very uneasy. We know that there is no debate in nominating conventions, no discussion of the merits of the respective candidates, at which the country can sit as audience and assess the wisdom of the final choice. If there is any talking to be done, aside from the formal addresses of the temporary and permanent chairmen and of those who present the platform and the names of the several aspirants for nomination, the assembly adjourns. The talking that is to decide the result must be done in private committee rooms and behind the closed doors of the headquarters of the several state delegations to the convention. The intervals between sessions are filled with a very feverish activity. Messengers run from one headquarters to another until the small hours of the morning. Conference follows conference in a way that is likely to bring newspaper correspondents to the verge of despair, it being next to impossible to put the rumors together into any coherent story of what is going on. Only at the rooms of the national committee of the party is there any clear knowledge of the situation as a whole; and the excitement of the members of the convention rises from session to session under the sheer pressure of uncertainty. The final majority is compounded no outsider and few members can tell how.

Many influences, too, play upon nominating conventions, which seem mere winds of feeling. They sit in great halls, with galleries into which crowd thousands of spectators from all parts of the country, but chiefly, of course, from the place at which the convention sits, and the feeling of the galleries is transmitted to the floor. The cheers of mere spectators echo the names of popular candidates, and every excitement on the floor is enhanced a hundred fold in the galleries. Sudden gusts of impulse are apt to change the whole feeling of the convention, and offset in a moment the most careful arrangements of managing politicians. It has come to be a commonly accepted opinion that if the Republican convention of 1860 had not met in Chicago, it would have nominated Mr. Seward and not Mr. Lincoln. Mr. Seward was the acknowledged leader of the new party; had been its most telling spokesman; had given its tenets definition and currency. Mr. Lincoln had not been brought within view of the country as a whole until the other day, when he had given Mr. Douglas so hard a fight to keep his seat in the Senate, and had but just now given currency among thoughtful men to the striking phrases of the searching speeches he had made in debate with his practised antagonist. But the convention met in Illinois, amidst throngs of Mr. Lincoln's ardent friends and advocates. His managers saw to it that the galleries were properly filled with men who would cheer every mention of his name until the hail was shaken. Every influence of the place worked for him and he was chosen.

Thoughtful critics of our political practices have not allowed the excellence of the choice to blind them to the danger of the method. They have known too many examples of what the galleries have done to supplement the efforts of managing politicians to feel safe in the presence of processes which seem rather those of intrigue and impulse than those of sober choice. They can cite instances, moreover, of sudden, unlooked-for excitements on the floor of such bodies which have swept them from the control of all sober influences and hastened them to choices which no truly deliberative assembly could ever have made. There is no training school for Presidents, unless, as some governors have wished, it be looked for in the governorships of states; and nominating conventions have confined themselves in their selections to no class, have demanded of aspirants no particular experience or knowledge of affairs. They have nominated lawyers without political experience, soldiers, editors of newspapers, newspaper correspondents, whom they pleased, without regard to their lack of contact with affairs. It would seem as if their choices were almost matters of chance.

In reality there is much more method, much more definite purpose, much more deliberate choice in the extraordinary process than there seems to be. The leading spirits of the national committee of each party could give an account of the matter which would put a very different face on it and make the methods of nominating conventions seem, for all the undoubted elements of chance there are in them, on the whole very manageable. Moreover, the party that expects to win may be counted on to make a much more conservative and thoughtful selection of a candidate than the party that merely hopes to win. The haphazard selections which seem to discredit the system are generally made by conventions of the party unaccustomed to success. Success brings sober calculation and a sense of responsibility.

And it must be remembered also that our political system is not so coördinated as to supply a training for presidential aspirants or even to make it absolutely necessary that they should have had extended experience in public affairs. Certainly the country has never thought of members of Congress as in any particular degree fitted for the presidency. Even the Vice President is not afforded an opportunity to learn the duties of the office. The men best prepared, no doubt, are those who have been governors of states or members of cabinets. And yet even they are chosen for their respective offices generally by reason of a kind of fitness and availability which does not necessarily argue in them the size and power that would fit them for the greater office. In our earlier practice cabinet officers were regarded as in the natural line of succession to the presidency. Mr. Jefferson had been in General Washington's cabinet, Mr. Madison in Mr. Jefferson's, Mr. Monroe in Mr. Madison's; and generally it was the Secretary of State who was taken. But those were days when English precedent was strong upon us, when cabinets were expected to be made up of the political leaders of the party in power; and from their ranks subsequent candidates for the presidency were most likely to be selected. The practice, as we look back to it, seems eminently sensible, and we wonder why it should have been so soon departed from and apparently forgotten. We wonder, too, why eminent senators have not sometimes been chosen; why members of the House have so seldom commanded the attention of nominating conventions; why public life has never offered itself in any definite way as a preparation for the presidential office.

If the matter be looked at a little more closely, it will be seen that the office of President, as we have used and developed it, really does not demand actual experience in affairs so much as particular qualities of mind and character which we are at least as likely to find outside the ranks of our public men as within them. What is it that a nominating convention wants in the man it is to present to the country for its suffrages? A man who will be and who will seem to the country in some sort an embodiment of the character and purpose it wishes its government to have,—a man who understands his own day and the needs of the country, and who has the personality and the initiative to enforce his views both upon the people and upon Congress. It may seem an odd way to get such a man. It is even possible that nominating conventions and those who guide them do not realize entirely what it is that they do. But in simple fact the convention picks out a party leader from the body of the nation. Not that it expects its nominee to direct the interior government of the party and to supplant its already accredited and experienced spokesmen in Congress and in its state and national committees; but it does of necessity expect him to represent it before public opinion and to stand before the country as its representative man, as a true type of what the country may expect of the party itself in purpose and principle. It cannot but be led by him in the campaign; if he be elected, it cannot but acquiesce in his leadership of the government itself. What the country will demand of the candidate will be, not that he be an astute politician, skilled and practised in affairs, but that he be a man such as it can trust, in character, in intention, in knowledge of its needs, in perception of the best means by which those needs may be met, in capacity to prevail by reason of his own weight and integrity. Sometimes the country believes in a party, but more often it believes in a man; and conventions have often shown the instinct to perceive which it is that the country needs in a particular presidential year, a mere representative partisan, a military hero, or some one who will genuinely speak for the country itself, whatever be his training and antecedents. It is in this sense that the President has the rôle of party leader thrust upon him by the very method by which he is chosen.

As legal executive, his constitutional aspect, the President cannot be thought of alone. He cannot execute laws. Their actual daily execution must be taken care of by the several executive departments and by the now innumerable body of federal officials throughout the country. In respect of the strictly executive duties of his office the President may be said to administer the presidency in conjunction with the members of his cabinet, like the chairman of a commission. He is even of necessity much less active in the actual carrying out of the law than are his colleagues and advisers. It is therefore becoming more and more true, as the business of the government becomes more and more complex and extended, that the President is becoming more and more a political and less and less an executive officer. His executive powers are in commission, while his political powers more and more centre and accumulate upon him and are in their very nature personal and inalienable.

Only the larger sort of executive questions are brought to him. Departments which run with easy routine and whose transactions bring few questions of general policy to the surface may proceed with their business for months and even years together without demanding his attention; and no department is in any sense under his direct charge. Cabinet meetings do not discuss detail: they are concerned only with the larger matters of policy or expediency which important business is constantly disclosing. There are no more hours in the President's day than in another man's. If he is indeed the executive, he must act almost entirely by delegation, and is in the hands of his colleagues. He is likely to be praised if things go well, and blamed if they go wrong; but his only real control is of the persons to whom he deputes the performance of executive duties. It is through no fault or neglect of his that the duties apparently assigned to him by the Constitution have come to be his less conspicuous, less important duties, and that duties apparently not assigned to him at all chiefly occupy his time and energy. The one set of duties it has proved practically impossible for him to perform; the other it has proved impossible for him to escape.

He cannot escape being the leader of his party except by incapacity and lack of personal force, because he is at once the choice of the party and of the nation. He is the party nominee, and the only party nominee for whom the whole nation votes. Members of the House and Senate are representatives of localities, are voted for only by sections of voters, or by local bodies of electors like the members of the state legislatures. There is no national party choice except that of President. No one else represents the people as a whole, exercising a national choice; and inasmuch as his strictly executive duties are in fact subordinated, so far at any rate as all detail is concerned, the President represents not so much the party's governing efficiency as its controlling ideals and principles. He is not so much part of its organization as its vital link of connection with the thinking nation. He can dominate his party by being spokesman for the real sentiment and purpose of the country, by giving direction to opinion, by giving the country at once the information and the statements of policy which will enable it to form its judgments alike of parties and of men.

For he is also the political leader of the nation, or has it in his choice to be. The nation as a whole has chosen him, and is conscious that it has no other political spokesman. His is the only national voice in affairs. Let him once win the admiration and confidence of the country, and no other single force can withstand him, no combination of forces will easily overpower him. His position takes the imagination of the country. He is the representative of no constituency, but of the whole people. When he speaks in his true character, he speaks for no special interest. If he rightly interpret the national thought and boldly insist upon it, he is irresistible; and the country never feels the zest of action so much as when its President is of such insight and calibre. Its instinct is for unified action, and it craves a single leader. It is for this reason that it will often prefer to choose a man rather than a party. A President whom it trusts can not only lead it, but form it to his own views.

It is the extraordinary isolation imposed upon the President by our system that makes the character and opportunity of his office so extraordinary. In him are centred both opinion and party. He may stand, if he will, a little outside party and insist as if it were upon the general opinion. It is with the instinctive feeling that it is upon occasion such a man that the country wants that nominating conventions will often nominate men who are not their acknowledged leaders, but only such men as the country would like to see lead both its parties. The President may also, if he will, stand within the party counsels and use the advantage of his power and personal force to control its actual programs. He may be both the leader of his party and the leader of the nation, or he may be one or the other. If he lead the nation, his party can hardly resist him. His office is anything he has the sagacity and force to make it.

That is the reason why it has been one thing at one time, another at another. The Presidents who have not made themselves leaders have lived no more truly on that account in the spirit of the Constitution than those whose force has told in the determination of law and policy. No doubt Andrew Jackson overstepped the bounds meant to be set to the authority of his office. It was certainly in direct contravention of the spirit of the Constitution that he should have refused to respect and execute decisions of the Supreme Court of the United States, and no serious student of our history can righteously condone what he did in such matters on the ground that his intentions were upright and his principles pure. But the Constitution of the United States is not a mere lawyers' document: it is a vehicle of life, and its spirit is always the spirit of the age. Its prescriptions are clear and we know what they are; a written document makes lawyers of us all, and our duty as citizens should make us conscientious lawyers, reading the text of the Constitution without subtlety or sophistication; but life is always your last and most authoritative critic.

Some of our Presidents have deliberately held themselves off from using the full power they might legitimately have used, because of conscientious scruples, because they were more theorists than statesmen. They have held the strict literary theory of the Constitution, the Whig theory, the Newtonian theory, and have acted as if they thought that Pennsylvania Avenue should have been even longer than it is; that there should be no intimate communication of any kind between the Capitol and the White House; that the President as a man was no more at liberty to lead the houses of Congress by persuasion than he was at liberty as President to dominate them by authority,—supposing that he had, what he has not, authority enough to dominate them. But the makers of the Constitution were not enacting Whig theory, they were not making laws with the expectation that, not the laws themselves, but their opinions, known by future historians to lie back of them, should govern the constitutional action of the country. They were statesmen, not pedants, and their laws are sufficient to keep us to the paths they set us upon. The President is at liberty, both in law and conscience, to be as big a man as he can. His capacity will set the limit; and if Congress be overborne by him, it will be no fault of the makers of the Constitution,—it will be from no lack of constitutional powers on its part, but only because the President has the nation behind him, and Congress has not. He has no means of compelling Congress except through public opinion.

That I say he has no means of compelling Congress will show what I mean, and that my meaning has no touch of radicalism or iconoclasm in it. There are illegitimate means by which the President may influence the action of Congress. He may bargain with members, not only with regard to appointments, but also with regard to legislative measures. He may use his local patronage to assist members to get or retain their seats. He may interpose his powerful influence, in one covert way or another, in contests for places in the Senate. He may also overbear Congress by arbitrary acts which ignore the laws or virtually override them. He may even substitute his own orders for acts of Congress which he wants but cannot get. Such things are not only deeply immoral, they are destructive of the fundamental understandings of constitutional government and, therefore, of constitutional government itself. They are sure, moreover, in a country of free public opinion, to bring their own punishment, to destroy both the fame and the power of the man who dares to practise them. No honorable man includes such agencies in a sober exposition of the Constitution or allows himself to think of them when he speaks of the influences of "life" which govern each generation's use and interpretation of that great instrument, our sovereign guide and the object of our deepest reverence. Nothing in a system like ours can be constitutional which is immoral or which touches the good faith of those who have sworn to obey the fundamental law. The reprobation of all good men will always overwhelm such influences with shame and failure. But the personal force of the President is perfectly constitutional to any extent to which he chooses to exercise it, and it is by the clear logic of our constitutional practice that he has become alike the leader of his party and the leader of the nation.

The political powers of the President are not quite so obvious in their scope and character when we consider his relations with Congress as when we consider his relations to his party and to the nation. They need, therefore, a somewhat more critical examination. Leadership in government naturally belongs to its executive officers, who are daily in contact with practical conditions and exigencies and whose reputations alike for good judgment and for fidelity are at stake much more than are those of the members of the legislative body at every turn of the law's application. The law-making part of the government ought certainly to be very hospitable to the suggestions of the planning and acting part of it. Those Presidents who have felt themselves bound to adhere to the strict literary theory of the Constitution have scrupulously refrained from attempting to determine either the subjects or the character of legislation, except so far as they were obliged to decide for themselves, after Congress had acted, whether they should acquiesce in it or not. And yet the Constitution explicitly authorizes the President to recommend to Congress "such measures as he shall deem necessary and expedient," and it is not necessary to the integrity of even the literary theory of the Constitution to insist that such recommendations should be merely perfunctory. Certainly General Washington did not so regard them, and he stood much nearer the Whig theory than we do. A President's messages to Congress have no more weight or authority than their intrinsic reasonableness and importance give them: but that is their only constitutional limitation. The Constitution certainly does not forbid the President to back them up, as General Washington did, with such personal force and influence as he may possess. Some of our Presidents have felt the need, which unquestionably exists in our system, for some spokesman of the nation as a whole, in matters of legislation no less than in other matters, and have tried to supply Congress with the leadership of suggestion, backed by argument and by iteration and by every legitimate appeal to public opinion. Cabinet officers are shut out from Congress; the President himself has, by custom, no access to its floor; many long-established barriers of precedent, though not of law, hinder him from exercising any direct influence upon its deliberations; and yet he is undoubtedly the only spokesman of the whole people. They have again and again, as often as they were afforded the opportunity, manifested their satisfaction when he has boldly accepted the rôle of leader, to which the peculiar origin and character of his authority entitle him. The Constitution bids him speak, and times of stress and change must more and more thrust upon him the attitude of originator of policies.

His is the vital place of action in the system, whether he accept it as such or not, and the office is the measure of the man,—of his wisdom as well as of his force. His veto abundantly equips him to stay the hand of Congress when he will. It is seldom possible to pass a measure over his veto, and no President has hesitated to use the veto when his own judgment of the public good was seriously at issue with that of the houses. The veto has never been suffered to fall into even temporary disuse with us. In England it has ceased to exist, with the change in the character of the executive. There has been no veto since Anne's day, because ever since the reign of Anne the laws of England have been originated either by ministers who spoke the king's own will or by ministers whom the king did not dare gainsay; and in our own time the ministers who formulate the laws are themselves the executive of the nation; a veto would be a negative upon their own power. If bills pass of which they disapprove, they resign and give place to the leaders of those who approve them. The framers of the Constitution made in our President a more powerful, because a more isolated, king than the one they were imitating; and because the Constitution gave them their veto in such explicit terms, our Presidents have not hesitated to use it, even when it put their mere individual judgment against that of large majorities in both houses of Congress. And yet in the exercise of the power to suggest legislation, quite as explicitly conferred upon them by the Constitution, some of our Presidents have seemed to have a timid fear that they might offend some law of taste which had become a constitutional principle.

In one sense their messages to Congress have no more authority than the letters of any other citizen would have. Congress can heed or ignore them as it pleases; and there have been periods of our history when presidential messages were utterly without practical significance, perfunctory documents which few persons except the editors of newspapers took the trouble to read. But if the President has personal force and cares to exercise it, there is this tremendous difference between his messages and the views of any other citizen, either outside Congress or in it: that the whole country reads them and feels that the writer speaks with an authority and a responsibility which the people themselves have given him.

The history of our cabinets affords a striking illustration of the progress of the idea that the President is not merely the legal head but also the political leader of the nation. In the earlier days of the government it was customary for the President to fill his cabinet with the recognized leaders of his party. General Washington even tried the experiment which William of Orange tried at the very beginning of the era of cabinet government. He called to his aid the leaders of both political parties, associating Mr. Hamilton with Mr. Jefferson, on the theory that all views must be heard and considered in the conduct of the government. That was the day in which English precedent prevailed, and English cabinets were made up of the chief political characters of the day. But later years have witnessed a marked change in our practice, in this as in many other things. The old tradition was indeed slow in dying out.

It persisted with considerable vitality at least until General Garfield's day, and may yet from time to time revive, for many functions of our cabinets justify it and make it desirable. But our later Presidents have apparently ceased to regard the cabinet as a council of party leaders such as the party they represent would have chosen. They look upon it rather as a body of personal advisers whom the President chooses from the ranks of those whom he personally trusts and prefers to look to for advice. Our recent Presidents have not sought their associates among those whom the fortunes of party contest have brought into prominence and influence, but have called their personal friends and business colleagues to cabinet positions, and men who have given proof of their efficiency in private, not in public, life,—bankers who had never had any place in the formal counsels of the party, eminent lawyers who had held aloof from politics, private secretaries who had shown an unusual sagacity and proficiency in handling public business; as if the President were himself alone the leader of his party, the members of his cabinet only his private advisers, at any rate advisers of his private choice. Mr. Cleveland may be said to have been the first President to make this conception of the cabinet prominent in his choices, and he did not do so until his second administration. Mr. Roosevelt has emphasized the idea.

Upon analysis it seems to mean this: the cabinet is an executive, not a political body. The President cannot himself be the actual executive; he must therefore find, to act in his stead, men of the best legal and business gifts, and depend upon them for the actual administration of the government in all its daily activities. If he seeks political advice of his executive colleagues, he seeks it because he relies upon their natural good sense and experienced judgment, upon their knowledge of the country and its business and social conditions, upon their sagacity as representative citizens of more than usual observation and discretion; not because they are supposed to have had any very intimate contact with politics or to have made a profession of public affairs. He has chosen, not representative politicians, but eminent representative citizens, selecting them rather for their special fitness for the great business posts to which he has assigned them than for their political experience, and looking to them for advice in the actual conduct of the government rather than in the shaping of political policy. They are, in his view, not necessarily political officers at all.

It may with a great deal of plausibility be argued that the Constitution looks upon the President himself in the same way. It does not seem to make him a prime minister or the leader of the nation's counsels. Some Presidents are, therefore, and some are not. It depends upon the man and his gifts. He may be like his cabinet, or he may be more than his cabinet. His office is a mere vantage ground from which he may be sure that effective words of advice and timely efforts at reform will gain telling momentum. He has the ear of the nation as of course, and a great person may use such an advantage greatly. If he use the opportunity, he may take his cabinet into partnership or not, as he pleases; and so its character may vary with his. Self-reliant men will regard their cabinets as executive councils; men less self-reliant or more prudent will regard them as also political councils, and will wish to call into them men who have earned the confidence of their party. The character of the cabinet may be made a nice index of the theory of the presidential office, as well as of the President's theory of party government; but the one view is, so far as I can see, as constitutional as the other.

One of the greatest of the President's powers I have not yet spoken of at all: his control, which is very absolute, of the foreign relations of the nation. The initiative in foreign affairs, which the President possesses without any restriction whatever, is virtually the power to control them absolutely. The President cannot conclude a treaty with a foreign power without the consent of the Senate, but he may guide every step of diplomacy, and to guide diplomacy is to determine what treaties must be made, if the faith and prestige of the government are to be maintained. He need disclose no step of negotiation until it is complete, and when in any critical matter it is completed the government is virtually committed. Whatever its disinclination, the Senate may feel itself committed also.

I have not dwelt upon this power of the President, because it has been decisively influential in determining the character and influence of the office at only two periods in our history; at the very first, when the government was young and had so to use its incipient force as to win the respect of the nations into whose family it had thrust itself, and in our own day when the results of the Spanish War, the ownership of distant possessions, and many sharp struggles for foreign trade make it necessary that we should turn our best talents to the task of dealing firmly, wisely, and justly with political and commercial rivals. The President can never again be the mere domestic figure he has been throughout so large a part of our history. The nation has risen to the first rank in power and resources. The other nations of the world look askance upon her, half in envy, half in fear, and wonder with a deep anxiety what she will do with her vast strength. They receive the frank professions of men like Mr. John Hay, whom we wholly trusted, with a grain of salt, and doubt what we were sure of, their truthfulness and sincerity, suspecting a hidden design under every utterance he makes. Our President must always, henceforth, be one of the great powers of the world, whether he act greatly and wisely or not, and the best statesmen we can produce will be needed to fill the office of Secretary of State. We have but begun to see the presidential office in this light; but it is the light which will more and more beat upon it, and more and more determine its character and its effect upon the politics of the nation. We can never hide our President again as a mere domestic officer. We can never again see him the mere executive he was in the thirties and forties. He must stand always at the front of our affairs, and the office will be as big and as influential as the man who occupies it.

How is it possible to sum up the duties and influence of such an office in such a system in comprehensive terms which will cover all its changeful aspects? In the view of the makers of the Constitution the President was to be legal executive; perhaps the leader of the nation; certainly not the leader of the party, at any rate while in office. But by the operation of forces inherent in the very nature of government he has become all three, and by inevitable consequence the most heavily burdened officer in the world. No other man's day is so full as his, so full of the responsibilities which tax mind and conscience alike and demand an inexhaustible vitality. The mere task of making appointments to office, which the Constitution imposes upon the President, has come near to breaking some of our Presidents down, because it is a never-ending task in a civil service not yet put upon a professional footing, confused with short terms of office, always forming and dissolving. And in proportion as the President ventures to use his opportunity to lead opinion and act as spokesman of the people in affairs the people stand ready to overwhelm him by running to him with every question, great and small. They are as eager to have him settle a literary question as a political; hear him as acquiescently with regard to matters of special expert knowledge as with regard to public affairs, and call upon him to quiet all troubles by his personal intervention. Men of ordinary physique and discretion cannot be Presidents and live, if the strain be not somehow relieved. We shall be obliged always to be picking our chief magistrates from among wise and prudent athletes,—a small class.

The future development of the presidency, therefore, must certainly, one would confidently predict, run along such lines as the President's later relations with his cabinet suggest. General Washington, partly out of unaffected modesty, no doubt, but also out of the sure practical instinct which he possessed in so unusual a degree, set an example which few of his successors seem to have followed in any systematic manner. He made constant and intimate use of his colleagues in every matter that he handled, seeking their assistance and advice by letter when they were at a distance and he could not obtain it in person. It is well known to all close students of our history that his greater state papers, even those which seem in some peculiar and intimate sense his personal utterances, are full of the ideas and the very phrases of the men about him whom he most trusted. His rough drafts came back to him from Mr. Hamilton and Mr. Madison in great part rephrased and rewritten, in many passages reconceived and given a new color. He thought and acted always by the light of counsel, with a will and definite choice of his own, but through the instrumentality of other minds as well as his own. The duties and responsibilities laid upon the President by the Constitution can be changed only by constitutional amendment,—a thing too difficult to attempt except upon some greater necessity than the relief of an overburdened office, even though that office be the greatest in the land; and it is to be doubted whether the deliberate opinion of the country would consent to make of the President a less powerful officer than he is. He can secure his own relief without shirking any real responsibility. Appointments, for example, he can, if he will, make more and more upon the advice and choice of his executive colleagues; every matter of detail not only, but also every minor matter of counsel or of general policy, he can more and more depend upon his chosen advisers to determine; he need reserve for himself only the larger matters of counsel and that general oversight of the business of the government and of the persons who conduct it which is not possible without intimate daily consultations, indeed, but which is possible without attempting the intolerable burden of direct control. This is, no doubt, the idea of their functions which most Presidents have entertained and which most Presidents suppose themselves to have acted on; but we have reason to believe that most of our Presidents have taken their duties too literally and have attempted the impossible. But we can safely predict that as the multitude of the President's duties increases, as it must with the growth and widening activities of the nation itself, the incumbents of the great office will more and more come to feel that they are administering it in its truest purpose and with greatest effect by regarding themselves as less and less executive officers and more and more directors of affairs and leaders of the nation,—men of counsel and of the sort of action that makes for enlightenment.

14

Inaugural Address, 1905*

Theodore Roosevelt

Theodore Roosevelt's convincing victory in the 1904 election reflected his broad appeal. From his support of the Sherman Anti-Trust Act to his active foreign policy that produced the Panama Canal and the Roosevelt Corollary, Roosevelt used the "bully pulpit" in both progressive and conservative causes. In the following selection, he calls upon the American people to address the pressing needs wrought by industrialization.

My fellow-citizens, no people on earth have more cause to be thankful than ours, and this is said reverently, in no spirit of boastfulness in our own strength, but with gratitude to the Giver of Good who has blessed us with the conditions which have enabled us to achieve so large a measure of well-being and of happiness. To us as a people it has been granted to lay the foundations of our national life in a new continent. We are the heirs of the ages, and yet we have had to pay few of the penalties which in old countries are exacted by the dead hand of a bygone civilization. We have not been obliged to fight for our existence against any alien race; and yet our life has called for the vigor and effort without which the manlier and hardier virtues wither away. Under such conditions it would be our own fault if we failed; and the success which we have had in the past, the success which we confidently believe the future will bring, should cause in us no feeling of vainglory, but rather a deep and abiding realization of all which life has offered us; a full acknowledgement of the responsibility

* Editors' Note: Theodore Roosevelt, "Inaugural Address, 1905," in *A Compilation of the Messages and Papers of the Presidents* 14, comp. James D. Richardson (Bureau of National Literature, Inc., 1917), 6930–32.

which is ours; and a fixed determination to show that under a free government a mighty people can thrive best, alike as regards the things of the body and the things of the soul.

Much has been given us, and much will rightfully be expected from us. We have duties to others and duties to ourselves; and we can shirk neither. We have become a great nation, forced by the fact of its greatness into relations with other nations of the earth, and we must behave as beseems a people with such responsibilities. Toward all other nations, large and small, our attitude must be one of cordial and sincere friendship. We must show not only in our words, but in our deeds, that we are earnestly desirous of securing their good will by acting toward them in a spirit of just and generous recognition of all their rights. But justice and generosity in a nation, as in an individual, count most when shown not by the weak but by the strong. While ever careful to refrain from wronging others, we must be no less insistent that we are not wronged ourselves. We wish peace, but we wish the peace of justice, the peace of righteousness. We wish it because we think it is right and not because we are afraid. No weak nation that acts manfully and justly should ever have cause to fear us, and no strong power should ever be able to single us out as a subject for insolent aggression.

Our relations with the other powers of the world are important; but still more important are our relations among ourselves. Such growth in wealth, in population, and in power as this nation has seen during the century and a quarter of its national life is inevitably accompanied by a like growth in the problems which are ever before every nation that rises to greatness. Power invariably means both responsibility and danger. Our forefathers faced certain perils which we have outgrown. We now face other perils, the very existence of which it was impossible that they should foresee. Modern life is both complex and intense, and the tremendous changes wrought by the extraordinary industrial development of the last half century are felt in every fiber of our social and political being. Never before have men tried so vast and formidable experiment as that of administering the affairs of a continent under the forms of a Democratic republic. The conditions which have told for our marvelous material well-being, which have developed to a very high degree our energy, self-reliance, and individual initiative, have also brought the care and anxiety inseparable from the accumulation of great wealth in industrial centers. Upon the success of our experiment much depends, not only as regards our own welfare, but as regards the welfare of mankind. If we fail, the cause of free self-government throughout the world will rock to its foundations, and therefore our responsibility is heavy, to ourselves, to the world as it is to-day, and to the generations yet unborn. There is no good reason why we should fear the future, but there is every reason why we should face it seriously, neither hiding from ourselves the gravity of the problems before us nor fearing to approach these problems with the unbending, unflinching purpose to solve them aright.

Yet, after all, though the problems are new, though the tasks set before us differ from the tasks set before our fathers who founded and preserved this Republic, the spirit in which these tasks must be undertaken and these problems faced, if our duty is to be well done, remains essentially unchanged. We know that self-government is difficult. We know that no people needs such high traits of character as that people which seeks to govern its affairs aright through the freely expressed will of the freemen who compose it. But we have faith that we shall not prove false to the memories of the men of the mighty past. They did their work, they left us the splendid heritage we now enjoy. We in our turn have an assured confidence that we shall be able to leave this heritage unwasted and enlarged to our children and our children's children. To do so we must show, not merely in great crises, but in the everyday affairs of life, the qualities of practical intelligence, of courage, of hardihood, and endurance, and above all the power of devotion to a lofty ideal, which made great the men who founded this Republic in the days of Washington, which made great the men who preserved this Republic in the days of Abraham Lincoln.

March 4, 1905.

15

The Presidency; Making an Old Party Progressive*

From *An Autobiography*, Chapter 10

Theodore Roosevelt

> Rich with reflections on his presidency, on the nature of presidential power in relation to the Constitution, and on leadership, this chapter from Theodore Roosevelt's *An Autobiography* may be best known for his explication of the so-called stewardship theory of executive power. Roosevelt's questionable reliance on Abraham Lincoln for this and other of his constitutional views is of particular interest.

On September 6, 1901, President McKinley was shot by an Anarchist in the city of Buffalo. I went to Buffalo at once. The President's condition seemed to be improving, and after a day or two we were told that he was practically out of danger. I then joined my family, who were in the Adirondacks, near the foot of Mount Tahawus. A day or two afterwards we took a long tramp through the forest, and in the afternoon I climbed Mount Tahawus. After reaching the top I had descended a few hundred feet to a shelf of land where there was a little lake, when I saw a guide coming out of the woods on our trail from below. I felt at once that he had bad news, and, sure enough, he handed me a telegram saying that the President's condition was much worse and that I must come to Buffalo immediately. It was late in the afternoon, and darkness had fallen by the time I reached the clubhouse where we were staying. It was some time afterwards before I could get a wagon to drive me out to the nearest railway station, North Creek, some forty or fifty miles distant.

* Editors' Note: Theodore Roosevelt, "The Presidency; Making an Old Party Progressive," in *An Autobiography* (New York: The Macmillan Company, 1913), 379–99. Excerpt. The author's footnotes have been omitted.

The roads were the ordinary wilderness roads and the night was dark. But we changed horses two or three times—when I say "we" I mean the driver and I, as there was no one else with us—and reached the station just at dawn, to learn from Mr. Loeb, who had a special train waiting, that the President was dead. That evening I took the oath of office, in the house of Ansley Wilcox, at Buffalo.

On three previous occasions the Vice-President had succeeded to the Presidency on the death of the President. In each case there had been a reversal of party policy, and a nearly immediate and nearly complete change in the personnel of the higher offices, especially the Cabinet. I had never felt that this was wise from any standpoint. If a man is fit to be President, he will speedily so impress himself in the office that the policies pursued will be his anyhow, and he will not have to bother as to whether he is changing them or not; while as regards the offices under him, the important thing for him is that his subordinates shall make a success in handling their several departments. The subordinate is sure to desire to make a success of his department for his own sake, and if he is a fit man, whose views on public policy are sound, and whose abilities entitle him to his position, he will do excellently under almost any chief with the same purposes.

I at once announced that I would continue unchanged McKinley's policies for the honor and prosperity of the country, and I asked all the members of the Cabinet to stay. There were no changes made among them save as changes were made among their successors whom I myself appointed. I continued Mr. McKinley's policies, changing and developing them and adding new policies only as the questions before the public changed and as the needs of the public developed. Some of my friends shook their heads over this, telling me that the men I retained would not be "loyal to me," and that I would seem as if I were "a pale copy of McKinley." I told them that I was not nervous on this score, and that if the men I retained were loyal to their work they would be giving me the loyalty for which I most cared; and that if they were not, I would change them anyhow; and that as for being "a pale copy of McKinley," I was not primarily concerned with either following or not following in his footsteps, but in facing the new problems that arose; and that if I were competent I would find ample opportunity to show my competence by my deeds without worrying myself as to how to convince people of the fact.

For the reasons I have already given in my chapter on the Governorship of New York, the Republican party, which in the days of Abraham Lincoln was founded as the radical progressive party of the Nation, had been obliged during the last decade of the nineteenth century to uphold the interests of popular government against a foolish and illjudged mock-radicalism. It remained the Nationalist as against the particularist or State's rights party, and in so far it remained absolutely sound; for little permanent good can be done by any party which worships the State's rights fetish or which fails to regard the State, like the county or the municipality, as merely a convenient unit for local self-government, while in all National matters, of importance to the whole people, the Nation is to be supreme over State, county, and town alike. But the State's rights fetish, although still effectively used at certain times by both courts and Congress to block needed National legislation directed against the huge corporations or in the interests of workingmen, was not a prime issue at the time of which I speak. In 1896, 1898, and 1900 the campaigns were waged on two great moral issues: (1) the imperative need of a sound and honest currency; (2) the need, after 1898, of meeting in manful and straightforward fashion the extraterritorial problems arising from the Spanish War. On these great moral issues the Republican party was right, and the men who were opposed to it, and who claimed to be the radicals, and their allies among the sentimentalists, were utterly and hopelessly wrong. This had, regrettably but perhaps inevitably, tended to throw the party into the hands not merely of the conservatives but of the reactionaries; of men who, sometimes for personal and improper reasons, but more often with entire sincerity and uprightness of purpose, distrusted anything that was progressive and dreaded radicalism. These men still from force of habit applauded what Lincoln had done in the way of radical dealing with the abuses of his day; but they did not apply the spirit in which Lincoln worked to the abuses of their own day. Both houses of Congress were controlled by these men. Their leaders in the Senate were Messrs. Aldrich and Hale. The Speaker of the House when I became President was Mr. Henderson, but in a little over a year he was succeeded by Mr. Cannon, who, although widely differing from Senator Aldrich in matters of detail, represented the same type of public sentiment. There were many points on which I agreed with Mr. Cannon and Mr. Aldrich, and some points on which I agreed with Mr. Hale. I made a resolute effort to get on with all three and with their followers, and I have no question that they made an equally resolute effort to get on with me. We succeeded in working together, although with increasing friction, for some years, I pushing forward and they hanging back. Gradually, however, I was forced to abandon the effort to persuade them to come my way, and then I achieved results only by appealing over the heads of the Senate and House leaders to the people, who were the masters of both of us. I continued in this way to get results until almost the close of my term; and the Republican party became once more the progressive and indeed the fairly radical progressive party of the Nation. When my successor was chosen, however, the leaders of the House and Senate, or most of them, felt that it was safe to come to a break with me, and the last or short session of Congress, held between the election of my successor and his inauguration four months later, saw a series of contests between the majorities in the two houses of Congress and the President,—myself,—quite as bitter as if they and I had belonged to opposite political parties. However, I held my own. I was not able to push through the legislation I desired during these four months, but I was able to prevent them doing anything I did not desire, or undoing anything that I had already succeeded in getting done.

There were, of course, many Senators and members of the lower house with whom up to the very last I continued to work in hearty accord, and with a growing understanding. I have not the space to enumerate, as I would like to, these men. For many years Senator Lodge had been my close personal and political friend, with whom I discussed all public questions, that arose, usually with agreement; and our intimately close relations were of course unchanged by my entry into the White House. He was of all our public men the man who had made the closest and wisest study of our foreign relations, and more clearly than almost any other man he understood the vital fact that the efficiency of our navy conditioned our national efficiency in foreign affairs. Anything relating to our international relations, from Panama and the navy to the Alaskan boundary question, the Algeciras negotiations, or the peace of Portsmouth, I was certain to discuss with Senator Lodge and also with certain other members of Congress, such as Senator Turner of Washington and Representative Hitt of Illinois. Anything relating to labor legislation and to measures for controlling big business or efficiently regulating the giant railway systems, I was certain to discuss with Senator Dolliver or Congressman Hepburn or Congressman Cooper. With men like Senator Beveridge, Congressman (afterwards Senator) Dixon, and Congressman Murdock, I was apt to discuss pretty nearly everything relating to either our internal or our external affairs[.] There were many, many others. The present President of the Senate, Senator Clark, of Arkansas, was as fearless and high-minded a representative of the people of the United States as I ever dealt with. He was one of the men who combined loyalty to his own State with an equally keen loyalty to the people of all the United States. He was politically opposed to me; but when the interests of the country were at stake, he was incapable of considering party differences; and this was especially his attitude in international matters—including certain treaties which most of his party colleagues, with narrow lack of patriotism, and complete subordination of National to factional interest, opposed. I have never anywhere met finer, more faithful, more disinterested, and more loyal public servants than Senator O. H. Platt, a Republican, from Connecticut, and Senator Cockrell, a Democrat, from Missouri. They were already old men when I came to the Presidency; and doubtless there were points on which I seemed to them to be extreme and radical; but eventually they found that our motives and beliefs were the same, and they did all in their power to help any movement that was for the interest of our people as a whole. I had met them when I was Civil Service Commissioner and Assistant Secretary of the Navy. All I ever had to do with either was to convince him that a given measure I championed was right, and he then at once did all he could to have it put into effect. If I could not convince them, why! that was my fault, or my misfortune; but if I could convince them, I never had to think again as to whether they would or would not support me. There were many other men of mark in both houses with whom I could work on some points, whereas on others we had to differ. There was one powerful leader—a burly, forceful man, of admirable traits—who had, however, been trained in the post-bellum school of business and politics, so that his attitude towards life, quite unconsciously, reminded me a little of Artemus Ward's view of the Tower of London—"If I like it, I'll buy it." There was a big governmental job in which this leader was much interested, and in reference to which he always wished me to consult a man whom he trusted, whom I will call Pitt Rodney. One day I answered him, "The trouble with Rodney is that he misestimates his relations to cosmos"; to which he responded, "Cosmos— Cosmos? Never heard of him. You stick to Rodney. He's your man!" Outside of the public servants there were multitudes of men, in newspaper offices, in magazine offices, in business or the professions or on farms or in shops, who actively supported the policies for which I stood and did work of genuine leadership which was quite as effective as any work done by men in public office. Without the active support of these men I would have been powerless. In particular, the leading newspaper correspondents at Washington were as a whole a singularly able, trustworthy, and public-spirited body of men, and the most useful of all agents in the fight for efficient and decent government.

As for the men under me in executive office, I could not overstate the debt of gratitude I owe them. From the heads of the departments, the Cabinet officers, down, the most striking feature of the Administration was the devoted, zealous, and efficient work that was done as soon as it became understood that the one bond of interest among all of us was the desire to make the Government the most effective instrument in advancing the interests of the people as a whole, the interests of the average men and women of the United States and of their children. I do not think I overstate the case when I say that most of the men who did the best work under me felt that ours was a partnership, that we all stood on the same level of purpose and service, and that it mattered not what position anyone of us held so long as in that position he gave the very best that was in him. We worked very hard; but I made a point of getting a couple of hours off each day for equally vigorous play. The men with whom I then played, whom we laughingly grew to call the "Tennis Cabinet," have been mentioned in a previous chapter of this book in connection with the gift they gave me at the last breakfast which they took at the White House. There were many others in the public service under me with whom I happened not to play, but who did their share of our common work just as effectively as it was done by us who did play. Of course nothing could have been done in my Administration if it had not been for the zeal, intelligence, masterful ability, and downright hard labor of these men in countless positions under me. I was helpless to do anything except as my thoughts and orders were translated into action by them; and, moreover, each of them, as he grew specially fit for his job, used to suggest to me the right thought to have, and the right order to give, concerning that job. It is of course hard for me to speak with cold and dispassionate partiality of these men, who were as close to me as were the men of my regiment. But the outside observers best fitted to pass judgment about them felt as I did. At the end of my Administration Mr. Bryce, the British Ambassador, told me that in a long life, during which he had studied intimately the government of many different countries, he had never in any country seen a more eager, high-minded, and efficient set of public servants, men more useful and more creditable to their country, than the men then doing the work of the American Government in Washington and in the field. I repeat this statement with the permission of Mr. Bryce.

At about the same time, or a little before, in the spring of 1908, there appeared in the English *Fortnightly Review* an article, evidently by a competent eye witness, setting forth more in detail the same views to which the British Ambassador thus privately gave expression. It was in part as follows:

"Mr. Roosevelt has gathered around him a body of public servants who are nowhere surpassed, I question whether they are anywhere equaled, for efficiency, self-sacrifice, and an absolute devotion to their country's interests. Many of them are poor men, without private means, who have voluntarily abandoned high professional ambitions and turned their backs on the rewards of business to serve their country on salaries that are not merely inadequate, but indecently so. There is not one of them who is not constantly assailed by offers of positions in the world of commerce, finance, and the law that would satisfy every material ambition with which he began life. There is not one of them who could not, if he chose, earn outside Washington from ten to twenty times the income on which he economizes as a State official. But these men are as indifferent to money and to the power that money brings as to the allurements of Newport and New York, or to merely personal distinctions, or to the commercialized ideals which the great bulk of their fellow-countrymen accept without question. They are content, and more than content, to sink themselves in the National service without a thought of private advancement, and often at a heavy sacrifice of worldly honors, and to toil on . . . sustained by their own native impulse to make of patriotism an efficient instrument of public betterment."

The American public rarely appreciate the high quality of the work done by some of our diplomats—work, usually entirely unnoticed and unrewarded, which redounds to the interest and the honor of all of us. The most useful man in the entire diplomatic service, during my presidency, and for many years before, was Henry White; and I say this having in mind the high quality of work done by such admirable ambassadors and ministers as Bacon, Meyer, Straus, O'Brien, Rockhill, and Egan, to name only a few among many. When I left the presidency White was Ambassador to France; shortly afterwards he was removed by Mr. Taft, for reasons unconnected with the good of the service.

The most important factor in getting the right spirit in my Administration, next to the insistence upon courage, honesty, and a genuine democracy of desire to serve the plain people, was my insistence upon the theory that the executive power was limited only by specific restrictions and prohibitions appearing in the Constitution or imposed by the Congress under its Constitutional powers. My view was that every executive officer, and above all every executive officer in high position, was a steward of the people bound actively and affirmatively to do all he could for the people, and not to content himself with the negative merit of keeping his talents undamaged in a napkin. I declined to adopt the view that what was imperatively necessary for the Nation could not be done by the President unless he could find some specific authorization to do it. My belief was that it was not only his right but his duty to do anything that the needs of the Nation demanded unless such action was forbidden by the Constitution or by the laws. Under this interpretation of executive power I did and caused to be done many things not previously done by the President and the heads of the departments. I did not usurp power, but I did greatly broaden the use of executive power. In other words, I acted for the public welfare, I acted for the common well-being of all our people, whenever and in whatever manner was necessary, unless prevented by direct constitutional or legislative prohibition. I did not care a rap for the mere form and show of power; I cared immensely for the use that could be made of the substance. The Senate at one time objected to my communicating with them in printing, preferring the expensive, foolish, and laborious practice of writing out the messages by hand. It was not possible to return to the outworn archaism of hand writing; but we endeavored to have the printing made as pretty as possible. Whether I communicated with the Congress in writing or by word of mouth, and whether the writing was by a machine, or a pen, were equally, and absolutely, unimportant matters. The importance lay in what I said and in the heed paid to what I said. So as to my meeting and consulting Senators, Congressmen, politicians, financiers, and labor men. I consulted all who wished to see me; and if I wished to see anyone, I sent for him; and where the consultation took place was a matter of supreme unimportance. I consulted every man with the sincere hope that I could profit by and follow his advice; I consulted every member of Congress who wished to be consulted, hoping to be able to come to an agreement of action with him; and I always finally acted as my conscience and common sense bade me act.

About appointments I was obliged by the Constitution to consult the Senate; and the long-established custom of the Senate meant that in practice this consultation was with individual Senators and even with big politicians who stood behind the Senators. I was only one-half the appointing power; I nominated; but the Senate confirmed. In practice, by what was called "the courtesy of the Senate," the Senate normally refused to confirm any appointment if the Senator from the State objected to it. In exceptional cases, where I could arouse public attention, I could force through the appointment in spite of the opposition of the Senators; in all ordinary cases this was impossible. On the other hand, the Senator could of course do nothing for any man unless I chose to nominate him. In consequence the Constitution itself forced the President and the Senators from each State to come to a working agreement on the appointments in and from that State.

My course was to insist on absolute fitness, including honesty, as a prerequisite to every appointment; and to remove only for good cause, and, where there was such cause, to refuse even to discuss with the Senator in interest the unfit servant's retention. Subject to these considerations, I normally accepted each Senator's recommendations for offices of a routine kind, such as most post-offices and the like, but insisted on myself choosing the men for the more important positions. I was willing to take any good man for postmaster; but in the case of a Judge or District Attorney or Canal Commissioner or Ambassador, I was apt to insist either on a given man or else on any man with a given class of qualifications. If the Senator deceived me, I took care that he had no opportunity to repeat the deception.

I can perhaps best illustrate my theory of action by two specific examples. In New York Governor Odell and Senator Platt sometimes worked in agreement and sometimes were at swords' points, and both wished to be consulted. To a friendly Congressman, who was also their friend, I wrote as follows on July 22, 1903:

"I want to work with Platt. I want to work with Odell. I want to support both and take the advice of both. But of course ultimately I must be the judge as to acting on the advice given. When, as in the case of the judgeship, I am convinced that the advice of both is wrong, I shall act as I did when I appointed Holt. When I can find a friend of Odell's like Cooley, who is thoroughly fit for the position I desire to fill, it gives me the greatest pleasure to appoint him. When Platt proposes to me a man like Hamilton Fish, it is equally a pleasure to appoint him."

This was written in connection with events which led up to my refusing to accept Senator Platt's or Governor Odell's sug[g]estions as to a Federal Judgeship and a Federal District Attorneyship, and insisting on the appointment, first of Judge Hough and later of District Attorney Stimson; because in each case I felt that the work to be done was of so high an order that I could not take an ordinary man.

The other case was that of Senator Fulton, of Oregon. Through Francis Heney I was prosecuting men who were implicated in a vast network of conspiracy against the law in connection with the theft of public land in Oregon. I had been acting on Senator Fulton's recommendations for office, in the usual manner. Heney had been insisting that Fulton was in league with the men we were prosecuting, and that he had recommended unfit men. Fulton had been protesting against my following Heney's advice, particularly as regards appointing Judge Wolverton as United States Judge. Finally Heney laid before me a report which convinced me of the truth of his statements. I then wrote to Fulton as follows, on November 20, 1905:

"My dear Senator Fulton: I inclose you herewith a copy of the report made to me by Mr. Heney. I have seen the originals of the letters from you and Senator Mitchell quoted therein. I do not at this time desire to discuss the report itself, which of course I must submit to the Attorney-General. But I have been obliged to reach the painful conclusion that your own letters as therein quoted tend to show that you recommended for the position of District Attorney B when you had good reason to believe that he had himself been guilty of fraudulent conduct; that you recommended C for the same position simply because it was for B's interest that he should be so recommended, and, as there is reason to believe, because he had agreed to divide the fees with B if he were appointed; and that you finally recommended the reappointment of H with the knowledge that if H were appointed he would abstain from prosecuting B for criminal misconduct, this being why B advocated H's claims for reappointment. If you care to make any statement in the matter, I shall of course be glad to hear it. As the District Judge of Oregon I shall appoint Judge Wolverton."

In the letter I of course gave in full the names indicated above by initials. Senator Fulton gave no explanation. I therefore ceased to consult him about appointments under the Department of Justice and the Interior, the two departments in which the crookedness had occurred—there was no question of crookedness in the other offices in the State, and they could be handled in the ordinary manner. Legal proceedings were undertaken against his colleague in the Senate, and one of his colleagues in the lower house, and the former was convicted and sentenced to the penitentiary.

In a number of instances the legality of executive acts of my Administration was brought before the courts. They were uniformly sustained. For example, prior to 1907 statutes relating to the disposition of coal lands had been construed as fixing the flat price at $10 to $20 per acre. The result was that valuable coal lands were sold for wholly inadequate prices, chiefly to big corporations. By executive order the coal lands were withdrawn and not opened for entry until proper classification was placed thereon by Government agents. There was a great clamor that I was usurping legislative power; but the acts were not assailed in court until we brought suits to set aside entries made by persons and associations to obtain larger areas than the statutes authorized. This position was opposed on the ground that the restrictions imposed were illegal; that the executive orders were illegal. The Supreme Court sustained the Government. In the same way our attitude in the water power question was sustained, the Supreme Court holding that the Federal Government had the rights we claimed over streams that are or may be declared navigable by Congress. Again, when Oklahoma became a State we were obliged to use the executive power to protect Indian rights and property, for there had been an enormous amount of fraud in the obtaining of Indian lands by white men. Here we were denounced as usurping power over a State as well as usurping power that did not belong to the executive. The Supreme Court sustained our action.

In connection with the Indians, by the way, it was again and again necessary to assert the position of the President as steward of the whole people. I had a capital Indian Commissioner, Francis E. Leupp. I found that I could rely on his judgment not to get me into fights that were unnecessary, and therefore I always backed him to the limit when he told me that a fight was necessary. On one occasion, for example, Congress passed a bill to sell to settlers about half a million acres of Indian land in Oklahoma at one and a half dollars an acre. I refused to sign it, and turned the matter over to Leupp. The bill was accordingly withdrawn, amended so as to safeguard the welfare of the Indians, and the minimum price raised to five dollars an acre. Then I signed the bill. We sold that land under sealed bids, and realized for the Kiowa, Comanche, and Apache Indians more than four million dollars—three millions and a quarter more than they would have obtained if I had signed the bill in its original form. In another case, where there had been a division among the Sac and Fox Indians, part of the tribe removing to Iowa, the Iowa delegation in Congress, backed by two Iowans who were members of my Cabinet, passed a bill awarding a sum of nearly a half million dollars to the Iowa seceders. They had not consulted the Indian Bureau. Leupp protested against the bill, and I vetoed it. A subsequent bill was passed on the lines laid down by the Indian Bureau, referring the whole controversy to the courts, and the Supreme Court in the end justified our position by deciding against the Iowa seceders and awarding the money to the Oklahoma stay-at-homes.

As to all action of this kind there have long been two schools of political thought, upheld with equal sincerity. The division has not normally been along political, but temperamental, lines. The course I followed, of regarding the executive as subject only to the people, and, under the Constitution, bound to serve the people affirmatively in cases where the Constitution does not explicitly forbid him to render the service, was substantially the course followed by both Andrew Jackson and Abraham Lincoln. Other honorable and well-meaning Presidents, such as James Buchanan, took the opposite and, as it seems to me, narrowly legalistic view that the President is the servant of Congress rather than of the people, and can do nothing, no matter how necessary it be to act, unless the Constitution explicitly commands the action. Most able lawyers who are past middle age take this view, and so do large numbers of well-meaning, respectable citizens. My successor in office took this, the Buchanan, view of the President's powers and duties.

For example, under my Administration we found that one of the favorite methods adopted by the men desirous of stealing the public domain was to carry the decision of the Secretary of the Interior into court. By vigorously opposing such action, and only by so doing, we were able to carry out the policy of properly protecting the public domain. My successor not only took the opposite view, but recommended to Congress the passage of a bill which would have given the courts direct appellate power over the Secretary of the Interior in these land matters. This bill was reported favorably by Mr. Mondell, Chairman of the House Committee on public lands, a Congressman who took the lead in every measure to prevent the conservation of our natural resources and the preservation of the National domain for the use of home-seekers. Fortunately, Congress declined to pass the bill. Its passage would have been a veritable calamity.

I acted on the theory that the President could at any time in his discretion withdraw from entry any of the public lands of the United States and reserve the same for forestry, for water-power sites, for irrigation, and other public purposes. Without such action it would have been impossible to stop the activity of the land thieves. No one ventured to test its legality by lawsuit. My successor, however, himself questioned it, and referred the matter to Congress. Again Congress showed its wisdom by passing a law which gave the President the power which he had long exercised, and of which my successor had shorn himself.

Perhaps the sharp difference between what may be called the Lincoln-Jackson and the Buchanan-Taft schools, in their views of the power and duties of the President, may be best illustrated by comparing the attitude of my successor toward his Secretary of the Interior, Mr. Ballinger, when the latter was accused of gross misconduct in office, with my attitude towards my chiefs of department and other subordinate officers. More than once while I was President my officials were attacked by Congress, generally because these officials did their duty well and fearlessly. In every such case I stood by the official and refused to recognize the right of Congress to interfere with me excepting by impeachment or in other Constitutional manner. On the other hand, wherever I found the officer unfit for his position I promptly removed him, even although the most influential men in Congress fought for his retention. The Jackson-Lincoln view is that a President who is fit to do good work should be able to form his own judgment as to his own subordinates, and, above all, of the subordinates standing highest and in closest and most intimate touch with him. My secretaries and their subordinates were responsible to me, and I accepted the responsibility for all their deeds. As long as they were satisfactory to me I stood by them against every critic or assailant, within or without Congress; and as for getting Congress to make up my mind for me about them, the thought would have been inconceivable to me. My successor took the opposite, or Buchanan, view when he permitted and requested Congress to pass judgment on the charges made against Mr. Ballinger as an executive officer. These charges were made to the President; the President had the facts before him and could get at them at any time, and he alone had power to act if the charges were true. However, he permitted and requested Congress to investigate Mr. Ballinger. The party minority of the committee that investigated him, and one member of the majority, declared that the charges were well founded and that Mr. Ballinger should be removed. The other members of the majority declared the charges ill founded. The President abode by the view of the majority. Of course believers in the Jackson-Lincoln theory of the Presidency would not be content with this town meeting majority and minority method of determining by another branch of the Government what it seems the especial duty of the President himself to determine for himself in dealing with his own subordinate in his own department.

There are many worthy people who reprobate the Buchanan method as a matter of history, but who in actual life reprobate still more strongly the Jackson-Lincoln method when it is put into practice. These persons conscientiously believe that the President should solve every doubt in favor of inaction as against action, that he should construe strictly and narrowly the Constitutional grant of powers both to the National Government, and to the President within the National Government. In addition, however, to the men who conscientiously believe in this course from high, although as I hold misguided, motives, there are many men who affect to believe in it merely because it enables them to attack and to try to hamper, for partisan or personal reasons, an executive whom they dislike. There are other men in whom, especially when they are themselves in office, practical adherence to the Buchanan principle represents not well-thought-out devotion to an unwise course, but simple weakness of character and desire to avoid trouble and responsibility. Unfortunately, in practice it makes little difference which class of ideas actuates the President, who by his action sets a cramping precedent. Whether he is high minded and wrongheaded or merely infirm of purpose, whether he means well feebly or is bound by a mischievous misconception of the powers and duties of the National Government and of the President, the effect of his actions is the same. The President's duty is to act so that he himself and his subordinates shall be able to do efficient work for the people, and this efficient work he and they cannot do if Congress is permitted to undertake the task of making up his mind for him as to how he shall [perform] what is clearly his sole duty[.]

. . .

V

NATIONAL ADMINISTRATION

16

The Study of Administration*

Woodrow Wilson

Perhaps Woodrow Wilson's most famous and influential scholarly essay, "The Study of Administration" introduces into American political thinking a central feature of administrative science that Wilson had learned from his extensive study of the theory and practice of Prussian bureaucracy: its separation from politics. Wilson here suggests that there are significant governmental powers — administrative powers — that exist, for the most part, outside of the boundaries of the Constitution and its separation-of-powers framework. This essay is credited by many public administration scholars as the launching point for their discipline in the United States.

I suppose that no practical science is ever studied where there is no need to know it. The very fact, therefore, that the eminently practical science of administration is finding its way into college courses in this country would prove that this country needs to know more about administration, were such proof of the fact required to make out a case. It need not be said, how ever, that we do not look into college programmes for proof of this fact. It is a thing almost taken for granted among us, that the present movement called civil service reform must, after the accomplishment of its first purpose, expand into efforts to improve, not the *personnel* only, but also the organization and methods of our government offices: because it is plain that their organization and methods need improvement only less than their *personnel*. It is the object

---

* Editors' Note: Woodrow Wilson, "The Study of Administration," *Political Science Quarterly* 2 (July 1887): 197–222.

of administrative study to discover, first, what government can properly and successfully do, and, secondly, how it can do these proper things with the utmost possible efficiency and at the least possible cost either of money or of energy. On both these points there is obviously much need of light among us; and only careful study can supply that light.

Before entering on that study, however, it is needful:

I. To take some account of what others have done in the same line; that is to say, of the history of the study.
II. To ascertain just what is its subject-matter.
III. To determine just what are the best methods by which to develop it, and the most clarifying political conceptions to carry with us into it.

Unless we know and settle these things, we shall set out without chart or compass.

I.

The science of administration is the latest fruit of that study of the science of politics which was begun some twenty-two hundred years ago. It is a birth of our own century, almost of our own generation.

Why was it so late in coming? Why did it wait till this too busy century of ours to demand attention for itself? Administration is the most obvious part of government; it is government in action; it is the executive, the operative, the most visible side of government, and is of course as old as government itself. It is government in action, and one might very naturally expect to find that government in action had arrested the attention and provoked the scrutiny of writers of politics very early in the history of systematic thought.

But such was not the case. No one wrote systematically of administration as a branch of the science of government until the present century had passed its first youth and had begun to put forth its characteristic flower of systematic knowledge. Up to our own day all the political writers whom we now read had thought, argued, dogmatized only about the *constitution* of government; about the nature of the state, the essence and seat of sovereignty, popular power and kingly prerogative; about the greatest meanings lying at the heart of government, and the high ends set before the purpose of government by man's nature and man's aims. The central field of controversy was that great field of theory in which monarchy rode tilt against democracy, in which oligarchy would have built for itself strongholds of privilege, and in which tyranny sought opportunity to make good its claim to receive submission from all competitors. Amidst this high warfare of principles, administration could command no pause for its own consideration. The question was always: Who shall make law, and what shall that law be? The other question, how law should be administered with enlightenment, with equity, with speed, and without friction, was put aside as "practical detail" which clerks could arrange after doctors had agreed upon principles.

That political philosophy took this direction was of course no accident, no chance preference or perverse whim of political philosophers. The philosophy of any time is, as Hegel says, "nothing but the spirit of that time expressed in abstract thought"; and political philosophy, like philosophy of every other kind, has only held up the mirror to contemporary affairs. The trouble in early times was almost altogether about the constitution of government; and consequently that was what engrossed men's thoughts. There was little or no trouble about administration,—at least little that was heeded by administrators. The functions of government were simple, because life itself was simple. Government went about imperatively and compelled men, without thought of consulting their wishes. There was no complex system of public revenues and public debts to puzzle financiers; there were, consequently, no financiers to be puzzled. No one who possessed power was long at a loss how to use it. The great and only question was: Who shall possess it? Populations were of manageable numbers; property was of simple sorts. There were plenty of farms, but no stocks and bonds: more cattle than vested interests.

I have said that all this was true of "early times"; but it was substantially true also of comparatively late times. One does not have to look back of the last century for the beginnings of the present complexities of trade and perplexities of commercial speculation, nor for the portentous birth of national debts. Good Queen Bess, doubtless, thought that the monopolies of the sixteenth century were hard enough to handle without burning her hands; but they are not remembered in the presence of the giant monopolies of the nineteenth century. When Blackstone lamented that corporations had no bodies to be kicked and no souls to be damned, he was anticipating the proper time for such regrets by full a century. The perennial discords between master and workmen which now so often disturb industrial society began before the Black Death and the Statute of Laborers; but never before our own day did they assume such ominous proportions as they wear now. In brief, if difficulties of governmental action are to be seen gathering in other centuries, they are to be seen culminating in our own.

This is the reason why administrative tasks have nowadays to be so studiously and systematically adjusted to carefully tested standards of policy, the reason why we are having now what we never had before, a science of administration. The weightier debates of constitutional principle are even yet by no means concluded; but they are no longer of more immediate practical moment than questions of administration. It is getting to be harder to *run* a constitution than to frame one.

Here is Mr. Bagehot's graphic, whimsical way of depicting the difference between the old and the new in administration:

> In early times, when a despot wishes to govern a distant province, he sends down a satrap on a grand horse, and other people on little horses; and very little is heard of the satrap again unless he send back some of the little people to tell what he has been doing. No great labour of superintendence is possible. Common rumour and casual report are the sources of intelligence. If it seems certain that the province is in a bad state, satrap No. 1 is recalled, and satrap No. 2 sent out in his stead. In civilized countries the process is different. You erect a bureau in the province you want to govern; you make it write letters and copy letters; it sends home eight reports *per diem* to the head bureau in St. Petersburg. Nobody does a sum in the province without some one doing the same sum in the capital, to "check" him, and see that he does it correctly. The consequence of this is, to throw on the heads of departments an amount of reading and labour which can only be accomplished by the greatest natural aptitude, the most efficient training, the most firm and regular industry.[1]

There is scarcely a single duty of government which was once simple which is not now complex; government once had but a few masters; it now has scores of masters. Majorities formerly only underwent government; they now conduct government. Where government once might follow the whims of a court, it must now follow the views of a nation.

And those views are steadily widening to new conceptions of state duty; so that, at the same time that the functions of government are every day becoming more complex and difficult, they are also vastly multiplying in number. Administration is everywhere putting its hands to new undertakings. The utility, cheapness, and success of the government's postal service, for instance, point towards the early establishment of governmental control of the telegraph system. Or, even if our government is not to follow the lead of the governments of Europe in buying or building both telegraph and railroad lines, no one can doubt that in some way it must make itself master of masterful corporations. The creation of national commissioners of railroads, in addition to the older state commissions, involves a very important and delicate extension of administrative functions. Whatever hold of authority state or federal governments are to take upon corporations, there must follow cares and responsibilities which will require not a little wisdom, knowledge, and experi-

---

1. Essay on William Pitt.

ence. Such things must be studied in order to be well done. And these, as I have said, are only a few of the doors which are being opened to offices of government. The idea of the state and the consequent ideal of its duty are undergoing noteworthy change; and "the idea of the state is the conscience of administration." Seeing every day new things which the state ought to do, the next thing is to see clearly how it ought to do them.

This is why there should be a science of administration which shall seek to straighten the paths of government, to make its business less unbusinesslike, to strengthen and purify its organization, and to crown its duties with dutifulness. This is one reason why there is such a science.

But where has this science grown up? Surely not on this side the sea. Not much impartial scientific method is to be discerned in our administrative practices. The poisonous atmosphere of city government, the crooked secrets of state administration, the confusion, sinecurism, and corruption ever and again discovered in the bureaux at Washington forbid us to believe that any clear conceptions of what constitutes good administration are as yet very widely current in the United States. No; American writers have hitherto taken no very important part in the advancement of this science. It has found its doctors in Europe. It is not of our making; it is a foreign science, speaking very little of the language of English or American principle. It employs only foreign tongues; it utters none but what are to our minds alien ideas. Its aims, its examples, its conditions, are almost exclusively grounded in the histories of foreign races, in the precedents of foreign systems, in the lessons of foreign revolutions. It has been developed by French and German professors, and is consequently in all parts adapted to the needs of a compact state, and made to fit highly centralized forms of government; whereas, to answer our purposes, it must be adapted, not to a simple and compact, but to a complex and multiform state, and made to fit highly decentralized forms of government. If we would employ it, we must Americanize it, and that not formally, in language merely, but radically, in thought, principle, and aim as well. It must learn our constitutions by heart; must get the bureaucratic fever out of its veins; must inhale much free American air.

If an explanation be sought why a science manifestly so susceptible of being made useful to all governments alike should have received attention first in Europe, where government has long been a monopoly, rather than in England or the United States, where government has long been a common franchise, the reason will doubtless be found to be twofold: first, that in Europe, just because government was independent of popular assent, there was more governing to be done; and, second, that the desire to keep government a monopoly made the monopolists interested in discovering the least irritating means of governing. They were, besides, few enough to adopt means promptly.

It will be instructive to look into this matter a little more closely. In speaking of European governments I do not, of course, include England. She has not refused to change with the times. She has simply tempered the severity of the transition from a polity of aristocratic privilege to a system of democratic power by slow measures of constitutional reform which, without preventing revolution, has confined it to paths of peace. But the countries of the continent for a long time desperately struggled against all change, and would have diverted revolution by softening the asperities of absolute government. They sought so to perfect their machinery as to destroy all wearing friction, so to sweeten their methods with consideration for the interests of the governed as to placate all hindering hatred, and so assiduously and opportunely to offer their aid to all classes of undertakings as to render themselves indispensable to the industrious. They did at last give the people constitutions and the franchise; but even after that they obtained leave to continue despotic by becoming paternal. They made themselves too efficient to be dispensed with, too smoothly operative to be noticed, too enlightened to be inconsiderately questioned, too benevolent to be suspected, too powerful to be coped with. All this has required study; and they have closely studied it.

On this side the sea we, the while, had known no great difficulties of government. With a new country, in which there was room and remunerative employment for everybody, with liberal principles of government and unlimited skill in practical politics, we were long exempted from the need of being anxiously careful about plans and methods of administration. We have naturally been slow to see the use or significance of those many volumes of learned research and painstaking examination into the ways and means of conducting government which the presses of Europe have been sending to our libraries. Like a lusty child, government with us has expanded in nature and grown great in stature, but has also become awkward in movement. The vigor and increase of its life has been altogether out of proportion to its skill in living. It has gained strength, but it has not acquired deportment. Great, therefore, as has been our advantage over the countries of Europe in point of ease and health of constitutional development, now that the time for more careful administrative adjustments and larger administrative knowledge has come to us, we are at a signal disadvantage as compared with the transatlantic nations; and this for reasons which I shall try to make clear.

Judging by the constitutional histories of the chief nations of the modern world, there may be said to be three periods of growth through which government has passed in all the most highly developed of existing systems, and through which it promises to pass in all the rest. The first of these periods is that of absolute rulers, and of an administrative system adapted to absolute rule; the second is that in which constitutions are framed to do away with absolute rulers and substitute popular control, and in which administration is neglected for these higher concerns; and the third is that in which the sovereign people undertake to develop administration under this new constitution which has brought them into power.

Those governments are now in the lead in administrative practice which had rulers still absolute but also enlightened when those modern days of political illumination came in which it was made evident to all but the blind that governors are properly only the servants of the governed. In such governments administration has been organized to subserve the general weal with the simplicity and effectiveness vouchsafed only to the undertakings of a single will.

Such was the case in Prussia, for instance, where administration has been most studied and most nearly perfected. Frederic the Great, stern and masterful as was his rule, still sincerely professed to regard himself as only the chief servant of the state, to consider his great office a public trust; and it was he who, building upon the foundations laid by his father, began to organize the public service of Prussia as in very earnest a service of the public. His no less absolute successor, Frederic William III, under the inspiration of Stein, again, in his turn, advanced the work still further, planning many of the broader structural features which give firmness and form to Prussian administration to-day. Almost the whole of the admirable system has been developed by kingly initiative.

Of similar origin was the practice, if not the plan, of modern French administration, with its symmetrical divisions of territory and its orderly gradations of office. The days of the Revolution—of the Constituent Assembly— were days of constitution-*writing*, but they can hardly be called days of constitution-*making*. The Revolution heralded a period of constitutional development,—the entrance of France upon the second of those periods which I have enumerated,—but it did not itself inaugurate such a period. It interrupted and unsettled absolutism, but did not destroy it. Napoleon succeeded the monarchs of France, to exercise a power as unrestricted as they had ever possessed.

The recasting of French administration by Napoleon is, therefore, my second example of the perfecting of civil machinery by the single will of an absolute ruler before the dawn of a constitutional era. No corporate, popular will could ever have effected arrangements such as those which Napoleon commanded. Arrangements so simple at the expense of local prejudice, so logical in their indifference to popular choice, might be decreed by a Constituent Assembly, but could be established only by the unlimited authority of a despot. The system of the year VIII was ruthlessly thorough and heartlessly perfect. It was, besides, in large part, a return to the despotism that had been overthrown.

Among those nations, on the other hand, which entered upon a season of constitution-making and popular reform before administration had received the impress of liberal principle, administrative improvement has been tardy and half-done. Once a nation has embarked in the business of manufacturing constitutions, it finds it exceedingly difficult to close out that business and open for the public a bureau of skilled, economical administration. There seems to be no end to the tinkering of constitutions. Your ordinary constitution will last you hardly ten years without repairs or additions; and the time for administrative detail comes late.

Here, of course, our examples are England and our own country. In the days of the Angevin kings, before constitutional life had taken root in the Great Charter, legal and administrative reforms began to proceed with sense and vigor under the impulse of Henry II's shrewd, busy, pushing, indomitable spirit and purpose; and kingly initiative seemed destined in England, as elsewhere, to shape governmental growth at its will. But impulsive, errant Richard and weak, despicable John were not the men to carry out such schemes as their father's. Administrative development gave place in their reigns to Constitutional struggles; and Parliament became king before any English monarch had had the practical genius or the enlightened conscience to devise just and lasting forms for the civil service of the state.

The English race, consequently, has long and successfully studied the art of curbing executive power to the constant neglect of the art of perfecting executive methods. It has exercised itself much more in controlling than in energizing government. It has been more concerned to render government just and moderate than to make it facile, well-ordered and effective. English and American political history has been a history, not of administrative development, but of legislative oversight,—not of progress in governmental organization, but of advance in law-making and political criticism. Consequently, we have reached a time when administrative study and creation are imperatively necessary to the well-being of our governments saddled with the habits of a long period of constitution-making. That period has practically closed, so far as the establishment of essential principles is concerned, but we cannot shake off its atmosphere. We go on criticizing when we ought to be creating. We have reached the third of the periods I have mentioned,—the period, namely, when the people have to develop administration in accordance with the Constitutions they won for themselves in a previous period of struggle with absolute power; but we are not prepared for the tasks of the new period.

Such an explanation seems to afford the only escape from blank astonishment at the fact that, in spite of our vast advantages in point of political liberty, and above all in point of practical political skill and sagacity, so many nations are ahead of us in administrative organization and administrative skill. Why, for instance, have we but just begun purifying a civil service which was rotten full fifty years ago? To say that slavery diverted us is but to repeat what I have said—that flaws in our constitution delayed us.

Of course all reasonable preference would declare for this English and American course of politics rather than for that of any European country. We should not like to have had Prussia's history for the sake of having Prussia's administrative skill; and Prussia's particular system of administration would quite suffocate us. It is better to be untrained and free than to be servile and systematic. Still there is no denying that it would be better yet to be both free in spirit and proficient in practice. It is this even more reasonable preference which impels us to discover what there may be to hinder or delay us in naturalizing this much-to-be-desired science of administration.

What, then, is there to prevent?

Well, principally, popular sovereignty. It is harder for democracy to organize administration than for monarchy. The very completeness of our most cherished political successes in the past embarrasses us. We have enthroned public opinion; and it is forbidden us to hope during its reign for any quick schooling of the sovereign in executive expertness or in the conditions of perfect functional balance in government. The very fact that we have realized popular rule in its fulness has made the task of *organizing* that rule just so much the more difficult. In order to make any advance at all we must instruct and persuade a multitudinous monarch called public opinion,—a much less feasible undertaking than to influence a single monarch called a king. An individual sovereign will adopt a simple plan and carry it out directly: he will have but one opinion, and he will embody that one opinion in one command. But this other sovereign, the people, will have a score of differing opinions. They can agree upon nothing simple: advance must be made through compromise, by a compounding of differences, by a trimming of plans and a suppression of too straightforward principles. There will be a succession of resolves running through a course of years, a dropping fire of commands running through a whole gamut of modifications.

In government, as in virtue, the hardest of hard things is to make progress. Formerly the reason for this was that the single person who was sovereign was generally either selfish, ignorant, timid, or a fool,—albeit there was now and again one who was wise. Nowadays the reason is that the many, the people, who are sovereign have no single ear which one can approach, and are selfish, ignorant, timid, stubborn, or foolish with the selfishness, the ignorances, the stubbornnesses, the timidities, or the follies of several thousand persons,—albeit there are hundreds who are wise. Once the advantage of the reformer was that the sovereign's mind had a definite locality, that it was contained in one man's head, and that consequently it could be gotten at; though it was his disadvantage that that mind learned only reluctantly or only in small quantities, or was under the influence of some one who let it learn only the wrong things. Now, on the contrary, the reformer is bewildered by the fact that the sovereign's mind has no definite locality, but is contained in a voting majority of several million heads; and embarrassed by the fact that the mind of this sovereign also is under the influence of favorites, who are none the less favorites in a good old-fashioned sense of the word because they are not persons but preconceived opinions; *i.e.*, prejudices which are not to be reasoned with because they are not the children of reason.

Wherever regard for public opinion is a first principle of government, practical reform must be slow and all reform must be full of compromises. For wherever public opinion exists it must rule. This is now an axiom half the world over, and will presently come to be believed even in Russia. Whoever would effect a change in a modern constitutional government must first educate his fellow-citizens to want *some* change. That done, he must persuade them to want the particular change he wants. He must first make public opinion willing to listen and then see to it that it listen to the right things. He must stir it up to search for an opinion, and then manage to put the right opinion in its way.

The first step is not less difficult than the second. With opinions, possession is more than nine points of the law. It is next to impossible to dislodge them. Institutions which one generation regards as only a makeshift approximation to the realization of a principle, the next generation honors as the nearest possible approximation to that principle, and the next worships as the principle itself. It takes scarcely three generations for the apotheosis. The grandson accepts his grandfather's hesitating experiment as an integral part of the fixed constitution of nature.

Even if we had clear insight into all the political past, and could form out of perfectly instructed heads a few steady, infallible, placidly wise maxims of government into which all sound political doctrine would be ultimately resolvable, *would the country act on them*? That is the question. The bulk of mankind is rigidly unphilosophical, and nowadays the bulk of mankind votes. A truth must become not only plain but also commonplace before it will be seen by the people who go to their work very early in the morning; and not to act upon it must involve great and pinching inconveniences before these same people will make up their minds to act upon it.

And where is this unphilosophical bulk of mankind more multifarious in its composition than in the United States? To know the public mind of this country, one must know the mind, not of Americans of the older stocks only, but also of Irishmen, of Germans, of negroes. In order to get a footing for new doctrine, one must influence minds cast in every mould of race, minds inheriting every bias of environment, warped by the histories of a score of different nations, warmed or chilled, closed or expanded by almost every climate of the globe.

So much, then, for the history of the study of administration, and the peculiarly difficult conditions under which, entering upon it when we do, we must undertake it. What, now, is the subject-matter of this study, and what are its characteristic objects?

II.

The field of administration is a field of business. It is removed from the hurry and strife of politics; it at most points stands apart even from the debatable ground of constitutional study. It is a part of political life only as the methods of the counting-house are a part of the life of society; only as machinery is part of the manufactured product. But it is, at the same time, raised very far above the dull level of mere technical detail by the fact that through its greater principles it is directly connected with the lasting maxims of political wisdom, the permanent truths of political progress.

The object of administrative study is to rescue executive methods from the confusion and costliness of empirical experiment and set them upon foundations laid deep in stable principle.

It is for this reason that we must regard civil-service reform in its present stages as but a prelude to a fuller administrative reform. We are now rectifying methods of appointment; we must go on to adjust executive functions more fitly and to prescribe better methods of executive organization and action. Civil-service reform is thus but a moral preparation for what is to follow. It is clearing the moral atmosphere of official life by establishing the sanctity of public office as a public trust, and, by making the service unpartisan, it is opening the way for making it businesslike. By sweetening its motives it is rendering it capable of improving its methods of work.

Let me expand a little what I have said of the province of administration. Most important to be observed is the truth already so much and so fortunately insisted upon by our civil-service reformers; namely, that administration lies outside the proper sphere of *politics*. Administrative questions are not political questions. Although politics sets the tasks for administration, it should not be suffered to manipulate its offices.

This is distinction of high authority; eminent German writers insist upon it as of course. Bluntschli,[2] for instance, bids us separate administration alike

2. [Johann K. Bluntschli,] *Politik* [*als Wissenschaft*], S[ection] 467.

from politics and from law. Politics, he says, is state activity "in things great and universal," while "administration, on the other hand," is "the activity of the state in individual and small things. Politics is thus the special province of the statesman, administration of the technical official." "Policy does nothing without the aid of administration"; but administration is not therefore politics. But we do not require German authority for this position; this discrimination between administration and politics is now, happily, too obvious to need further discussion.

There is another distinction which must be worked into all our conclusions, which, though but another side of that between administration and politics, is not quite so easy to keep sight of: I mean the distinction between *constitutional* and administrative questions, between those governmental adjustments which are essential to constitutional principle and those which are merely instrumental to the possibly changing purposes of a wisely adapting convenience.

One cannot easily make clear to every one just where administration resides in the various departments of any practicable government without entering upon particulars so numerous as to confuse and distinctions so minute as to distract. No lines of demarcation, setting apart administrative from non-administrative functions, can be run between this and that department of government without being run up hill and down dale, over dizzy heights of distinction and through dense jungles of statutory enactment, hither and thither around "ifs" and "buts," "whens" and "howevers," until they become altogether lost to the common eye not accustomed to this sort of surveying, and consequently not acquainted with the use of the theodolite of logical discernment. A great deal of administration goes about *incognito* to most of the world, being confounded now with political "management," and again with constitutional principle.

Perhaps this ease of confusion may explain such utterances as that of Niebuhr's: "Liberty," he says, "depends incomparably more upon administration than upon constitution." At first sight this appears to be largely true. Apparently facility in the actual exercise of liberty does depend more upon administrative arrangements than upon constitutional guarantees; although constitutional guarantees alone secure the existence of liberty. But—upon second thought—is even so much as this true? Liberty no more consists in easy functional movement than intelligence consists in the ease and vigor with which the limbs of a strong man move. The principles that rule within the man, or the constitution, are the vital springs of liberty or servitude. Because independence and subjection are without chains, are lightened by every easy-working device of considerate, paternal government, they are not thereby transformed into liberty. Liberty cannot live apart from constitutional principle; and no administration, however perfect and liberal its methods, can give men more than a poor counterfeit of liberty if it rest upon illiberal principles of government.

A clear view of the difference between the province of constitutional law and the province of administrative function ought to leave no room for misconception; and it is possible to name some roughly definite criteria upon which such a view can be built. Public administration is detailed and systematic execution of public law. Every particular application of general law is an act of administration. The assessment and raising of taxes, for instance, the hanging of a criminal, the transportation and delivery of the mails, the equipment and recruiting of the army and navy, *etc.*, are all obviously acts of administration; but the general laws which direct these things to be done are as obviously outside of and above administration. The broad plans of governmental action are not administrative; the detailed execution of such plans is administrative. Constitutions, therefore, properly concern themselves only with those instrumentalities of government which are to control general law. Our federal constitution observes this principle in saying nothing of even the greatest of the purely executive offices, and speaking only of that President of the Union who was to share the legislative and policy-making functions of government, only of those judges of highest jurisdiction who were to interpret and guard its principles, and not of those who were merely to give utterance to them.

This is not quite the distinction between Will and answering Deed, because the administrator should have and does have a will of his own in the choice of means for accomplishing his work. He is not and ought not to be a mere passive instrument. The distinction is between general plans and special means.

There is, indeed, one point at which administrative studies trench on constitutional ground—or at least upon what seems constitutional ground. The study of administration, philosophically viewed, is closely connected with the study of the proper distribution of constitutional authority. To be efficient it must discover the simplest arrangements by which responsibility can be unmistakably fixed upon officials; the best way of dividing authority without hampering it, and responsibility without obscuring it. And this question of the distribution of authority, when taken into the sphere of the higher, the originating functions of government, is obviously a central constitutional question. If administrative study can discover the best principles upon which to base such distribution, it will have done constitutional study an invaluable service. Montesquieu did not, I am convinced, say the last word on this head.

To discover the best principle for the distribution of authority is of greater importance, possibly, under a democratic system, where officials serve many masters, than under others where they serve but a few. All sovereigns are suspicious of their servants, and the sovereign people is no exception to the rule; but how is its suspicion to be allayed by *knowledge*? If that suspicion could but be clarified into wise vigilance, it would be altogether salutary; if that vigilance could be aided by the unmistakable placing of responsibility, it would be altogether beneficent. Suspicion in itself is never healthful either in the private or in the public mind. *Trust is strength* in all relations of life; and, as it is the office of the constitutional reformer to create conditions of trustfulness, so it is the office of the administrative organizer to fit administration with conditions of clear-cut responsibility which shall insure trustworthiness.

And let me say that large powers and unhampered discretion seem to me the indispensable conditions of responsibility. Public attention must be easily directed, in each case of good or bad administration, to just the man deserving of praise or blame. There is no danger in power, if only it be not irresponsible. If it be divided, dealt out in shares to many, it is obscured; and if it be obscured, it is made irresponsible. But if it be centred in heads of the service and in heads of branches of the service, it is easily watched and brought to book. If to keep his office a man must achieve open and honest success, and if at the same time he feels himself intrusted with large freedom of discretion, the greater his power the less likely is he to abuse it, the more is he nerved and sobered and elevated by it. The less his power, the more safely obscure and unnoticed does he feel his position to be, and the more readily does he relapse into remissness.

Just here we manifestly emerge upon the field of that still larger question,— the proper relations between public opinion and administration.

To whom is official trustworthiness to be disclosed, and by whom is it to be rewarded? Is the official to look to the public for his meed of praise and his push of promotion, or only to his superior in office? Are the people to be called in to settle administrative discipline as they are called in to settle constitutional principles? These questions evidently find their root in what is undoubtedly the fundamental problem of this whole study. That problem is: What part shall public opinion take in the conduct of administration?

The right answer seems to be, that public opinion shall play the part of authoritative critic.

But the *method* by which its authority shall be made to tell? Our peculiar American difficulty in organizing administration is not the danger of losing liberty, but the danger of not being able or willing to separate its essentials from its accidents. Our success is made doubtful by that besetting error of ours, the error of trying to do too much by vote. Self-government does not consist in having a hand in everything, any more than housekeeping consists necessarily in cooking dinner with one's own hands. The cook must be trusted with a large discretion as to the management of the fires and the ovens.

In those countries in which public opinion has yet to be instructed in its privileges, yet to be accustomed to having its own way, this question as to the province of public opinion is much more readily soluble than in this country, where public opinion is wide awake and quite intent upon having its own way anyhow. It is pathetic to see a whole book written by a German professor of political science for the purpose of saying to his countrymen, "Please try to have an opinion about national affairs"; but a public which is so modest may at least be expected to be very docile and acquiescent in learning what things it has *not* a right to think and speak about imperatively. It may be sluggish, but it will not be meddlesome. It will submit to be instructed before it tries to instruct. Its political education will come before its political activity. In trying to instruct our own public opinion, we are dealing with a pupil apt to think itself quite sufficiently instructed beforehand.

The problem is to make public opinion efficient without suffering it to be meddlesome. Directly exercised, in the oversight of the daily details and in the choice of the daily means of government, public criticism is of course a clumsy nuisance, a rustic handling delicate machinery. But as superintending the greater forces of formative policy alike in politics and administration, public criticism is altogether safe and beneficent, altogether indispensable. Let administrative study find the best means for giving public criticism this control and for shutting it out from all other interference.

But is the whole duty of administrative study done when it has taught the people what sort of administration to desire and demand, and how to get what they demand? Ought it not to go on to drill candidates for the public service?

There is an admirable movement towards universal political education now afoot in this country. The time will soon come when no college of respectability can afford to do without a well-filled chair of political science. But the education thus imparted will go but a certain length. It will multiply the number of intelligent critics of government, but it will create no competent body of administrators. It will prepare the way for the development of a sure-footed understanding of the general principles of government, but it will not necessarily foster skill in conducting government. It is an education which will equip legislators, perhaps, but not executive officials. If we are to improve public opinion, which is the motive power of government, we must prepare better officials as the *apparatus* of government. If we are to put in new boilers and to mend the fires which drive our governmental machinery, we must not leave the old wheels and joints and valves and bands to creak and buzz and clatter on as best they may at bidding of the new force. We must put

in new running parts wherever there is the least lack of strength or adjustment. It will be necessary to organize democracy by sending up to the competitive examinations for the civil service men definitely prepared for standing liberal tests as to technical knowledge. A technically schooled civil
service will presently have become indispensable.

I know that a corps of civil servants prepared by a special schooling and
drilled, after appointment, into a perfected organization, with appropriate hierarchy and characteristic discipline, seems to a great many very thoughtful
persons to contain elements which might combine to make an offensive official class,—a distinct, semi-corporate body with sympathies divorced from
those of a progressive, free-spirited people, and with hearts narrowed to the
meanness of a bigoted officialism. Certainly such a class would be altogether
hateful and harmful in the United States. Any measures calculated to produce
it would for us be measures of reaction and of folly.

But to fear the creation of a domineering, illiberal officialism as a result of
the studies I am here proposing is to miss altogether the principle upon which
I wish most to insist. That principle is, that administration in the United States
must be at all points sensitive to public opinion. A body of thoroughly trained
officials serving during good behavior we must have in any case: that is a
plain business necessity. But the apprehension that such a body will be anything un-American clears away the moment it is asked, What is to constitute
good behavior? For that question obviously carries its own answer on its face.
Steady, hearty allegiance to the policy of the government they serve will constitute good behavior. That *policy* will have no taint of officialism about it. It
will not be the creation of permanent officials, but of statesmen whose responsibility to public opinion will be direct and inevitable. Bureaucracy can
exist only where the whole service of the state is removed from the common
political life of the people, its chiefs as well as its rank and file. Its motives,
its objects, its policy, its standards, must be bureaucratic. It would be difficult
to point out any examples of impudent exclusiveness and arbitrariness on the
part of officials doing service under a chief of department who really served
the people, as all our chiefs of departments must be made to do. It would be
easy, on the other hand, to adduce other instances like that of the influence of
Stein in Prussia, where the leadership of one statesman imbued with true public spirit transformed arrogant and perfunctory bureaux into public-spirited
instruments of just government.

The ideal for us is a civil service cultured and self-sufficient enough to act
with sense and vigor, and yet so intimately connected with the popular
thought, by means of elections and constant public counsel, as to find arbitrariness of class spirit quite out of the question.

III.

Having thus viewed in some sort the subject-matter and the objects of this study of administration, what are we to conclude as to the methods best suited to it—the points of view most advantageous for it?

Government is so near us, so much a thing of our daily familiar handling, that we can with difficulty see the need of any philosophical study of it, or the exact point of such study, should it be undertaken. We have been on our feet too long to study now the art of walking. We are a practical people, made so apt, so adept in self-government by centuries of experimental drill that we are scarcely any longer capable of perceiving the awkwardness of the particular system we may be using, just because it is so easy for us to use any system. We do not study the art of governing: we govern. But mere unschooled genius for affairs will not save us from sad blunders in administration. Though democrats by long inheritance and repeated choice, we are still rather crude democrats. Old as democracy is, its organization on a basis of modern ideas and conditions is still an unaccomplished work. The democratic state has yet to be equipped for carrying those enormous burdens of administration which the needs of this industrial and trading age are so fast accumulating. Without comparative studies in government we cannot rid ourselves of the misconception that administration stands upon an essentially different basis in a democratic state from that on which it stands in a non-democratic state.

After such study we could grant democracy the sufficient honor of ultimately determining by debate all essential questions affecting the public weal, of basing all structures of policy upon the major will; but we would have found but one rule of good administration for all governments alike. So far as administrative functions are concerned, all governments have a strong structural likeness; more than that, if they are to be uniformly useful and efficient, they *must* have a strong structural likeness. A free man has the same bodily organs, the same executive parts, as the slave, however different may be his motives, his services, his energies. Monarchies and democracies, radically different as they are in other respects, have in reality much the same business to look to.

It is abundantly safe nowadays to insist upon this actual likeness of all governments, because these are days when abuses of power are easily exposed and arrested, in countries like our own, by a bold, alert, inquisitive, detective public thought and a sturdy popular self-dependence such as never existed before. We are slow to appreciate this; but it is easy to appreciate it. Try to imagine personal government in the United States. It is like trying to imagine a national worship of Zeus. Our imaginations are too modern for the feat.

But, besides being safe, it is necessary to see that for all governments alike the legitimate ends of administration are the same, in order not to be frightened at the idea of looking into foreign systems of administration for instruction and suggestion; in order to get rid of the apprehension that we might perchance blindly borrow something incompatible with our principles. That man is blindly astray who denounces attempts to transplant foreign systems into this country. It is impossible: they simply would not grow here. But why should we not use such parts of foreign contrivances as we want, if they be in any way serviceable? We are in no danger of using them in a foreign way. We borrowed rice, but we do not eat it with chopsticks. We borrowed our whole political language from England, but we leave the words "king" and "lords" out of it. What did we ever originate, except the action of the federal government upon individuals and some of the functions of the federal supreme court?

We can borrow the science of administration with safety and profit if only we read all fundamental differences of condition into its essential tenets. We have only to filter it through our constitutions, only to put it over a slow fire of criticism and distil away its foreign gases.

I know that there is a sneaking fear in some conscientiously patriotic minds that studies of European systems might signalize some foreign methods as better than some American methods; and the fear is easily to be understood. But it would scarcely be avowed in just any company.

It is the more necessary to insist upon thus putting away all prejudices against looking anywhere in the world but at home for suggestions in this study, because nowhere else in the whole field of politics, it would seem, can we make use of the historical, comparative method more safely than in this province of administration. Perhaps the more novel the forms we study the better. We shall the sooner learn the peculiarities of our own methods. We can never learn either our own weaknesses or our own virtues by comparing ourselves with ourselves. We are too used to the appearance and procedure of our own system to see its true significance. Perhaps even the English system is too much like our own to be used to the most profit in illustration. It is best on the whole to get entirely away from our own atmosphere and to be most careful in examining such systems as those of France and Germany. Seeing our own institutions through such *media*, we see ourselves as foreigners might see us were they to look at us without preconceptions. Of ourselves, so long as we know only ourselves, we know nothing.

Let it be noted that it is the distinction, already drawn, between administration and politics which makes the comparative method so safe in the field of administration. When we study the administrative systems of France and Germany, knowing that we are not in search of *political* principles, we need not care a peppercorn for the constitutional or political reasons which Frenchmen or Germans give for their practices when explaining them to us. If I see a murderous fellow sharpening a knife cleverly, I can borrow his way of sharpening the knife without borrowing his probable intention to commit murder with it; and so, if I see a monarchist dyed in the wool managing a public bureau well, I can learn his business methods without changing one of my republican spots. He may serve his king; I will continue to serve the people; but I should like to serve my sovereign as well as he serves his. By keeping this distinction in view,—that is, by studying administration as a means of putting our own politics into convenient practice, as a means of making what is democratically politic towards all administratively possible towards each,—we are on perfectly safe ground, and can learn without error what foreign systems have to teach us. We thus devise an adjusting weight for our comparative method of study. We can thus scrutinize the anatomy of foreign governments without fear of getting any of their diseases into our veins; dissect alien systems without apprehension of blood-poisoning.

Our own politics must be the touchstone for all theories. The principles on which to base a science of administration for America must be principles which have democratic policy very much at heart. And, to suit American habit, all general theories must, as theories, keep modestly in the background, not in open argument only, but even in our own minds,—lest opinions satisfactory only to the standards of the library should be dogmatically used, as if they must be quite as satisfactory to the standards of practical politics as well. Doctrinaire devices must be postponed to tested practices. Arrangements not only sanctioned by conclusive experience elsewhere but also congenial to American habit must be preferred without hesitation to theoretical perfection. In a word, steady, practical statesmanship must come first, closet doctrine second. The cosmopolitan what-to-do must always be commanded by the American how-to-do-it.

Our duty is, to supply the best possible life to a *federal* organization, to systems within systems; to make town, city, county, state, and federal governments live with a like strength and an equally assured healthfulness, keeping each unquestionably its own master and yet making all interdependent and co-operative, combining independence with mutual helpfulness. The task is great and important enough to attract the best minds.

This interlacing of local self-government with federal self-government is quite a modern conception. It is not like the arrangements of imperial federation in Germany. There local government is not yet, fully, local *self-*government. The bureaucrat is everywhere busy. His efficiency springs out of *esprit de corps*, out of care to make ingratiating obeisance to the authority of a superior, or, at best, out of the soil of a sensitive conscience. He serves, not the public, but an irresponsible minister. The question for us is, how shall our series of governments within governments be so administered that it shall always be to the interest of the public officer to serve, not his superior alone but the community also, with the best efforts of his talents and the soberest service of his conscience? How shall such service be made to his commonest interest by contributing abundantly to his sustenance, to his dearest interest by furthering his ambition, and to his highest interest by advancing his honor and establishing his character? And how shall this be done alike for the local part and for the national whole?

If we solve this problem we shall again pilot the world. There is a tendency—is there not?—a tendency as yet dim, but already steadily impulsive and clearly destined to prevail, towards, first the confederation of parts of empires like the British, and finally of great states themselves. Instead of centralization of power, there is to be wide union with tolerated divisions of prerogative. This is a tendency towards the American type—of governments joined with governments for the pursuit of common purposes, in honorary equality and honorable subordination. Like principles of civil liberty are everywhere fostering like methods of government; and if comparative studies of the ways and means of government should enable us to offer suggestions which will practically combine openness and vigor in the administration of such governments with ready docility to all serious, well-sustained public criticism, they will have approved themselves worthy to be ranked among the highest and most fruitful of the great departments of political study. That they will issue in such suggestions I confidently hope.

17

The New Nationalism*

Theodore Roosevelt

Given by Theodore Roosevelt in 1910, the themes of this speech, "The New Nationalism," would serve as the foundation for his presidential campaign in 1912. The speech is perhaps the clearest concession from Roosevelt that achieving his progressive policy goals would require a radical expansion of governmental power into the private sphere. Indeed, the very concept of private property would have to reconceived, Roosevelt suggests, with the national government to determine if private property was of genuine benefit to the community at large.

We come here to-day to commemorate one of the epoch-making events of the long struggle for the rights of man—the long struggle for the uplift of humanity. Our country—this great republic—means nothing unless it means the triumph of a real democracy, the triumph of popular government, and, in the long run, of an economic system under which each man shall be guaranteed the opportunity to show the best that there is in him. That is why the history of America is now the central feature of the history of the world; for the world has set its face hopefully toward our democracy; and, O my fellow citizens, each one of you carries on your shoulders not only the burden of doing well for the sake of your own country, but the burden of doing well and of seeing that this nation does well for the sake of mankind.

There have been two great crises in our country's history: first, when it was formed, and then, again, when it was perpetuated; and, in the second of these

* Editors' Note: Theodore Roosevelt, "The New Nationalism," in *The New Nationalism* (New York: The Outlook Company, 1910), 3–33.

great crises—in the time of stress and strain which culminated in the Civil War, on the outcome of which depended the justification of what had been done earlier, you men of the Grand Army, you men who fought through the Civil War, not only did you justify your generation, not only did you render life worth living for our generation, but you justified the wisdom of Washington and Washington's colleagues. If this Republic had been founded by them only to be split asunder into fragments when the strain came, then the judgment of the world would have been that Washington's work was not worth doing. It was you who crowned Washington's work, as you carried to achievement the high purpose of Abraham Lincoln.

Now, with this second period of our history the name of John Brown will be forever associated; and Kansas was the theater upon which the first act of the second of our great national life dramas was played. It was the result of the struggle in Kansas which determined that our country should be in deed as well as in name devoted to both union and freedom; that the great experiment of democratic government on a national scale should succeed and not fail. In name we had the Declaration of Independence in 1776; but we gave the lie by our acts to the words of the Declaration of Independence until 1865; and words count for nothing except in so far as they represent acts. This is true everywhere; but, O my friends, it should be truest of all in political life. A broken promise is bad enough in private life. It is worse in the field of politics. No man is worth his salt in public life who makes on the stump a pledge which he does not keep after the election; and, if he makes such as pledge and does not keep it, hunt him out of public life. I care for the great deeds of the past chiefly as spurs to drive us onward in the present. I speak of the men of the past partly that they may be honored by our praise of them, but more that they may serve as examples for the future.

It was a heroic struggle; and, as is inevitable with all such struggles, it had also a dark and terrible side. Very much was done of good, and much also of evil; and, as was inevitable in such a period of revolution, often the same man did both good and evil. For our great good fortune as a nation, we, the people of the United States as a whole, can now afford to forget the evil, or, at least, to remember it without bitterness, and to fix our eyes with pride only on the good that was accomplished. Even in ordinary times there are very few of us who do not see the problems of life as through a glass, darkly; and when the glass is clouded by the murk of furious popular passion, the vision of the best and the bravest is dimmed. Looking back, we are all of us now able to do justice to the valor and the disinterestedness and the love of the right, as to each it was given to see the right, shown both by the men of the North and the men of the South in that contest which was finally decided by the attitude of the West. We can admire the heroic valor, the sincerity, the self-devotion shown alike by the men who wore the blue and the men who wore the gray; and our sadness that such men should have had to fight one another is tempered by the glad knowledge that ever hereafter their descendants shall be found fighting side by side, struggling in peace as well as in war for the uplift of their common country, all alike resolute to raise to the highest pitch of honor and usefulness the nation to which they all belong. As for the veterans of the Grand Army of the Republic, they deserve honor and recognition such as is paid to no other citizens of the republic; for to them the republic owes its all; for to them it owes its very existence. It is because of what you and your comrades did in the dark years that we of to-day walk, each of us, head erect, and proud that we belong, not to one of a dozen little squabbling contemptible commonwealths, but to the mightiest nation upon which the sun shines.

I do not speak of this struggle of the past merely from the historic standpoint. Our interest is primarily in the application to-day of the lessons taught by the contest of half a century ago. It is of little use for us to pay lip loyalty to the mighty men of the past unless we sincerely endeavor to apply to the problems of the present precisely the qualities which in other crises enabled the men of that day to meet those crises. It is half melancholy and half amusing to see the way in which well-meaning people gather to do honor to the men who, in the company with John Brown, and under the lead of Abraham Lincoln, faced and solved the great problems of the nineteenth century, while, at the same time, these same good people nervously shrink from, or frantically denounce, those who are trying to meet the problems of the twentieth century in the spirit which was accountable for the successful solution of the problems of Lincoln's time.

Of that generation of men to whom we owe so much, the man to whom we owe most is, of course, Lincoln. Part of our debt to him is because he forecast our present struggle and saw the way out. He said: —

["]I hold that while man exists it is his duty to improve not only his own condition, but to assist in ameliorating mankind.["]

And again: —

["]Labor is prior to, and independent of, capital. Capital is only the fruit of labor, and could never have existed if labor had not first existed. Labor is the superior of capital, and deserves much the higher consideration.["]

If that remark was original with me, I should be even more strongly denounced as a communist agitator than I shall be anyhow. It is Lincoln's. I am only quoting it; and that is one side, that is the side the capitalist should hear. Now, let the workingman hear his side.

["]Capital has its rights, which are as worthy of protection as any other rights. . . . Nor should this lead to a war upon the owners of property. Property is the fruit of labor; . . . property is desirable; is a positive good in the world.["]

And then comes a thoroughly Lincolnlike sentence: —

["]Let not him who is houseless pull down the house of another, but let him work diligently and build one for himself, thus by example assuring that his own shall be safe from violence when built.["]

It seems to me that, in these words, Lincoln took substantially the attitude that we ought to take; he showed the proper sense of proportion in his relative estimates of capital and labor, of human rights and property rights. Above all, in this speech, as in many others, he taught a lesson in wise kindliness and charity; an indispensable lesson to us of to-day. But this wise kindliness and charity never weakened his arm or numbed his heart. We cannot afford weakly to blind ourselves to the actual conflict which faces us to-day. The issue is joined, and we must fight or fail.

In every wise struggle for human betterment one of the main objects, and often the only object, has been to achieve in large measure equality of opportunity. In the struggle for this great end, nations rise from barbarism to civilization, and through it people press forward from one stage of enlightenment to the next. One of the chief factors in progress is the destruction of special privilege. The essence of any struggle for healthy liberty has always been, and must always be, to take from some one man or class of men the right to enjoy power, or wealth, or position, or immunity, which has not been earned by service to his or their fellows. That is what you fought for in the Civil War, and that is what we strive for now.

At many stages in the advance of humanity, this conflict between the men who possess more than they have earned and the men who have earned more than they possess is the central condition of progress. In our day it appears as the struggle of free men to gain and hold the right of self-government as against the special interests, who twist the methods of free government into machinery for defeating the popular will. At every stage, and under all circumstances, the essence of the struggle is to equalize opportunity, destroy privilege, and give to the life and citizenship of every individual the highest possible value both to himself and to the commonwealth. That is nothing new. All I ask in civil life is what you fought for in the Civil War. I ask that civil life be carried on according to the spirit in which the army was carried on. You never get perfect justice, but the effort in handling the army was to bring to the front the men who could do the job. Nobody grudged promotion to

Grant, or Sherman, or Thomas, or Sheridan, because they earned it. The only complaint was when a man got promotion which he did not earn.

Practical equality of opportunity for all citizens, when we achieve it, will have two great results. First, every man will have a fair chance to make of himself all that in him lies; to reach the highest point to which his capacities, unassisted by special privilege of his own and unhampered by the special privilege of others, can carry him, and to get for himself and his family substantially what he has earned. Second, equality of opportunity means that the commonwealth will get from every citizen the highest service of which he is capable. No man who carries the burden of the special privileges of another can give to the commonwealth that service to which it is fairly entitled.

I stand for the square deal. But when I say that I am for the square deal, I mean not merely that I stand for fair play under the present rules of the game, but that I stand for having those rules changed so as to work for a more substantial equality of opportunity and of reward for equally good service. One word of warning, which, I think, is hardly necessary in Kansas. When I say I want a square deal for the poor man, I do not mean that I want a square deal for the man who remains poor because he has not got the energy to work for himself. If a man who has had a chance will not make good, than he has got to quit. And you men of the Grand Army, you want justice for the brave man who fought, and punishment for the coward who shirked his work. Is not that so?

Now, this means that our government, national and state, must be freed from the sinister influence or control of special interests. Exactly as the special interests of cotton and slavery threatened our political integrity before the Civil War, so now the great special business interests too often control and corrupt the men and methods of government for their own profit. We must drive the special interests out of politics. That is one of our tasks to-day. Every special interest is entitled to justice—full, fair, and complete,—and, now, mind you, if there were any attempt by mob violence to plunder and work harm to the special interest, whatever it may be, that I most dislike, and the wealthy man, whomsoever he may be, for whom I have the greatest contempt, I would fight for him, and you would if you were worth your salt. He should have justice. For every special interest is entitled to justice, but not one is entitled to a vote in Congress, to a voice on the bench, or to representation in any public office. The Constitution guarantees protection to property, and we must make that promise good. But it does not give the right of suffrage to any corporation.

The true friend of property, the true conservative, is he who insists that property shall be the servant and not the master of the commonwealth; who insists that the creature of man's making shall be the servant and not the master of the man who made it. The citizens of the United States must effectively control the mighty commercial forces which they have themselves called into being.

There can be no effective control of corporations while their political activity remains. To put an end to it will be neither a short nor an easy task, but it can be done.

We must have complete and effective publicity of corporate affairs, so that the people may know beyond peradventure whether the corporations obey the law and whether their management entitles them to the confidence of the public. It is necessary that laws should be passed to prohibit the use of corporate funds directly or indirectly for political purposes; it is still more necessary that such laws should be thoroughly enforced. Corporate expenditures for political purposes, and especially such expenditures by public service corporations, have supplied one of the principal sources of corruption in our political affairs.

It has become entirely clear that we must have government supervision of the capitalization, not only of public service corporations, including, particularly, railways, but of all corporations doing an interstate business. I do not wish to see the nation forced into the ownership of the railways if it can possibly be avoided, and the only alternative is thoroughgoing and effective regulation, which shall be based on a full knowledge of all the facts, including a physical valuation of property. This physical valuation is not needed, or, at least, is very rarely needed, for fixing rates; but it is needed as the basis of honest capitalization.

We have come to recognize that franchises should never be granted except for a limited time, and never without proper provision for compensation to the public. It is my personal belief that the same kind and degree of control and supervision which should be exercised over public service corporations should be extended also to combinations which control necessaries of life, such as meat, oil, and coal, or which deal in them on an important scale. I have no doubt that the ordinary man who has control of them is much like ourselves. I have no doubt he would like to do well, but I want to have enough supervision to help him realize that desire to do well.

I believe that the officers, and, especially, the directors, of corporations should be held personally responsible when any corporation breaks the law.

Combinations in industry are the result of an imperative economic law which cannot be repealed by political legislation. The effort at prohibiting all combination has substantially failed. The way out lies, not in attempting to prevent such combinations, but in completely controlling them in the interest of the public welfare. For that purpose the Federal Bureau of Corporations is an agency of first importance. Its powers, and, therefore, its efficiency, as well as that of the Interstate Commerce Commission, should be largely increased. We have a right to expect from the Bureau of Corporations and from the Interstate Commerce Commission a very high grade of public service. We should be as sure of the proper conduct of the interstate railways and the proper management of interstate business as we are now sure of the conduct and management of the national banks, and we should have as effective supervision in one case as in the other. The Hepburn Act, and the amendment to the Act in the shape in which it finally passed Congress at the last session, represent a long step in advance, and we must go yet further.

There is a widespread belief among our people that, under the methods of making tariffs which have hitherto obtained, the special interests are too influential. Probably this is true of both the big special interests and the little special interests. These methods have put a premium on selfishness, and, naturally, the selfish big interests have gotten more than their smaller, though equally selfish, brothers. The duty of Congress is to provide a method by which the interest of the whole people shall be all that receives consideration. To this end there must be an expert tariff commission, wholly removed from the possibility of political pressure or of improper business influence. Such a commission can find the real difference between cost of production, which is mainly the difference of labor cost here and abroad. As fast as its recommendations are made, I believe in revising one schedule at a time. A general revision of the tariff almost inevitably leads to log-rolling and the subordination of the general public interest to local and special interests.

The absence of effective state, and, especially, national, restraint upon unfair money getting has tended to create a small class of enormously wealthy and economically powerful men, whose chief object is to hold and increase their power. The prime need is to change the conditions which enable these men to accumulate power which it is not for the general welfare that they should hold or exercise. We grudge no man a fortune which represents his own power and sagacity, when exercised with entire regard to the welfare of his fellows. Again, comrades over there, take the lesson from your own experience. Not only did you not grudge, but you gloried in the promotion of the great generals who gained their promotion by leading the army to victory. So it is with us. We grudge no man a fortune in civil life if it is honorably obtained and well used. It is not even enough that it should have been gained without doing damage to the community. We should permit it to be gained only so long as the gaining represents benefit to the community. This, I know, implies a policy of a far more active governmental interference with social and economic conditions in this country than we have yet had, but I think we have got to face the fact that such an increase in governmental control is now necessary.

No man should receive a dollar unless that dollar has been fairly earned. Every dollar received should represent a dollar's worth of service rendered—not gambling in stocks, but service rendered. The really big fortune, the swollen fortune, by the mere fact of its size acquires qualities which differentiate it in kind as well as in degree from what is possessed by men of relatively small means. Therefore, I believe in a graduated income tax on big fortunes, and in another tax which is far more easily collected and far more effective—a graduated inheritance tax on big fortunes, properly safeguarded against evasion and increasing rapidly in amount with the size of the estate.

The people of the United States suffer from periodical financial panics to a degree substantially unknown among the other nations which approach us in financial strength. There is no reason why we should suffer what they escape. It is of profound importance that our financial system should be promptly investigated, and so thoroughly and effectively revised as to make it certain that hereafter our currency will no longer fail at critical times to meet our needs.

It is hardly necessary for me to repeat that I believe in an efficient army and a navy large enough to secure for us abroad that respect which is the surest guarantee of peace. A word of special warning to my fellow citizens who are as progressive as I hope I am. I want them to keep up their interest in our internal affairs; and I want them also continually to remember Uncle Sam's interests abroad. Justice and fair dealing among nations rest upon principles identical with those which control justice and fair dealing among the individuals of which nations are composed, with the vital exception that each nation must do its own part in international police work. If you get into trouble here, you can call for the police; but if Uncle Sam gets into trouble, he has got to be his own policeman, and I want to see him strong enough to encourage the peaceful aspirations of other peoples in connection with us. I believe in national friendships and heartiest good will to all nations; but national friendships, like those between men, must be founded on respect as well as on liking, on forbearance as well as upon trust. I should be heartily ashamed of any American who did not try to make the American government act as justly toward the other nations in international relations as he himself would act toward any individual in private relations. I should be heartily ashamed to see us wrong a weaker power, and I should hang my head forever if we tamely suffered wrong from a stronger power.

Of conservation I shall speak more at length elsewhere. Conservation means development as much as it does protection. I recognize the right and duty of this generation to develop and use the natural resources of our land; but I do not recognize the right to waste them, or to rob, by wasteful use, the generations that come after us. I ask nothing of the nation except that it so behave as each farmer here behaves with reference to his own children. That farmer is a poor creature who skins the land and leaves it worthless to his children. The farmer is a good farmer who, having enabled the land to support himself and to provide for the education of his children, leaves it to them a little better than he found it himself. I believe the same thing of a nation.

Moreover, I believe that the natural resources must be used for the benefit of all our people, and not monopolized for the benefit of the few, and here again is another case in which I am accused of taking a revolutionary attitude. People forget now that one hundred years ago there were public men of good character who advocated the nation selling its public lands in great quantities, so that the nation could get the most money out of it, and giving it to the men who could cultivate it for their own uses. We took the proper democratic ground that the land should be granted in small sections to the men who were actually to till it and live on it. Now, with the water power, with the forests, with the mines, we are brought face to face with the fact that there are many people who will go with us in conserving the resources only if they are to be allowed to exploit them for their benefit. That is one of the fundamental reasons why the special interests should be driven out of politics. Of all the questions which can come before this nation, short of the actual preservation of its existence in a great war, there is none which compares in importance with the great central task of leaving this land even a better land for our descendants than it is for us, and training them into a better race to inhabit the land and pass it on. Conservation is a great moral issue, for it involves the patriotic duty of insuring the safety and continuance of the nation. Let me add that the health and vitality of our people are at least as well worth conserving as their forests, waters, lands, and minerals, and in this great work the national government must bear a most important part.

I have spoken elsewhere also of the great task which lies before the farmers of the country to get for themselves and their wives and children not only the benefits of better farming, but also those of better business methods and better conditions of life on the farm. The burden of this great task will fall, as it should, mainly upon the great organizations of the farmers themselves. I am glad it will, for I believe they are all well able to handle it. In particular, there are strong reasons why the Departments of Agriculture of the various states, the United States Department of Agriculture, and the agricultural colleges and experiment stations should extend their work to cover all phases of farm life, instead of limiting themselves, as they have far too often limited themselves in the past, solely to the question of the production of crops. And now a special word to the farmer. I want to see him make the farm as fine a farm as it can be made; and let him remember to see that the improvement goes on indoors as well as out; let him remember that the farmer's wife should have her share of thought and attention just as much as the farmer himself.

Nothing is more true than that excess of every kind is followed by reaction; a fact which should be pondered by reformer and reactionary alike. We are face to face with new conceptions of the relations of property to human welfare, chiefly because certain advocates of the rights of property as against the rights of men have been pushing their claims too far. The man who wrongly holds that every human right is secondary to his profit must now give way to the advocate of human welfare, who rightly maintains that every man holds his property subject to the general right of the community to regulate its use to whatever degree the public welfare may require it.

But I think we may go still further. The right to regulate the use of wealth in the public interest is universally admitted. Let us admit also the right to regulate the terms and conditions of labor, which is the chief element of wealth, directly in the interest of the common good. The fundamental thing to do for every man is to give him a chance to reach a place in which he will make the greatest possible contribution to the public welfare. Understand what I say there. Give him a chance, not push him up if he will not be pushed. Help any man who stumbles; if he lies down, it is a poor job to try to carry him; but if he is a worthy man, try your best to see that he gets a chance to show the worth that is in him. No man can be a good citizen unless he has a wage more than sufficient to cover the bare cost of living, and hours of labor short enough so that after his day's work is done he will have time and energy to bear his share in the management of the community, to help in carrying the general load. We keep countless men from being good citizens by the conditions of life with which we surround them. We need comprehensive workmen's compensation acts, both state and national laws to regulate child labor and work for women, and, especially, we need in our common schools not merely education in book learning, but also practical training for daily life and work. We need to enforce better sanitary conditions for our workers and to extend the use of safety appliances for our workers in industry and commerce, both within and between the states. Also, friends, in the interest of the workingman himself we need to set our faces like flint against mob violence just as against corporate greed; against violence and injustice and lawlessness by wage workers just as much as against lawless cunning and greed and selfish arrogance of employers. If I could ask but one thing of my fellow countrymen, my request would be that, whenever they go in for reform, they remember the two sides, and that they always exact justice from one side as much as from the other. I have small use for the public servant who can always see and denounce the corruption of the capitalist, but who cannot persuade himself, especially before election, to say a word about lawless mob violence. And I have equally small use for the man, be he a judge on the bench, or editor of a great paper, or wealthy and influential private citizen, who can see clearly enough and denounce the lawlessness of mob violence, but whose eyes are closed so that he is blind when the question is one of corruption in business on a gigantic scale. Also remember what I said about excess in reformer and reactionary alike. If the reactionary man, who thinks of nothing but the rights of property, could have his way, he would bring about a revolution; and one of my chief fears in connection with progress comes because I do not want to see our people, for lack of proper leadership, compelled to follow men whose intentions are excellent, but whose eyes are a little too wild to make it really safe to trust them. Here in Kansas there is one paper which habitually denounces me as the tool of Wall Street, and at the same time frantically repudiates the statement that I am a Socialist on the ground that that is an unwarranted slander of the Socialists.

National efficiency has many factors. It is a necessary result of the principle of conservation widely applied. In the end it will determine our failure or success as a nation. National efficiency has to do, not only with natural resources and with men, but it is equally concerned with institutions. The state must be made efficient for the work which concerns only the people of the state; and the nation for that which concerns all the people. There must remain no neutral ground to serve as a refuge for lawbreakers, and especially for lawbreakers of great wealth, who can hire the vulpine legal cunning which will teach them how to avoid both jurisdictions. It is a misfortune when the national legislature fails to do its duty in providing a national remedy, so that the only national activity is the purely negative activity of the judiciary forbidding the state to exercise power in the premises.

I do not ask for over centralization; but I do ask that we work in a spirit of broad and far-reaching nationalism when we work for what concerns our people as a whole. We are all Americans. Our common interests are as broad as the continent. I speak to you here in Kansas exactly as I would speak in New York or Georgia, for the most vital problems are those which affect us all alike. The national government belongs to the whole American people, and where the whole American people are interested, that interest can be guarded effectively only by the national government. The betterment which we seek must be accomplished, I believe, mainly through the national government.

The American people are right in demanding that New Nationalism, without which we cannot hope to deal with new problems. The New Nationalism puts the national need before sectional or personal advantage. It is impatient of the utter confusion that results from local legislatures attempting to treat national issues as local issues. It is still more impatient of the impotence which springs from overdivision of governmental powers, the impotence which makes it possible for local selfishness or for legal cunning, hired by wealthy special interests, to bring national activities to a deadlock. This New Nationalism regards the executive power as the steward of the public welfare. It demands of the judiciary that it shall be interested primarily in human welfare rather than in property, just as it demands that the representative body shall represent all the people rather than any one class or section of the people.

I believe in shaping the ends of government to protect property as well as human welfare. Normally, and in the long run, the ends are the same; but whenever the alternative must be faced, I am for men and not for property, as you were in the Civil War. I am far from underestimating the importance of dividends; but I rank dividends below human character. Again, I do not have any sympathy with the reformer who says he does not care for dividends. Of course, economic welfare is necessary, for a man must pull his own weight and be able to support his family. I know well that the reformers must not bring upon the people economic ruin, or the reforms themselves will go down in the ruin. But we must be ready to face temporary disaster, whether or not brought on by those who will war against us to the knife. Those who oppose all reform will do well to remember that ruin in its worst form is inevitable if our national life brings us nothing better than swollen fortunes for the few and the triumph in both politics and business of a sordid and selfish materialism.

If our political institutions were perfect, they would absolutely prevent the political domination of money in any part of our affairs. We need to make our political representatives more quickly and sensitively responsive to the people whose servants they are. More direct action by the people in their own affairs under proper safeguards is vitally necessary. The direct primary is a step in this direction, if it is associated with a corrupt practices act effective to prevent the advantage of the man willing recklessly and unscrupulously to spend money over his more honest competitor. It is particularly important that all moneys received or expended for campaign purposes should be publicly accounted for, not only after election, but before election as well. Political action must be made simpler, easier, and freer from confusion for every citizen. I believe that the prompt removal of unfaithful or incompetent public servants should be made easy and sure in whatever way experience shall show to be most expedient in any given class of cases.

One of the fundamental necessities in a representative government such as ours is to make certain that the men to whom the people delegate their power shall serve the people by whom they are elected, and not the special interests. I believe that every national officer, elected or appointed, should be forbidden to perform any service or receive any compensation, directly or indirectly, from interstate corporations; and a similar provision could not fail to be useful within the states.

The object of government is the welfare of the people. The material progress and prosperity of a nation are desirable chiefly so far as they lead to the moral and material welfare of all good citizens. Just in proportion as the average man and woman are honest, capable of sound judgment and high ideals, active in public affairs,—but, first of all, sound in their home life, and the father and mother of healthy children whom they bring up well,—just so far, and no farther, we may count our civilization a success. We must have— I believe we have already—a genuine and permanent moral awakening, without which no wisdom of legislation or administration really means anything; and, on the other hand, we must try to secure the social and economic legislation without which any improvement due to purely moral agitation is necessarily evanescent. Let me again illustrate by a reference to the Grand Army. You could not have won simply as a disorderly and disorganized mob. You needed generals; you needed careful administration of the most advanced type; and a good commissary—the cracker line. You well remember that success was necessary in many different lines in order to bring about general success. You had to have the administration at Washington good, just as you had to have the administration in the field; and you had to have the work of the generals good. You could not have triumphed without that administration and leadership; but it would all have been worthless if the average soldier had not had the right stuff in him. He had to have the right stuff in him, or you could not get it out of him. In the last analysis, therefore, vitally necessary though it was to have the right kind of organization and the right kind of generalship, it was even more vitally necessary that the average soldier should have the fighting edge, the right character. So it is in our civil life. No matter how honest and decent we are in our private lives, if we do not have the right kind of law and the right kind of administration of the law, we cannot go forward as a nation. That is imperative; but it must be an addition to, and not a substitution for, the qualities that make us good citizens. In the last analysis, the most important elements in any man's career must be the sum of those qualities which, in the aggregate, we speak of as character. If he has not got it, then no law that the wit of man can devise, no administration of the law by the boldest and strongest executive, will avail to help him. We must have the right kind of character—character that makes a man, first of all, a good man in the home, a good father, a good husband—that makes a man a good neighbor. You must have that, and, then, in addition, you must have the kind of law and the kind of administration of the law which will give to those qualities in the private citizen the best possible chance for development. The prime problem of our nation is to get the right type of good citizenship, and, to get it, we must have progress, and our public men must be genuinely progressive.

VI

PARTIES AND DIRECT DEMOCRACY

18

Progressive Government Produces Business Prosperity*

From *La Follette's Autobiography*, Chapter 8

Robert M. La Follette

Author of the "Wisconsin Idea" of efficiency in government, Robert M. La Follette (1855–1925) challenged the state Republican organization in Wisconsin, eventually winning the gubernatorial contest in 1900. After five years as governor, La Follette was elected to the U.S. Senate where he quickly became known for his advocacy of progressive reform. He established a magazine, *La Follette's Weekly Magazine* (1909), which popularized such progressive devices as "The Roll Call" in order to publicize voting records of senators and representatives. In the following selection, La Follette details the innovative means by which he defeated the Republican party machine in Wisconsin and introduced substantial regulation of business in his state.

Reformers often stop fighting before the battle is really won: before the new territory is completely occupied. I felt that the campaign of 1904 was the very crux of our whole movement. We had passed our railroad taxation and direct primary measures in 1903; but the railroad taxation law would be a barren victory until it was supplemented by a commission to control railroad rates; and the direct nomination of candidates would fail unless we carried the election and secured the adoption of the primary bill at the referendum that fall. Without the direct primary law it would be an easy matter for the old machine to regain control of the legislature and not only prevent

* Editors' Note: Robert M. La Follete, "Progressive Government Produces Business Prosperity: What Was Accomplished in Wisconsin," in *La Follette's Autobiography: A Personal Narrative of Political Experiences* (Madison, Wisc.: The Robert M. La Follette Co., 1911), 319–26, 335–40, 348–56, 359–62, 367–69. Excerpt.

further progressive legislation, but undo part, if not all, of the work already accomplished.

I felt absolutely sure that another term, with another legislature, would securely ground and bulwark self-government in Wisconsin. I knew that the opposition understood this too, and that they would make the most desperate fight in that campaign that they had ever made. I began, therefore, delivering speeches both inside and outside the state as early as December, 1903—nearly a year before the election. As for the old machine, Congressman Joseph W. Babcock early came forward as commander-in-chief. He criticized the methods adopted by Phillipp, Pfister, and others in the campaign of 1902 as being too open and noisy. He came right to Madison, rented some rooms and began what he called a "gumshoe campaign." Men were sent quietly about the state, arrangements were made for controlling the employees of the railroads and the big industries, and the federal office-holders were marshaled for duty.

Upon our part the campaign of 1904 was the most comprehensive of the whole series. We went straight to the people with the same facts—the same dry statistics—which we had used so effectively upon the legislature in 1903. We prepared ten different pamphlets and distributed over 1,600,000 separate pieces of mail. Some of the pamphlets contained comparative tables showing transportation rates upon all the principal products shipped to market from *every county seat in the state.* It placed side by side with these items the cost of shipping the same products an equal distance from stations in Illinois and Iowa. In that way it was brought home to every citizen in every county just what he was sacrificing in dollars and cents as the result of the negligence of his representatives in affording him the same protection which his neighbors in Iowa and Illinois had secured many years before. Even in those two states the railroads had controlled the commissions for a long period and the rates had not been lowered in many years, though the volume of traffic had enormously increased and railway profits had more than kept pace with the big tonnage. In this connection I want to credit the Bureau of Labor and Industrial Statistics, Mr. Erickson particularly, as its head, and his assistant, Walter Drew, with the aid rendered in constructing these rate sheets. It was Mr. Erickson's mastery of this subject which suggested to my mind his fitness as a member of the Wisconsin Railway Commission when it was later established and upon which he has served with distinction.

Two or three weeks before the close of the nominating campaign we were surprised by an entirely new tack taken by the old leaders. Word came that in many counties second sets of Republican delegates were being elected under such circumstances that it could have but one meaning—that the opposition was laying the foundation either for stealing the state convention or else bolting it and placing a third ticket in the field. They were desperate: they knew that it was their last chance to win the state under the old system, that the approaching convention would probably be the last ever held in the state for the nomination of candidates, as indeed it proved to be.

When the time arrived for the convention to meet, at Madison, they brought in a veritable army of men. All their leaders were there: Babcock, Pfister, Phillip, Spooner and Quarles. We realized that we were facing a crisis; that all we had been struggling for in Wisconsin might be lost if we permitted these men by force or by confusion to cast doubt upon the action of the convention.

The convention was called to meet in the university gymnasium, the largest auditorium in Madison. We felt it necessary to protect the doorkeepers from being rushed and swept aside by a crowd of men not entitled to seats as delegates. So during the night before we had constructed at the delegates' entrance a barbed wire passage which would admit of the delegates entering only in single file. Stationed along the line of this fence we had twelve or fifteen of the old university football men—fine, clean, upright fellows who were physically able to meet any emergency. Among them were Arne Lerum, "Norsky" Larson, "Bill" Hazard, and Fred Kull. The machine crowd formed in a body on the capitol square, a mile from the university, and marched down in large numbers, prepared to take possession of the convention hall. They had printed "fake" badges and delegates' tickets exactly duplicating those issued by the State Central Committee to all regularly elected delegates—theirs as well as ours. It was only by placing initials on the genuine badges and tickets at a late hour that our men stationed at the gymnasium entrance were able to distinguish the genuine from the spurious. When this army appeared at the gymnasium they discovered that provision had been made against a rush and that they had to enter in single file. Whenever a man presented a counterfeit credential he was promptly set outside of the wire fence. All these men, however, came in later with the spectators at the front entrance and found seats in that portion of the hall which had been separated by roping off from the portion occupied by delegates; and along that roping they found another sturdy lot of "Norsky" Larsons. So well was all this preliminary work arranged that the convention organized regularly and in the best of order.

The critical moment came when Mr. Rosenberry, a machine member of the State Central Committee, arose to make his minority report regarding the election contests. The state committee, which was composed partly of our men and partly of their men, had tried out all of these contests before the convention met and they had *unanimously* seated enough of our delegates to give Progressives a comfortable majority of the convention. After the meeting of the committee and before the convention was called to order the machine

leaders evidently planned to repudiate the report of the state committee, to ignore the roll of delegates entitled to seats for the preliminary organization of
the convention in accord with all precedent, and to seat their "delegates,"
which the committee had unanimously rejected, and thus get control of the
convention—which they knew would probably result in a row.

As I say, Rosenberry came forward to make a speech. It had leaked out that
the conclusion of his speech was to be the signal for action; that Rosenberry
would then be on the platform, in a good position to seize the gavel, and take
possession of the chair, with the fellows down on the floor all primed to have
him declared elected chairman. They were simply going to gavel it through,
no matter how much protest there might be. The convention was crowded, but
we reserved three or four seats close to the front of the platform and near the
speaker's chair, where we planted some more "Norsky" Larsons and "Bill"
Hazzards. The result of all this precaution was that they dared make no move,
and the convention went forward in the most orderly way. Not an unparlia-
mentary thing was done. They voted upon the contests and even upon the
nominations, and of course were beaten.

. . .

It was not possible for one man to cover, during the caucus period, all of the
seventy-two counties of the state, but I did as well as I could; and in those
senatorial and assembly districts which I was unable to reach and in which
Republican candidates secured renomination whose records would have defeated them if they had been properly placed before their constituents, I now
resolved to make the contest against them at the election, although they were
nominally members of my own party. Wherever I found a Democratic nominee for the assembly or senate whose standing was such as to warrant confidence in his pledges, and who was willing to come into my meetings and give
assurance of his support of the measures for the public good embodied in the
Republican platform, I besought the voters of such legislative districts to support him and defeat the Republican nominee who had betrayed them in the
preceding legislatures. I utterly ignored the campaign for my own election. In
nearly one half of the counties of the state I never held a single meeting in
that campaign. But I picked out those legislative districts that were the bat-
tleground for the accomplishment of legislation and I campaigned those as
they had never been campaigned before. I spoke forty-eight days in succession, never missing one single day, excepting Sundays. I averaged eight and
one quarter hours a day on the platform. We had two automobiles, so that if
one broke down or got out of order in any way I could transfer to the other. I
began speaking about nine o'clock in the morning. I would go into a county
and speak at every little hamlet or crossroads, talking to small groups of men

during the day, often from the automobile, and sometimes in a store. Then we would have a meeting in the evening, probably at the county seat, where I always had a large audience, finishing my work about eleven o'clock at night. Some of those night meetings were enormous; when I closed the campaign at Milwaukee I spoke to about 10,000 people for four hours.

I took only one meal a day at the table during those forty-eight days. My noon luncheon consisted of a bottle of good rich milk and two slices of the crust of bread buttered, and sometimes a little well-cured cheese shaved off and put in between. For my supper I duplicated my luncheon. I got the bread and milk at the farmhouses along the road, and ate it on the way. It was a real whirlwind campaign, and I came out of it weighing only two pounds less than when I went in. The opposition tried for a time to follow me and catch my crowds, but they were soon worn out, and their reception, just after I had furnished my audiences with the ammunition for asking concrete questions, was discouraging, so that they soon desisted.

I discussed chiefly freight rates. I would tell them how much it cost them to ship a carload of hogs from that town to Chicago, and how much it would cost an Iowa farmer to ship a carload of hogs from his town the same distance to market. And then I would tell them that we were trying to create in Wisconsin a railroad commission to which appeal could be made, instead of to a railroad official, for fair freight rates and adequate service. Then I would take the record of the last legislature on that question. I would say: "Now, I think you are entitled to know how your representative voted on this question. I am going to make no personal attack upon any individual, but he is your servant, and the servant of all the people of this state. His vote counts not only against your interests, but against the interests of the district in which I live as well, and I am here to-day to lay before you his record, and let you then decide whether that is the sort of service you want. There is no politics in this thing; it does not matter whether you get this legislation upon the vote of a Republican or a Democrat." Then I would tell them that I had interviewed the candidate on the Democratic side, and found him to be a man of integrity, that I had received from him assurance that he would support the important legislation pledged in the Republican platform, and submitted to them whether the promise of this man was not better than the performance of the man who had betrayed them in the preceding session.

And I cleaned up the legislature. That was the origin of the "roll call" which I have since used with such effectiveness. It is simply a form of publicity, of letting the light in on dark records. I have developed a department called "The Roll Call" in *La Follette's Magazine* which has presented accurately the records of many Senators and Congressmen, and has been instrumental, I am positive, in putting more than one bad Congressman and Senator out of business. In my Chautauqua work also I have found the roll call a most potent instrument for political regeneration.

I was elected by about 50,000, and the direct primary law, for which we had campaigned vigorously, carried by about the same majority. We also elected a safe majority of both houses of the legislature.

. . .

As soon as the legislature passed our regulation law I appointed the three commissioners. I had contended all along for an appointive rather than an elective commission. I felt that the state should have the best experts in the country in these positions, whether residents of Wisconsin or not, for much would depend upon the way in which our new law was administered. They would have to match wits with the highly skilled, highly paid agents of the railroads, and they would have to make their work pass the critical consideration of the courts. Now, the men best equipped by study and experience for such work might, if the commission were elective, prove very poor campaigners. If pitted against brilliant talkers or good "mixers" they might stand no show at all. The submission also of a large number of candidates to the voter to be selected at a time when his mind is occupied with the consideration of questions under discussion, as well as candidates, tends still further to lessen the chances of the selection of the best man for particular service. For these reasons I have always strongly advocated the appointive method for filling all places requiring the services of trained experts.

I tried to persuade Commissioner Prouty of the Interstate Commerce Commission to come to Wisconsin, organize our commission, and take the chairmanship, but failing in that, I turned at once to the head of the transportation department of the University of Wisconsin, B. H. Meyer. A native of Wisconsin and a graduate of the university, Professor Meyer had made himself an authority upon railroad affairs in the country. He served upon our commission with great distinction, resigning in January of last year (1911) to accept a position upon the Interstate Commerce Commission at Washington. As another commissioner I appointed John Barnes, a Democrat, one of the foremost lawyers of the state, who sacrificed much in taking the place at the salary we paid. He has since been elected to the Supreme Court of the State. The third member was Halford Erickson, who had rendered invaluable service as Commissioner of Industrial and Labor Statistics. He had practical knowledge of railroading and has steadily grown in power until to-day he has no superior as a railroad authority on any state commission in the country.

The commission proceeded with wisdom. Though under great pressure at first, it refused to consider complaints until it had laid a broad foundation of scientific knowledge. Expert engineers and contractors were employed and many months were spent in making a physical valuation of all railroad property in the state. This is the logical first step if you are going to fix rates. It then became necessary to determine the actual cost of maintenance and operation—a very difficult matter in our case—because the railroads of Wisconsin are parts of great systems.

When all this immense work was done, the commission had the wisdom and foresight to submit its findings to the railroad officials, who went over them and approved them. This prevented disputes in the future upon fundamental facts.

Having all this data, the commissioners began to entertain complaints, and to fix rates upon a basis which they knew positively was fair to the public and fair to the railroads. They so reduced transportation charges as to effect a saving of over $2,000,000 per year to the people of the state, and they have only made a beginning. Generally the rates of public utility corporations have been reduced, but in some cases the investigation showed that the rates were too low already and the commission raised them. The result is that individuals may be found in communities where rates have been increased or have not been promptly or radically reduced who declare that the Railroad Commission has not met expectations by "going after" the corporations.

All through our fight for railroad control the lobbyists and the railroad newspapers made the most mournful prophecies of disaster: they predicted that capital would fly from the state, that new construction would stop, that equipment would deteriorate, and so on and so on. What are the facts?

The object of our legislation was not to "smash" corporations, but to drive them out of politics, and then to treat them exactly the same as other people are treated. Equality under the law was our guiding star. It is the special discriminations and unjust rates that are being corrected; the privileges, unfair advantages, and political corruption that have been abolished. Where these do not exist the object has been to foster and encourage business activity. Consequently, no state in the union to-day offers better security for the savings of its people than Wisconsin. The honest investor, or business man, or farmer, or laborer, who simply wants equal opportunity with others and security for what he honestly earns, is protected and encouraged by the laws. The mere speculator, or monopolist, or promoter, who wants to take advantage of others under protection of law, is held down or driven out. The result is that instead of falling behind, the state has actually gone forward more rapidly than the rest of the country. This may be shown by incontrovertible facts and figures in practically every direction where there has been progressive legislation affecting business.

The Railroad Commission keeps accurate account of all the business of every railroad and public utility in the state. It has jurisdiction over property whose total value amounts to $450,000,000. The books are kept exactly as the commission orders them to be kept. These accounts show that while during the first five years of its existence the commission reduced rates by more than $2,000,000 a year, the *net earnings* of the railroads of Wisconsin increased relatively just a little more than the net earnings for all railways in the United States. The increase in Wisconsin was 18.45 per cent., and in the United States it was 18.41 per cent.

How did this come about? Simply from the fact that the decrease in rates for freight and passengers was followed by an enormous increase in the amount of freight and number of passengers carried. So it happened that, notwithstanding the *reduction in rates*, there was an actual increase of nearly 20 per cent. in the revenue, while the increase of revenue of all the railroads in the United States was only 16 per cent.

This remarkable increase took place notwithstanding the fact that, mainly on account of the greatly improved service which the commission required the railroads to perform, the expense of railroad operation in Wisconsin increased 33 per cent. more than the average rate of increase in the entire United States.

Much of what the railroads lost in the reduction of open rates that everybody shares they recovered by being compelled to abolish free passes and secret cut rates that went only to insiders and grafters. The special examiners whom I appointed in 1903 uncovered $5,992,731.58 as Wisconsin's share of rebates paid by twelve roads during the six years 1898 to 1903. By stopping rebates alone the railroads have gained at least $1,000,000 a year toward offsetting $2,000,000 they lost by reduction of rates. They must also have gained largely by the stoppage of political contributions and expenses. The railroads to-day are gaining far more by treating everybody on an equality than they could have gained if their old methods of politics and secret favoritism had continued.

It is not claimed that railroads are both *making* and *keeping* more money in Wisconsin than they did before the progressive legislation began. Indeed, they are *making more but keeping a smaller proportion of it*. They are now paying taxes the same as other people on exactly what their property is worth. This they began to do in 1904. Under the old system of unequal taxation, in 1903, when the railroads practically assessed themselves, they paid taxes in the state amounting to $1,711,900. Under the new system, in 1910, when the State Tax Commission assessed them exactly like farms and other property, they paid $3,142,886. This was an increase of 83 per cent. in the amount of their taxes. But during the years 1903 to 1909 the taxes of all railroads in the United States increased only 41 percent. That is, railroad taxation in Wisconsin has been increased by the progressive legislation in six years nearly twice as much as the increase for all of the United States. If this increase in taxation is a hardship on the railroads, it is simply because equal taxation is always a hardship on those who had not been formerly paying their equal share of taxes.

Nor did progressive legislation stop new construction: During the years 1903 to 1909 the railroads invested in new construction in Wisconsin an amount estimated by the Railroad Commission at $39,000,000, an increase of 15 per cent. over 1903. This is not a fictitious increase in capitalization. It is *actual cash paid out* for new road and equipment. A cash investment by railroads of $6,500,000 a year for six years of progressive legislation refutes their prophecies of disaster.

. . .

How has it been possible that both the people of Wisconsin and the investors in public utilities have been so greatly benefited by this regulation? *Simply because the regulation is scientific.* The Railroad Commission has found out through its engineers, accountants, and statisticians what it actually cost to build and operate the road and utilities. Watered stock and balloon bonds get no consideration. On the other hand, since the commission knows the costs, it knows exactly the point below which rates cannot be reduced. It even raises rates when they are below the cost, including reasonable profit.

The people are benefited because they are not now paying profits on inflated capital. The investors are benefited because the commission has all the facts needed to prevent a reduction of rates below a fair profit on their true value. So honestly, capably, and scientifically has the work of our commission been done that the railroads and other utility corporations have accepted their reductions without any contest at all. Our law makes it perfectly easy for the railroads to seek redress in the courts if they feel wronged in any way. Yet it is significant that there has never been an appeal taken in any railroad rate case decided by the Railroad Commission. The corporations know that the Railroad Commission has all the data for making rates that they (the railroads) have, and that it can go into court and show that it is making rates not by guess, not by estimate, but by the most careful calculation based upon definite information. Thus while the railroad companies do not enjoy having their rates cut down, they are not over-eager to advertise the Wisconsin system of rate-making. When the other states of the country and the federal government make rates as we do in Wisconsin, the shippers of the country will be saved millions of dollars every year in excessive transportation charges.

In Wisconsin we regulate services as well as rates. When the services of a railroad are not satisfactory to the public, complaint can be made to the Railroad Commission. Under our law that complaint does not need to be a formal legal document, but a simple statement of grievance by letter or postal card. In 1906 I rode over the branch of the Chicago, Milwaukee and St. Paul road which runs from Madison to Prairie du Chien. The train was not so very crowded when I got on two or three stations east of Prairie du Chien, but it kept filling up and pretty soon I found myself standing in the aisle. I kept being crowded back and back until when I got to Madison I was sitting on the tail end of the train, and I was thoroughly angry. I had a canvass made of the regular patrons of the train who were aboard, to find out how the service that morning compared with the average service. I found it was the usual thing, and I wrote at once on the back of an envelope which I took from my pocket something like this:

"Mr. Commissioner: I call your attention to the bad service on the Prairie du Chien division of the Chicago, Milwaukee and St. Paul road. It is not adequately equipped either with cars or trains. Passenger train so-and-so crowded to the platforms. I think the matter should be investigated by your commission."

I think inside of ten days there was a new train running on that road. The traveling men called it the "Bob" train in honor of me, but I am sure that no more attention was paid to my complaint than would have been paid to one from any other source.

. . .

These are a few of the conclusive proofs that progressive legislation in Wisconsin has not been destructive, as its enemies predicted. Instead of driving capital out of the state it has attracted capital more than other states. It has made investments safe for all, instead of speculative for a few. It has been conservative and constructive as well as progressive. Only one of the progressive laws—a law passed in 1911, declaring flowing water public property—has been overturned by the supreme court of the state, and not one has been carried into the federal courts.

No account of the long and successful struggle in Wisconsin would be fair and complete that did not record the splendid services of the men who led the fight for progressive principles. I regret that I cannot here give to each the individual recognition that is merited. That must wait for a more detailed history of the Wisconsin movement. It was a day-and-night service with them; they left their offices and business interests and devoted years to the great constructive work which has made Wisconsin the safest guide in dealing with the political, economic and social problems of our time.

This closes the account of my services in Wisconsin—a time full of struggle, and yet a time that I like to look back upon. It has been a fight supremely worth making, and I want it to be judged, as it will be ultimately, by results actually attained. If it can be shown that Wisconsin is a happier and better state to live in, that its institutions are more democratic, that the opportunities of all its people are more equal, that social justice more nearly prevails, that human life is safer and sweeter—then I shall rest content in the feeling that the Progressive movement has been successful. And I believe all these things can really be shown, and that there is no reason now why the movement should not expand until it covers the entire nation. While much has been accomplished, there is still a world of problems yet to be solved; we have just begun; there is hard fighting, and a chance for the highest patriotism, still ahead of us. The fundamental problem as to which shall rule, men or property, is still unsettled; it will require the highest qualities of heroism, the profoundest devotion to duty in this and in the coming generation, to reconstruct our institutions to meet the requirements of a new age. May such brave and true leaders develop that the people will not be led astray.

19

*Progressive Democracy**

Chapters 12 and 13

Herbert Croly

Herbert Croly (1869–1930) was a founding editor of *The New Republic*, which became the chief organ for progressive opinion in the United States. His influence was wide, most notably with Theodore Roosevelt, who adopted Croly's "new nationalism" theme as Roosevelt turned to a more radical brand of progressivism following his presidency. In addition to his scores of essays for *The New Republic*, Croly authored two substantial books: *The Promise of American Life* (1909) and *Progressive Democracy* (1914), the latter of which is considered to contain the more mature and comprehensive of its author's reflections on liberty and democracy. In the following chapters from *Progressive Democracy*, Croly outlines the principles of direct democracy, various mechanisms of which had been springing up as the hallmarks of the progressive movement across the United States.

CHAPTER XII: "THE ADVENT OF DIRECT GOVERNMENT"

. . .

If economic, social, political and technical conditions had remained very much as they were at the end of the eighteenth century, the purely democratic political aspirations might never have obtained the chance of expression. Some form of essentially representative government was at that time apparently the only dependable kind of liberal political organization. It was imposed by the physical and technical conditions under which government had

---

* Editors' Note: Herbert Croly, *Progressive Democracy* (New York: The Macmillan Company, 1914), 262–83. Excerpt.

to be conducted. Direct government did not seem to be possible outside of city or tribal states, whose population and area was sufficiently small to permit the actual assemblage of the body politic at some particular place, either at regular intervals or in case of an emergency. But in the case of states chiefly devoted to agriculture, whose free citizens were distributed over a wide area, and were, in any event, too numerous for actual assemblage in anyone spot, it seemed necessary for the people to delegate to a body of representatives the power required not merely for public administration, but for the discussion of public questions, the adoption of public policies and the supervising of the administration itself. Some form of a responsible representative government, that is, was prescribed by fundamental economic and social conditions. The function was performed in the several states according to the method best adapted to local traditions and by the class which had proved itself capable of leadership.

In the twentieth century, however, these practical conditions of political association have again changed, and have changed in a manner which enables the mass of the people to assume some immediate control of their political destinies. While it is more impossible than ever for the citizens of a modern industrial and agricultural state actually to assemble after the manner of a New England town-meeting, it is no longer necessary for them so to assemble. They have abundant opportunities of communication and consultation without any actual meeting at one time and place. They are kept in constant touch with one another by means of the complicated agencies of publicity and intercourse which are afforded by the magazines, the press and the like. The active citizenship of the country meets every morning and evening and discusses the affairs of the nation with the newspaper as an impersonal interlocutor. Public opinion has a thousand methods of seeking information and obtaining definite and effective expression which it did not have four generations ago. The community is broken up into innumerable smaller communities, each of which is united by common interests and ideas and each of which is seeking to bring a larger number of people under the influence of its interests and ideas. Under such conditions the discussions which take place in a Congress or a Parliament no longer possess their former function. They no longer create and guide what public opinion there is. Their purpose rather is to provide a mirror for public opinion, to advertise and illuminate its constituent ideas and purposes, and to confront the advocates of those ideas with the discipline of effective resistance and, perhaps, with the responsibilities of power. Phases of public opinion form, develop, gather to a head, assert their power and find their place chiefly by the activity of other more popular unofficial agencies. Thus the democracy has at its disposal a mechanism of developing and exchanging opinions, and of reaching decisions, which is independent of representative assemblies, and which is, or may become, superior to that which it formerly obtained by virtue of occasional popular assemblages.

The adoption of the machinery of direct government is a legitimate expression of this change. After centuries of political development, in which certain forms of representation were imposed upon progressive nations by conditions of practical efficiency, and in which these representative forms grew continually in variety and complexity, underlying conditions have again shifted. Pure democracy has again become not merely possible, but natural and appropriate. The attempt to return to it is no more retrogressive than was the attempt to recover classic humanism after its eclipse during the Middle Ages. Society has been passing through a period of prodigious fertility, during which new social aspirations, purposes, instruments and activities have multiplied with unprecedented rapidity. If these new interests and activities are to be assimilated, they must be recognized and incorporated into the system of government. As a consequence of the attempt to incorporate them into the system of government, society may seem to be yielding to the power of disintegrating economic and social forces. This appears to be the beginning of a reverse process of denationalization which will be equivalent to dissolution. Those who place any such interpretation upon the facts of modern social development and the corresponding political changes fail to understand their meaning. Increasing direct popular political action is coming to have a function in the political organization of a modern society, because only in this way can the nation again become a master in its own house. Its very fecundity, and the enormous power which many of its offspring obtain, have compelled a democratic nation to adopt a more thoroughgoing method of promoting its integrity. As yet it is not making very much headway. It is distracted and disconcerted by its own fertility. It is terrified in particular by the capitalist and labor organizations to which it has given birth. But it will not continue to be disconcerted and terrified. It is adopting the very political instruments which are necessary for the purpose of keeping control of the increasingly numerous and increasingly powerful agencies of its own life. The attempt, far from being a reactionary reversion to an earlier political and social type, prepares the way, it may be hoped, for an advance towards a better and deeper social and political union, associated with direct popular political action and responsibility.

CHAPTER XIII:
"DIRECT *VERSUS* REPRESENTATIVE GOVERNMENT"

In the preceding chapter I have submitted some reasons for believing that direct government is not retrogressive merely because its methods exhibit certain analogies to those used in city and tribal states. Neither does the fact that the electorate in a directly governed state has certain positive functions to perform in relation to legislation place upon such a state the stigma of reaction. Direct government cannot be fairly condemned as reactionary unless the exercise of the broad general responsibilities which it imposes upon the electorate proves inimical to the delegation of sufficient and specific additional responsibilities to other departments of the government. This second aspect of the matter still remains to be discussed. Will the advent of direct democracy result in any increase of the confusion and disorganization which prevails in the mechanism of American state representation? Or will the draught of self-confidence, which our local democracies are by way of swallowing, be communicated to the behavior of the rest of the political mechanism and invigorate the whole system? Will direct popular government commit the same fatal mistake which, to a greater or smaller extent, has already been committed by the national monarchies, by parliamentary government and by democratic legalism? Will it seek to appropriate or emasculate legislative or administrative functions which need to be delegated to other human agencies?

The critics of direct democracy can hardly be blamed for considering doubtful the answers to the foregoing questions. The American experiment in direct democracy is still in its early youth. Its meaning and its tendencies cannot be demonstrated from experience. If the active political responsibilities which it grants to the electorate are redeemed in the negative and suspicious spirit which characterized the attitude of the American democracy towards its official organization during its long and barren alliance with legalism, direct democracy will merely become a source of additional confusion and disorganization. On the other hand, if, as a consequence of its rupture with legalism, the American democracy undergoes a change of spirit, if the attempt to discharge new and responsible activities in connection with its own government brings with it a positive inspiration and genuine social energy, the result may be to renovate American representative institutions and afford novel and desirable opportunities for effective political leadership. I prefer the second of these alternatives, but the preference can hardly be justified by a consideration of the results which have already been achieved in the directly governed states. It is born of an examination of the history, the needs and the ideals of the American local democracies.

The more dogmatic partisans of direct government do not help us very much in making a decision between the foregoing alternatives. In fact, they seem not to understand that any such alternatives exist. They usually attach much the same automatic efficacy to the system of direct government that the Fathers attached to constitutionalism and checks and balances. They have not, indeed, any declared intention of substituting direct for representative government. They admit verbally the necessity in a pure democracy of some effective delegation of specific governmental functions. But as a rule they devote very little attention and thought to the problem of a more powerful and efficient mechanism of legislation and administration. They are preoccupied by the flagrant betrayal of the popular interest which took place under the traditional system, and they seem to think that the adoption of the initiative, referendum and the recall will not merely protect the popular interest, but liberate the popular will—even though the popular will lacks, as much as it has lacked in the past, the impulse of positive social purposes.

Such an attitude toward the instruments of direct government is merely another expression of the old superstitious belief in political mechanics against which progressive democracy is bound to protest. If the people in the directly governed states consider the new instruments of democracy as fundamentally a safeguard against abuse and oppression, they may succeed in abolishing one kind of abuse and oppression, but only at the price of its being succeeded by other kinds. If they do not impose limits on their use of the instruments of direct government, based upon the conditions of their profitable service, it will prove to be a barren and mischievous addition to the stock of democratic political institutions. The success of the new instruments as negative safeguards will be commensurate with their success as agencies for the realization of positive popular political purposes. Their serviceability as agencies for the realization of popular political purposes will depend upon the ability of democratic law-givers to associate with them an efficient method of delegating popular political authority. Direct democracy, that is, has little meaning except in a community which is resolutely pursuing a vigorous social program. It must become one of a group of political institutions, whose object is fundamentally to invigorate and socialize the action of American public opinion.

The salient reasons which make it necessary to associate the advent of direct democracy with the attempt to realize a positive social program have already been indicated. They are derived from the profound alterations in the balance of a political organization which is substituting a positive for a negative social policy. The abstract legalistic individualism of the Jeffersonian democracy had in theory no need of any machinery of direct popular control. The activity of government was restricted, and its organs were emasculated, in the interest of a specific formulation of individual rights. Government was considered to be merely a form of temporary police supervision. Such a political system was placed in irons by the Law and lacked the power to do any harm. It really needed to operate somewhat independently of public opinion. Fermentation of public opinion and active political and social experimentation could not accomplish anything of real social value. The essential popular needs were already safeguarded in the Law, which deserved vigilant protection and unquestioning obedience on the part of all good citizens. Effective popular control of such a government was unnecessary. Government was not intended to be the instrument of important popular social purposes.

In its actual historical development the government soon became the instrument of important popular social purposes, and it was obliged to develop a corresponding method of popular control. But the popular social purposes which the state and Federal governments formerly attempted to realize were derived from the old individualistic social economy, and the control supposed to be exercised by the partisan organizations was ineffective. A wholly new situation was created when the local democracies came to need and possess a genuinely social policy, which threw increased burdens upon the government, and commensurately increased its power. Under such conditions direct popular control over the mechanism of government became of essential importance. A negative individualistic social policy implies a weak and irresponsible government. A positive comprehensive social policy implies a strong, efficient and responsible government. But a strong and efficient government, which exercises a large part of the authority of the state and which is not bound by the substantive provisions of the fundamental Law, might well be dangerous not only to individual civil rights, but to popular political rights. Every precaution should be adopted to keep it in sensitive touch with public opinion. A lack of responsiveness to public opinion would tempt it to become domineering and oppressive, and would in the long run make its own work abortive as well as dangerous. A social policy is concerned in the most intimate and comprehensive way with the lives of the people. In order to be successful, it must rest on the basis of abundant and cordial popular support.

The mechanism of direct government has, consequently, an essential function to perform in the organization of a social democracy. The realization of a genuine social policy necessitates the aggrandizement of the administrative and legislative branches of the government. Progressive democracy recognizes the need of these instruments, but it recognizes the need of keeping control of them. A strong government with an affirmative policy and effective popular control are supplementary rather than hostile one to another. The realization of such a policy will in the long run demand both an efficient system of representation and an efficient method of direct popular supervision.

The friends of direct government do not usually advocate it, for the reasons indicated in the preceding paragraph. An exclusively representative government is to many of them a perfectly satisfactory form of democratic political organization. It is objectionable only because it has failed to be really representative. A recent convert to pure democracy, President Woodrow Wilson, has expressed in the following words the reasons for his conversion: "If we felt we had genuine representative government in our state legislatures, no one would propose the initiative and the referendum in the United States. Our most ardent and successful advocates regard them as a sobering means of obtaining genuine representative action on the part of legislative bodies. They do not mean to set anything aside. They mean to restore and to reinvigorate rather." And a much more radical critic of our traditional system, Professor J. Allen Smith, who also favors direct popular political action, asserts that "a government of the representative type, if responsive to public sentiment, would answer all the requirements of a democratic state."

The adoption of direct government may, it is true, end by reinvigorating representative government; but if so, the result will not be accomplished by refusing "to set anything aside." The first thing which must be set aside is the method of representation which has passed in this country under the name of representative government. Direct government will never reinvigorate our existing state of political institutions. What it may accomplish is to supply energy to a new and better method of delegating popular political authority.

A statesman whose dominant object was the reorganization of existing state representative government would be foolish to depend upon the initiative and the referendum for the accomplishment of his purpose. There are a score of ways in which American state government could be made more representative without any invocation of the instrument of direct government. The first condition of effective representation is the bestowal upon the representative body of some effective power and responsibility, which, as all admit, is precisely the condition which has been largely and increasingly absent from our so-called representative institutions. Direct government does not automatically satisfy this need. On the contrary, as the experience of the state of Oregon sufficiently proves, its merely external addition to the existing machinery of representation tends, if anything, to attenuate still further the meag[er] responsibilities officially conferred on our state representative agencies.

So far as these state representative agencies are concerned, a representative value cannot be restored to them, because they were never intended to be and never have been representative in any self-respecting meaning of the word. A thoroughly representative government is essentially government by men rather than by Law. The active exercise of effective political responsibility is confided to a body of the elect. They assume the same responsibility for the ultimate welfare of the state that the American system delegates to the Law and its official expounders. True, the legislative body may govern, just as the Law was permitted to govern, by virtue of an explicit or implied popular consent, but in a representative system popular power is exercised only to be delegated. For the time being, complete legal responsibility for the public weal is conferred upon the legislature. Quite obviously no such responsibility has been conferred by the American system either upon the legislature or upon the legislature and executive together; and, to my mind, it cannot be expected that any exclusively representative system will be even fairly successful on any other terms.

The Progressive Republicans, who are advocating an increase of executive power and a closer cooperation between the executive and the legislature as the most effective means of reinvigorating the representative system, can make a very strong argument in its favor. They can make a stronger argument than can those advocates of "pure" democracy who expect to develop a genuinely representative government by grafting the instruments of direct government on an essentially and fatally unrepresentative system. But they cannot make a strong enough argument. The cooperation between an executive and a legislature, each of which derives its authority directly from the people, cannot be made properly operative except by some method of referring disputes to the common master—which means a considerable measure of direct government. Moreover, an American electorate would not submit for long to the increased power of the organs of government which would result from their cooperative action, without the creation of some means of effective popular control. But even if these difficulties could be overcome, it is doubtful how far any system can be considered really representative which does not bestow complete responsibility for the public welfare upon the government. The government must have the power to determine the Law instead of being circumscribed by the Law. Just in so far as its authority was curtailed, its sense of responsibility would be relaxed and its integrity would be undermined.

A purely representative system, such as that of the United Kingdom, seeks to accomplish the fundamental objects of government by a method opposed to that of the traditional American system. The former bestows complete legal responsibility for the welfare of the state and the course of its development upon the elect in the expectation that thereby society will obtain the boon of rational guidance. "Representation is not," says Guizot, who was one of its most ardent advocates, "an arithmetical means employed to count individual wills, but a natural process, whereby public reason, which alone has the right to govern modern society, may be extracted from the bosom of society itself." This account of the ultimate meaning of a purely representative system was accepted substantially by John Stuart Mill, although with certain significant modifications; and it manifestly constitutes the only justification for the enormous power and responsibility bestowed upon the legislative body. As the result of their deliberations the action of the representatives must embody a program based upon the enduring and the binding interests of the nation.

The American constitutional system did not need to create a powerful organ of government whose wise leadership would help to extract reason from the bosom of society. That desirable result had already been accomplished. Reason had been printed on the bosom of society in indelible ink by virtue of the embodiment in the Constitution of the great principles of legal morals. Its human purveyors were rather the judges than the legislature; and the business of the courts was not merely to declare the Word, but to keep the fire of political reason glowing in the political hearth. Under such a system executives and legislatures were not supposed, and did not need, to be particularly reasonable—which is certainly a proof of the wisdom of the Fathers of the Republic. They needed most of all to be obedient and self-restrained. For if any effective method exists of extracting reason from the bosom of society, the human purveyors of this rational extract certainly require some oracular writing for their guidance; and the more authoritative this oracle can be made, the better. So far as the object of political organization is to bring to the surface an already existing fund of reason, the method adopted by the founders of the American constitutional system may be preferred to the method characteristic of a purely representative system. The latter leaves the secretion and extraction of reason much more to the operation of a clumsy mechanism. As an edifice of political rationalism, the record of the discussion and action of the British Parliament during the past century cannot be compared to the constitutional decisions of the Supreme Court of the United States; and this is true notwithstanding the fact that even in the latter some traces may be occasionally discovered of the fallibility of that sovereign faculty.

Thus the difficulty with a purely representative government is similar to the difficulty which is involved in government by Law. The assumption made by the advocates of both of these systems is that society possesses at anyone time a fund of social reason which, by virtue of its superiority to interested, inexperienced and perverse counsel, is entitled to determine social action. The state should be organized chiefly for the purpose of giving control to this fund of social reason. The means whereby this control is exercised differs radically in the two systems; but we need not bother about their respective advantages or disadvantages. Neither of them meets the needs of a progressive democratic society, because in a society of this kind no such fund of really authoritative social reason can be held to exist. There is a fund of social reason which should possess some authority; but it is so small compared to social aspirations and needs that a democratic society must be organized less to obey than to increase it. The work of extracting the stores of reason from the bosom of society must be subordinated to the more fundamental object of augmenting the supply of social reason and improving its distribution. Legalism and purely representative government are unsuited to the needs of a thoroughgoing democracy, because their method of organization depends on popular obedience rather than popular education. The promotion and the diffusion of social reason cannot be brought about without a reverence for orderly procedure and without the leadership of the elect; but the erection of legalism alone or of representation alone into a system is not sufficient to secure this most important of all political objects. The best chance of securing it opens up as a result a more thoroughly popular organization of the state. The electorate must be required as the result of its own actual experience and unavoidable responsibilities to develop those very qualities of intelligence, character, faith and sympathy which are necessary for the success of the democratic experiment.

Thus neither representative government nor government by law nor any combination between the two is competent to meet all the requirements of a democratic polity. A clear-sighted, self-confident and loyal democracy will keep in its own hands the active control of all the agents and instruments of its own fulfil[l]ment. The instinctive repugnance which the American democracy has always exhibited to the delegation of too much power to anyone of the separate departments of government is explicable and justifiable. No plebiscite can bestow authenticity upon an ostensibly democratic political system which approximates in practice to the exercise of executive omnipotence. No intermittent appeals to the people for their approbation can wholly democratize a system which approximates in practice to the exercise of legislative omnipotence. No reverence for the law can guarantee political and social liberty to a body of democrats who confide their collective destiny to written formulas as expounded by a ruling body of lawyers. In practice each of these systems develops into a method of class government. The men to whom the enormous power is delegated will use it, in part at least, to perpetuate the system which is so beneficial to themselves. But even if they were as wise as Solomon and as gallant and disinterested as Sir Galahad, the systems for which they spoke and acted would still be evading rather than meeting the democratic problem. None of these systems make the people actively responsible for their own reasonableness and welfare. The people do not reap the advantages to which they are entitled, but if they did receive every possible advantage, they would not be earning it and could not keep what they received.

In all three of the principal departments of government, there are essential functions to be performed which must be delegated by a democracy to selected men under conditions which make for technical efficiency and individual independence and self-respect. The Fathers of the Republic were fully justified both in keeping the powers distinguished, and in seeking to balance one against the other. Their mistake consisted in the methods adopted for preserving or readjusting the balance. The preservation of a balance depends upon the harmonious development of several elements which enter into it; and as in the course of nature harmonious development is rare, the preservation of any such balance must usually be contrived by human insistence and intelligence. Only one part of a democratic system is entitled to exercise any such function—the electorate itself. The whole of a democratic political system is divided into three parts, not merely or primarily as a protection to individual and popular liberties, but rather to provide an essential positive function for the people to perform—the function of recreating the unity which is necessarily compromised by the no less necessary specialization of governmental function. Such is the part which the people, or the closest possible approximation to the people, have to play in the process of their own nationalization or socialization. They must divide in order to act, to think, to rule, to move on and to aspire; but they must not impose upon anyone of the resulting classifications or subdivisions the responsibility of ultimate social cohesion. That responsibility rests with the whole people, and its fulfil[l]ment depends upon popular intelligence, sympathy and faith.

Many sincere social democrats in this country, as well as in England or France, regard any such dependence upon direct government with the utmost repugnance. The industrial and social program of a democracy can, in their opinion, be accomplished with less friction and delay through the agency of an authoritative representative body. They are probably right in expecting that in the near future direct popular government will increase the difficulty of securing the adoption of many items in a desirable social program. But reformers of this class, like the conservatives, attach too much importance to the accomplishment and maintenance of specific results, and too little to the permanent moral welfare of the democracy. They are willing to have the people imposed upon in the interest of what is or is intended to be the popular benefit. An authoritative representative government, particularly one which is associated with inherited leadership and a strong party system, carries with it an enormous prestige. It is frequently in a position either to ignore, to circumvent or to wear down popular opposition. But a social program purchased at such a price is not worth what it costs. It makes no difference how benevolent the intention of the government may be or how wise its legislation. The program which is carried out by such means will do nothing to make the people worthy of their advantages. The result will either be popular servility or organized popular resistance or both. The country in which a benevolent government has succeeded in carrying out the most comprehensive social policy of modern times is the country in which a social democratic party, organized to overthrow the government, has succeeded in obtaining the support of a third of the electorate.

Social reformers must, consequently, be patient as well as eager and tenacious. A moderate program which is well understood and cordially supported by public opinion, and upon which the electorate has been in some measure specifically consulted, will be much more beneficial than a more extensive program which is not so well understood, and which does not represent a genuine popular affirmation. From the beginning of civilization the people have been constantly imposed upon by moral or social or physical force in the real or supposed interest of their own welfare. The process will doubtless have to continue in some measure; but if democracy means anything, it means popular liberation in precisely this respect. It means that social reformers must present their arguments primarily to the electorate, and welcome every good opportunity of allowing the electorate to pass judgment upon their proposals.

Our conclusion, then, is double-faced. Democracy implies and needs some method of representation which will be efficient and responsible enough to carry out a social policy, but which does not imply the delegation of its own ultimate discretionary power to any body of men or body of law. No such representative system can be found in the provisions of existing state constitutions. An organization of the executive and legislative powers, which will give increased energy to both of them and which is adjusted to their cooperation both one with another and with a sufficient measure of direct government, is what is needed and must be contrived. The new organization will be intended first, last and always to promote political education. It must be adapted to action, but the action must merely be the decisive temporary result of widespread popular fermentation. It must have the chance to be efficient, but only for the purpose of being educational. It must be able to educate, but primarily by the road of efficient action. The new system can accomplish nothing without human energy, intelligence, sacrifice and faith, but if those qualities are present, it will make the best use of them.

20

The Right of the People to Rule*

Theodore Roosevelt

Given just after he had entered the presidential race in 1912, Theodore Roosevelt uses this address to outline his support for the various mechanisms of direct democracy that had become an important part of the progressive program: the initiative, referendum, recall, direct primary, and popular override of state judicial decisions. Roosevelt grounds his call for direct democracy in an endorsement of nearly unfettered majority rule and an attack on the notion that indirect government could be a means of protecting minority rights.

The great fundamental issue now before the Republican party and before our people can be stated briefly. It is, Are the American people fit to govern themselves, to rule themselves, to control themselves? I believe they are. My opponents do not. I believe in the right of the people to rule. I believe the majority of the plain people of the United States will, day in and day out, make fewer mistakes in governing themselves than any smaller class or body of men, no matter what their training, will make in trying to govern them. I believe, again, that the American people are, as a whole, capable of self-control and of learning by their mistakes. Our opponents pay lip-loyalty to this doctrine; but they show their real beliefs by the way in which they champion every device to make the nominal rule of the people a sham.

I have scant patience with this talk of the tyranny of the majority. Whenever there is tyranny of the majority, I shall protest against it with all my heart

* Editors' Note: Theodore Roosevelt, "The Right of the People to Rule," in *The Outlook* 100 (March 1912): 618–23. Excerpt.

and soul. But we are today suffering from the tyranny of minorities. It is a small minority that is grabbing our coal deposits, our water powers, and our harbor fronts. A small minority is battening on the sale of adulterated foods and drugs. It is a small minority that lies behind monopolies and trusts. It is a small minority that stands behind the present law of master and servant, the sweat-shops, and the whole calendar of social and industrial injustice. It is a small minority that is to-day using our convention system to defeat the will of a majority of the people in the choice of delegates to the Chicago Convention. The only tyrannies from which men, women, and children are suffering in real life are the tyrannies of minorities.

If the majority of the American people were in fact tyrannous over the minority, if democracy had no greater self-control than empire, then indeed no written words which our forefathers put into the Constitution could stay that tyranny.

No sane man who has been familiar with the government of this country for the last twenty years will complain that we have had too much of the rule of the majority. The trouble has been a far different one—that, at many times and in many localities, there have held public office in the States and in the Nation men who have, in fact, served not the whole people, but some special class or special interest. I am not thinking only of those special interests which by grosser methods, by bribery and crime, have stolen from the people. I am thinking as much of their respectable allies and figureheads, who have ruled and legislated and decided as if in some way the vested rights of privilege had a first mortgage on the whole United States, while the rights of all the people were merely an unsecured debt. Am I overstating the case? Have our political leaders always, or generally, recognized their duty to the people as anything more than a duty to disperse the mob, see that the ashes are taken away, and distribute patronage? Have our leaders always, or generally, worked for the benefit of human beings, to increase the prosperity of all the people, to give to each some opportunity of living decently and bringing up his children well? The questions need no answer.

Now there has sprung up a feeling deep in the hearts of the people—not of the bosses and professional politicians, not of the beneficiaries of special privilege—a pervading belief of thinking men that when the majority of the people do in fact, as well as theory, rule, then the servants of the people will come more quickly to answer and obey, not the commands of the special interests, but those of the whole people. To reach toward that end the Progressives of the Republican party in certain States have formulated certain proposals for change in the form of the State government—certain new "checks and balances" which may check and balance the special interests and their allies. That is their purpose. Now turn for a moment to their proposed methods.

First, there are the "initiative and referendum," which are so framed that if the Legislatures obey the command of some special interest, and obstinately refuse the will of the majority, the majority may step in and legislate directly. No man would say that it was best to conduct all legislation by direct vote of the people—it would mean the loss of deliberation, of patient consideration— but, on the other hand, no one whose mental arteries have not long since hardened can doubt that the proposed changes are needed when the Legislatures refuse to carry out the will of the people. The proposal is a method to reach an undeniable evil. Then there is the recall of public officers—the principle that an officer chosen by the people who is unfaithful may be recalled by vote of the majority before he finishes his term. I will speak of the recall of judges in a moment—leave that aside—but as to the other officers, I have heard no argument advanced against the proposition, save that it will make the public officer timid and always currying favor with the mob. That argument means that you can fool all the people all the time, and is an avowal of disbelief in democracy. If it be true—and I believe it is not—it is less important than to stop those public officers from currying favor with the interests. Certain States may need the recall, others may not; where the term of elective office is short it may be quite needless; but there are occasions when it meets a real evil, and provides a needed check and balance against the special interests.

Then there is the direct primary—the real one, not the New York one—and that, too, the Progressives offer as a check on the special interests. Most clearly of all does it seem to me that this change is wholly good—for every State. The system of party government is not written in our Constitutions, but it is none the less a vital and essential part of our form of government. In that system the party leaders should serve and carry out the will of their own party. There is no need to show how far that theory is from the facts, or to rehearse the vulgar thieving partnerships of the corporations and the bosses, or to show how many times the real government lies in the hands of the boss, protected from the commands and the revenge of the voters by his puppets in office and the power of patronage. We need not be told how he is thus intrenched nor how hard he is to overthrow. The facts stand out in the history of nearly every State in the Union. They are blots on our political system. The direct primary will give the voters a method ever ready to use, by which the party leader shall be made to obey their command. The direct primary, if accompanied by a stringent corrupt-practices act, will help break up the corrupt partnership of corporations and politicians.

My opponents charge that two things in my programme are wrong because they intrude into the sanctuary of the judiciary. The first is the recall of judges; and the second, the review by the people of judicial decisions on certain constitutional questions. I have said again and again that I do not advocate the recall of judges in all States and in all communities. In my own State I do not advocate it or believe it to be needed, for in this State our trouble lies not with corruption on the bench, but with the effort by the honest but wrong headed judges to thwart the people in their struggle for social justice and fair-dealing. The integrity of our judges from Marshall to White and Holmes—and to Cullen and many others in our own State—is a fine page of American history. But—I say it soberly—democracy has a right to approach the sanctuary of the courts when a special interest has corruptly found sanctuary there; and this is exactly what has happened in some of the States where the recall of the judges is a living issue. I would far more willingly trust the whole people to judge such a case than some special tribunal—perhaps appointed by the same power that chose the judge—if that tribunal is not itself really responsible to the people and is hampered and clogged by the technicalities of impeachment proceedings.

I have stated that the courts of the several States—not always but often— have construed the "due process" clause of the State Constitutions as if it prohibited the whole people of the State from adopting methods of regulating the use of property so that human life, particularly the lives of the working men, shall be safer, freer, and happier. No one can successfully impeach this statement. I have insisted that the true construction of "due process" is that pronounced by Justice Holmes in delivering the unanimous opinion of the Supreme Court of the United States, when he said:

> The police power extends to all the great public needs. It may be put forth in aid of what is sanctioned by usage, or held by the prevailing morality or strong and preponderant opinion to be greatly and immediately necessary to the public welfare.

I insist that the decision of the New York Court of Appeals in the Ives case, which set aside the will of the majority of the people as to the compensation of injured workmen in dangerous trades, was intolerable and based on a wrong political philosophy. I urge that in such cases where the courts construe the due process clause as if property rights, to the exclusion of human rights, had a first mortgage on the Constitution, the people may, after sober deliberation, vote, and finally determine whether the law which the court set aside shall be valid or not. By this method can be clearly and finally ascertained the preponderant opinion of the people which Justice Holmes makes the test of due process in the case of laws enacted in the exercise of the police power. The ordinary methods now in vogue of amending the Constitution have in actual practice proved wholly inadequate to secure justice in such cases with reasonable speed, and cause intolerable delay and injustice, and those who stand against the changes I propose are champions of wrong and injustice, and of tyranny by the wealthy and the strong over the weak and the helpless.

So that no man may misunderstand me, let me recapitulate:

(1) I am not proposing anything in connection with the Supreme Court of the United States, or with the Federal Constitution.
(2) I am not proposing anything having any connection with ordinary suits, civil or criminal, as between individuals.
(3) I am not speaking of the recall of judges.
(4) I am proposing merely that in a certain class of cases involving the police power, when a State court has set aside as unconstitutional a law passed by the Legislature for the general welfare, the question of the validity of the law—which should depend, as Justice Holmes so well phrases it, upon the prevailing morality or preponderant opinion—be submitted for final determination to a vote of the people, taken after due time for consideration. And I contend that the people, in the nature of things, must be better judges of what is the preponderant opinion than the courts, and that the courts should not be allowed to reverse the political philosophy of the people. My point is well illustrated by a recent decision of the Supreme Court, holding that the Court would not take jurisdiction of a case involving the constitutionality of the initiative and referendum laws of Oregon. The ground of the decision was that such a question was not judicial in its nature, but should be left for determination to the other co-ordinate departments of the Government. Is it not equally plain that the question whether a given social policy is for the public good is not of a judicial nature, but should be settled by the Legislature, or in the final instance by the people themselves?

The President of the United States, Mr. Taft, devoted most of a recent speech to criticism of this proposition. He says that it "is utterly without merit or utility, and, instead of being . . . in the interest of all the people, and of the stability of popular government, is sowing the seeds of confusion and tyranny." (By this he of course means the tyranny of the majority, that is, the tyranny of the American people as a whole.) He also says that my proposal (which, as he rightly sees, is merely a proposal to give the people a real, instead of only a nominal, chance to construe and amend a State Constitution with reasonable rapidity) would make such amendment and interpretation "depend on the feverish, uncertain, and unstable determination of successive votes on different laws by temporary and changing majorities;" and that "it lays the axe at the foot of the tree of well-ordered freedom, and subjects the guaranties of life, liberty, and property without remedy to the fitful impulse of a temporary majority of an electorate."

This criticism is really less a criticism of my proposal than a criticism of all popular government. It is wholly unfounded, unless it is founded on the belief that the people are fundamentally untrustworthy. If the Supreme Court's definition of due process in relation to the police power is sound, then an act of the Legislature to promote the collective interests of the community must be valid, if it embodies a policy held by the prevailing morality or a preponderant opinion to be necessary to the public welfare. This is the question that I propose to submit to the people. How can the prevailing morality or a preponderant opinion be better and more exactly ascertained than by a vote of the people? The people must know better than the court what their own morality and their own opinion is. I ask that you, here, you and the others like you, you the people, be given the chance to state your own views of justice and public morality, and not sit meekly by and have your views announced for you by well-meaning adherents of outworn philosophies, who exalt the pedantry of formulas above the vital needs of human life.

The object I have in view could probably be accomplished by an amendment of the State Constitutions taking away from the courts the power to review the Legislature's determination of a policy of social justice, by defining due process of law in accordance with the views expressed by Justice Holmes of the Supreme Court. But my proposal seems to me more democratic and, I may add, less radical. For under the method I suggest the people may sustain the court as against the Legislature, whereas, if due process were defined in the Constitution, the decision of the Legislature would be final.

Mr. Taft's position is the position that has been held from the beginning of our Government, although not always so openly held, by a large number of reputable and honorable men who, down at bottom, distrust popular government, and, when they must accept it, accept it with reluctance, and hedge it around with every species of restriction and check and balance, so as to make the power of the people as limited and as ineffective as possible. Mr. Taft fairly defines the issue when he says that our Government is and should be a government of all the people by a representative part of the people. This is an excellent and moderate description of an oligarchy. It defines our Government as a government of all the people by a few of the people.

Mr. Taft, in his able speech, has made what is probably the best possible presentation of the case for those who feel in this manner. Essentially this view differs only in its expression from the view nakedly set forth by one of his supporters, Congressman Campbell. Congressman Campbell, in a public speech in New Hampshire, in opposing the proposition to give the people real and effective control over all their servants, including the judges, stated that this was equivalent to allowing an appeal from the umpire to the bleachers. Doubtless Congressman Campbell was not himself aware of the cynical truthfulness with which he was putting the real attitude of those for whom he spoke. But it unquestionably is their real attitude. Mr. Campbell's conception of the part the American people should play in self-government is that they should sit on the bleachers and pay the price of admission, but should have nothing to say as to the contest which is waged in the arena by the professional politicians. Apparently Mr. Campbell ignores the fact that the American people are not mere onlookers at a game, that they have a vital stake in the contest, and that democracy means nothing unless they are able and willing to show that they are their own masters.

I am not speaking jokingly, nor do I mean to be unkind; for I repeat that many honorable and well-meaning men of high character take this view, and have taken it from the time of the formation of the Nation. Essentially this view is that the Constitution is a straight-jacket to be used for the control of an unruly patient—the people. Now I hold that this view is not only false but mischievous, that our Constitutions are instruments designed to secure justice by securing the deliberate but effective expression of the popular will, that the checks and balances are valuable as far, and only so far, as they accomplish that deliberation, and that it is a warped and unworthy and improper construction of our form of government to see in it only a means of thwarting the popular will and of preventing justice. Mr. Taft says that "every class" should have a "voice" in the government. That seems to me a very serious misconception of the American political situation. The real trouble with us is that some classes have had too much voice. One of the most important of all the lessons to be taught and to be learned is that a man should vote, not as a representative of a class, but merely as a good citizen, whose prime interests are the same as those of all other good citizens. The belief in different classes, each having a voice in the Government, has given rise to much of our present difficulty; for whosoever believes in these separate classes, each with a voice, inevitably, even although unconsciously, tends to work, not for the good of the whole people, but for the protection of some special class—usually that to which he himself belongs.

The same principle applies when Mr. Taft says that the judiciary ought not to be "representative" of the people in the sense that the Legislature and the Executive are. This is perfectly true of the judge when he is performing merely the ordinary functions of a judge in suits between man and man. It is not true of the judge engaged in interpreting, for instance, the due process clause—where the judge is ascertaining the preponderant opinion of the people (as Judge Holmes states it). When he exercises that function he has no right to let his political philosophy reverse and thwart the will of the majority. In that function the judge must represent the people or he fails in the test the Supreme Court has laid down. Take the Workmen's Compensation Act here in New York. The legislators gave us a law in the interest of humanity and decency and fair dealing. In so doing they represented the people, and represented them well. Several judges declared that law Constitutional in our State, and several courts in other States declared similar laws Constitutional, and the Supreme Court of the Nation declared a similar law affecting men in inter-State business constitutional; but the highest court in the State of New York, the Court of Appeals, declared that we, the people of New York, could not have such a law. I hold that in this case the legislators and the judges alike occupied representative positions; the difference was merely that the former represented us well and the latter represented us ill. Remember that the legislators promised that law, and were returned by the people partly in consequence of such promise. That judgment of the people should not have been set aside unless it were irrational. Yet in the Ives case the New York Court of Appeals praised the policy of the law and the end it sought to obtain; and then declared that the people lacked power to do justice!

Mr. Taft again and again, in quotations I have given and elsewhere through his speech, expresses his disbelief in the people when they vote at the polls. In one sentence he says that the proposition gives "powerful effect to the momentary impulse of a majority of an electorate and prepares the way for the possible exercise of the grossest tyranny." Elsewhere he speaks of the "feverish uncertainty" and "unstable determination" of laws by "temporary and changing majorities;" and again he says that the system I propose "would result in suspension or application of Constitutional guaranties according to popular whim," which would destroy "all possible consistency" in Constitutional interpretation. I should much like to know the exact distinction that is to be made between what Mr. Taft calls "the fitful impulse of a temporary majority" when applied to a question such as that I raise and any other question. Remember that under my proposal to review a rule of decision by popular vote, amending or construing, to that extent, the Constitution, would certainly take at least two years from the time of the election of the Legislature which passed the act. Now, only four months elapse between the nomination and the election of a man as President, to fill for four years the most important office in the land. In one of Mr. Taft's speeches he speaks of "the voice of the people as coming next to the voice of God." Apparently, then, the decision of the people about the Presidency, after four months' deliberation, is to be treated as "next to the voice of God;" but if, after two years of sober thought, they decide that women and children shall be protected in industry, or men protected from excessive hours of labor under unhygienic conditions, or wage-workers compensated when they lose life or limb in the service of others, then their decision forthwith becomes a "whim" and "feverish" and "unstable" and an exercise of "the grossest tyranny" and the "laying of the axe to the foot of the tree of freedom." It seems absurd to speak of a conclusion reached by the people after two years' deliberation, after threshing the matter out before the Legislature, after threshing it out before the Governor, after threshing it out before the court and by the court, and then after full debate for four or six months, as "the fitful impulse of a temporary majority." If Mr. Taft's language correctly describes such action by the people, then he himself and all other Presidents have been elected by "the fitful impulse of a temporary majority;" then the Constitution of each State, and the Constitution of the Nation, have been adopted, and all amendments thereto have been adopted, by "the fitful impulse of a temporary majority." If he is right, it was "the fitful impulse of a temporary majority" which founded, and another fitful impulse which perpetuated, this Nation. Mr. Taft's position is perfectly clear. It is that we have in this country a special class of persons wiser than the people, who are above the people, who cannot be reached by the people, but who govern them and ought to govern them; and who protect various classes of the people from the whole people. That is the old, old doctrine which has been acted upon for thousands of years abroad; and which here in America has been acted upon sometimes openly, sometimes secretly, for forty years by many men in public and in private life, and I am sorry to say by many judges; a doctrine which has in fact tended to create a bulwark for privilege, a bulwark unjustly protecting special interests against the rights of the people as a whole. This doctrine is to me a dreadful doctrine; for its effect is, and can only be, to make the courts the shield of privilege against popular rights. Naturally, every upholder and beneficiary of crooked privilege loudly applauds the doctrine. It is behind the shield of that doctrine that crooked clauses creep into laws, that men of wealth and power control legislation. The men of wealth who praise this doctrine, this theory, would do well to remember that to its adoption by the courts is due the distrust so many of our wage-workers now feel for the courts. I deny that that theory has worked so well that we should continue it. I most earnestly urge that the evils and abuses it has produced cry aloud for remedy; and the only remedy is in fact to restore the power to govern directly to the people, and to make the public servant directly responsible to the whole people — and to no part of them, to no "class" of them.

Mr. Taft is very much afraid of the tyranny of majorities. For twenty-five years here in New York State, in our efforts to get social and industrial justice, we have suffered from the tyranny of a small minority. We have been denied, now by one court, now by another, as in the Bakeshop Case, where the courts set aside the law limiting the hours of labor in bakeries — the "due process" clause again — as in the workmen's compensation act, as in the tenement-house cigar factory case — in all these and many other cases we have been denied by small minorities, by a few worthy men of wrong political philosophy on the bench, the right to protect our people in their lives, their liberty, and their pursuit of happiness. As for "consistency"—why, the record of the courts, in such a case as the income tax for instance, is so full of inconsistencies as to make the fear expressed of "inconsistency" on the part of the people seem childish.

. . .

21

Executive *versus* Partisan Responsibility*

From *Progressive Democracy*, Chapter 16

Herbert Croly

Along with Theodore Roosevelt, Herbert Croly called for the abolition of the party system (which, strangely enough, was to be effected by the establishment of a Progressive Party). This call for abolition distinguished Croly from some other progressives, like Woodrow Wilson, who believed that the aims of the movement could best be accomplished by reforming—as opposed to abolishing—the current party system. In this chapter from *Progressive Democracy*, Croly explains that the fundamental problem with the party system was grounded in its interrupting the direct link between the people and their government, and in its siphoning off the complete devotion that the individual should have toward the state.

. . .

The national political system is, no doubt, beginning to feel the effects of the trend towards direct democracy, which is doing so much to modify the state political systems; but the acid is working much more slowly in one case than in the other. There is every reason why it should work more slowly. The central government has been far more successful than the state governments. It has never exhibited the same uneasiness, the same constant need of internal readjustment. It has been modified, of course, at once by amendment, by judicial construction, by the aggrandizement of one or the other of its departments and by extra-official additions; but up to date its development has not tended either to disintegrate the traditional system or to substitute for it a

* Editors' Note: Herbert Croly, *Progressive Democracy* (New York: The Macmillan Company, 1914), 332–45. Excerpt.

more frankly democratic system. It has retained throughout the four generations of our national political history a tenacious integrity, and it has exhibited an equally stubborn power of resistance to external attack. Its persistent
vitality is a sufficient indication of its service ability and its future endurance.

The one way in which this government by Law can be democratized is, as
has already been pointed out, to amend the amending clause of the Constitution. But it will be many years before this result can be accomplished. The
friends of the "gateway amendment" are still scarce in Congress. Even after
they have become numerous they will be obliged to overcome a strong and
obstinate resistance which may well be proof against all assaults, until some
crisis in our national affairs necessitates the calling of a constitutional convention. In the meantime the prevailing system will persist with only minor
modifications. The prevailing system is not workable without being supplemented by an extra-official system of partisan organization. But if an extra-
official system of partisan government is necessary for an indefinite period,
it must be made effective; and the effective method of partisan government is
a two-party system.

A conviction of the persistent practical importance of the party system was
an influential consideration with many progressives who contributed to the
formation of a Progressive party in the summer of 1912. Their argument ran
as follows: The future of progressivism as an idea demands the formation of
a party exclusively devoted to the interests of that idea. Neither the Democratic nor the Republican parties can be depended upon to be sincerely and
radically progressive. They both contain a large number of adherents who are
essentially conservative. Even if these conservatives do not constitute a majority of either party, they form a strong and able minority. As long as progressives remain associated with conservatives in a partisan organization,
progressivism will be hampered by unnecessary and demoralizing compromises. If partisan loyalty and partisan patriotism mean anything, they mean
that progressive Republicans or Democrats should be willing at times to
abandon or to postpone their own political purposes in the interest of party
harmony. Admitting that all effective practical political association demands
some such sacrifices, do not the sacrifices which a progressive is obliged to
make as the price of his alliance with conservatives cost too much? Why remain in political association with a group of men when your points of difference with them are more fundamental than your points of agreement? A progressive who remains politically affiliated with conservative Republicans and
conservative Democrats is acting as if Republicanism and Democracy were
of greater value to the American people than is progressivism.

Thus the formation of a Progressive party made a strong appeal to many
radicals, to whom progressivism meant more than did Democracy or Repub-

licanism, and who appreciated the importance of partisan organizations in the operation of the national political system. The progressive democratic program was considered to be indispensable to the welfare of the American people. It demanded the organization of a party united fundamentally by their devotion to that program. The whole history of political and social reform in the United States could be cited as a proof of the way in which the partisan organizations adopted reforms only for the purpose of neutralizing them. Ballot reform, civil service reform, primary reform and the like had been taken up by the party organizations in response to public opinion and had been made the subject of legislation; but this legislation was not framed in good faith by sincere men who were determined to make it successful. It went just far enough to placate public opinion, but it always stopped short of seeking to accomplish effective results. If progressivism was not constantly to be betrayed by its ostensible friends, it needed a partisan organization whose dominant purpose was the advancement of progressive policies.

A Progressive party was organized, and polled for its presidential candidate a larger vote than that received by his Republican competitor. Whatever the future history of this party, it has in one respect lived up to the expectations of its organizers. It has done more to make the progressive idea count at its proper value in American public opinion, and to make possible the realization of a certain portion of the progressive program, than has any other agency of progressive expression.

Its weakness in the state and national legislative bodies has prevented it from having any direct effect on legislation; but the fact that it holds the balance between the two older political parties has given to the program of those parties a stronger progressive tendency and has strengthened the hands of their more progressive members. President Wilson owes his nomination and probably his election to the creation of a third party. His ability to exercise an effective influence over his Democratic associates is partly due to the necessity which a governing minority is under to stick together and submit to discipline. If the Progressive party were to disintegrate, the President's situation with respect to his party would be altered very much for the worse. The Democrats would be less in need of emphatically progressive leadership, to which they are obliged to submit in order to keep the sincere progressives in their own party true to their partisan allegiance, and would not be placed so very much on their good behavior. In the same way the Republicans are obliged to wear a mask of progressivism in order to win back the progressive seceders. The conservative element in both parties would be very much strengthened as soon as a living partisan progressive alternative ceased to exist.

The resulting situation is curiously paradoxical. The future of the Progressive party depends on its ability to convince the American people that

Herbert Croly

progressivism is so novel and important a political idea and so jealous a master that it is incompatible with traditional Democracy and traditional Republicanism. Both the Democrats and the Republicans repudiate any such aggrandizement of progressivism in theory; but they are both becoming as progressive as they know how to be in practice in order to keep their own members out of the Progressive party. Republican and Democratic progressives, that is, are struggling to make a Progressive party unnecessary, and in so far as they succeed, their own influence in their own parties will be considerably diminished. On the other hand, if the Progressive party should be right in its contention that the realization of the progressive program cannot be intrusted to half-hearted friends or covert enemies, and if it gradually wins the support of the social and political radicals of both parties, it will be confronted by the almost hopeless task of reconciling loyalty to the progressive ideal with loyalty to a particular partisan organization. The logic of the progressive democratic principle will count against it. Just in so far as a progressive political program is carried out, progressive social democracy will cease to need a national political party as an instrument.

For the present, however, the machinery of the Federal government can be operated only by national parties which are bound together by common memories and traditions as well as common ideas, and whose members are under obligation to sacrifice their convictions of what the public welfare requires for the sake of partisan harmony. President Wilson is making a most significant, intelligent and gallant attempt to give renewed vitality to partisan government and to convert it into an agency of what he understands by progressivism. He has frankly assumed the leadership of his partisan associates, and by virtue of that leadership has conferred upon his party unprecedented powers of effective action. Discipline is enforced and opposition stamped out by the constant use of the caucus; but no dangerous ill-feeling seems to result. The Democrats in Congress accept his leadership at least as willingly as their forbears accepted that of Jefferson and Jackson. They are so surprised and delighted with their own partisan efficiency and with the privileges, emoluments and prestige of office that they are glad to pay the market rate for these boons. Up to date they have had few individual convictions which they were not entirely ready to sacrifice at the bidding of the President and of the caucus. Under Mr. Wilson's leadership they have passed the only tariff bill of the last seventy years which represented an honest attempt to subordinate special interests to the national economic welfare. Their currency legislation was an intelligent, a painstaking and, on the whole, a fair compromise between the local and the national financial needs. Considering the tendency which the Democratic party in the past has exhibited towards dubious financial doctrine, their passage of this bill was a most notable and reassuring event. For the first time in their history the Democrats placed on the statute book a piece of really constructive legislation. No wonder they are willing to accept the leadership of a man who can convert the party into a positively useful and purposeful political organization.

President Wilson has done more than to help the Democratic party to become a united, self-confident and efficient political association. He has tried to persuade the American people that the Democracy is peculiarly entitled to be the instrument of progressivism. In his "New Freedom" he has placed an interpretation on progressivism which associates it with a revival of the old Jeffersonian individualism and expressly distinguishes it from a social democracy. The object of the "New Freedom" as a program is to remove the impediments which have hampered the individual in the exercise of his political and economic rights. The emancipation is to be accomplished chiefly by negative means—that is, by destroying excesses of political and economic power in private hands and by imposing restraints which will prevent the reappearance of any such undesirable company. The legislative program of the party has only in part conformed to the theories of its leader. In practice the "New Freedom" has approximated in certain respects to the "New Nationalism." But the Democratic party has never been very much interested in squaring its behavior with its theories. President Wilson's "New Freedom" has served its purpose in enabling his party to believe for a few years in the existence of a friendly relation between traditional Democracy and the legislative needs of a modern democratic progressivism.

The attempt which President Wilson is making with so much ability and tenacity to prevent progressivism from escaping from the confines of the old party system is fraught with weighty consequences. If he succeeds for a sufficiently long time in keeping the leadership of the Democratic progressives without breaking with the Democratic conservatives, he will make the position of the Progressive party extremely precarious. It may fall to pieces and its membership be divided among the Democrats, the Republicans and the Socialists. He seems to have, moreover, a certain chance of success—chiefly because of the peculiar nature of Democratic conservatism. It is a conservatism of local interest rather than definite economic and political conviction. Its habitation is for the most part in the southern states. As long as their dominant local interest is safeguarded, the southern conservatives will make any sacrifice of less important matters for the sake of partisan harmony. They will accept progressive leadership, partly because they are enjoying so many of the fruits of partisan success, but chiefly because they have no political alternative outside of the Democratic party. No doubt they have had small reason to protest against any progressive legislation which has been hitherto enacted. The tariff, currency and trust bills were aimed chiefly at northern rather than southern conservative interests. But they will dutifully accept a far larger dose of repugnant progressive legislation than any they have been obliged to accept without raising any irreconcilable opposition to it. They cannot afford to permit a split in the Democratic party, because the consequences of such a split would be fatal to their own political influence. They could not ally themselves with a northern and western conservative party, which would consist for the most part of former Republicans; and if they formed a separate sectional organization, they would always remain in a hopeless minority. In so far as their Democracy is inevitable, the persistence of the old dual partisan system is essential for them.

The inability of southern Democratic conservatives to make any effective protest against northern Democratic progressivism will artificially prolong the efficiency of the two-party system. President Wilson and his immediate advisers will be able to dictate the policy of the party. They will not be obliged to compromise with their conservative partisan associates to at all the same extent as would Republican progressives. Of course, the progressive Democrats will go through the form of consulting their conservative associates. They will have to use tact, forbearance and even conciliation; but when it comes to an important difference of opinion, they will rarely have to yield. They can depend upon the southern Democratic votes just as Bryan always could—in spite of the fact that the southerners were never very much interested in Bryanism. This gives them an enormous advantage over progressive Republicans. If progressive Democrats can live up to this opportunity, it should enable them to keep the upper hand in a continuation of the duel with their traditional opponents. Their eventual failure, if and when it takes place, will be due chiefly to the poverty of their own progressivism ideal, and to their inability to make their program conform to the demands of a genuinely progressive democracy.

The enforced partisan loyalty of southern conservative Democrats may well enable progressive Democrats to prevent progressivism from undermining Democracy. But the old two-party system will merely be prolonged rather than really resurrected. Associated as it is with representation by law, it cannot survive the advent of an official representative system based upon direct popular government. The two-party system, like other forms of representative democracy, proposes to accomplish for the people a fundamental political task which they ought to accomplish for themselves. It seeks to interpose two authoritative partisan organizations between the people and their government. It demands of them that they act and think in politics not under the influence of their natural class or personal convictions, but according to the necessities of an artificial partisan classification. In this way it demands and obtains for a party an amount of loyal service and personal sacrifice which a public-spirited democrat should lavish only on the state. The unity of purpose and the effective power of joint action which results from the action of partisan discipline and patriotism should accrue to the benefit not of Republicanism or Democracy, but to that of the nation and of the really significant social ingredients which enter into the national composition.

The two-party system is a semi-democratic device which was intended to democratize an undemocratic political organization. For a couple of generations it was an effective agency of American national democracy. That it has ceased to be an agency of democracy is sufficiently proved by the means which are now being taken to reform it. The parties which were organized for the purpose of making an undemocratic government responsive to the popular will are now being reorganized by the law for the purpose of democratizing the supposed instruments of democracy. The reorganization is mechanical and is merely following the lines of the least resistance. It recognizes the peculiar importance of partisan allegiance in American practical politics, converts parties from unofficial into official instruments of popular government and seeks to democratize them by forcing their members to select their regular candidates by popular vote. Direct primaries have resulted in making the domination of the machine in defiance of partisan public opinion much more difficult; but by popularizing the mechanism of partisan government the state has thrust a sword into the vitals of its former master. Under the influence of direct primaries national parties will no longer continue to be an effective method for organizing the rule of the majority.

A party is essentially a voluntary association for the promotion of certain common political and economic objects. It presupposes a substantial agreement of opinion and interest among the members of the party, and a sufficient amount of mutual confidence. If they differ vitally in interest and opinion, and have little or no confidence in one another, the association should not be regulated; it should to that extent be dissolved. By regulating it and by forcing it to select its leaders in a certain way, the state is sacrificing the valuable substance of partisan loyalty and allegiance to the mere mechanism of partisan association. Direct primaries will necessarily undermine partisan discipline and loyalty. They will make it more necessary for every voter to belong nominally to either one of the two dominant parties; but the increasing importance of a formal allegiance will be accompanied by diminished community of spirit and purpose. Such is the absurd and contradictory result of legalizing and regularizing a system of partisan government. If the two-party system is breaking down as an agency for democratizing an undemocratic government, the remedy is not to democratize the party which was organized to democratize the government, but to democratize the government itself. Just in proportion as the official political organization becomes genuinely democratic, it can dispense with the services of national parties.

The state governments are, as we have seen, by way of being reorganized into more effective and representative instruments of popular rule. In the case of the central government, the corresponding process has not been carried very far; but it is being carried far enough to indicate the gradual devitalizing of the partisan system. In spite of the praiseworthy record which the Democrats are now making of partisan efficiency, the prediction may be confidently ventured that it will not be continued. Partisan government at Washington will remain necessary for a long time; but it will become increasingly less effective. The system of direct presidential primaries will result in intense and bitter contests for the nomination, and in the consequent undermining of party cohesion. The party, instead of being organized in order to enable its members to consult one another and reach an agreement upon differences of opinion, will be organized chiefly as an official machinery of naming candidates. The candidate, after having been named by a majority of the voting members of his party, becomes comparatively independent of its other leaders. He has the power to write his own platform and practically to repudiate the official platform of his party. He becomes the leader, almost the dictator, of his party, as no President has been between Andrew Jackson and Woodrow Wilson. A wise, firm, yet conciliatory man like President Wilson can so exercise his enormous power as to make his party a more rather than a less effective instrument of government, just as a monarchy may become, in the hands of an exceptionally able, independent, energetic and humane administrator, a temporarily beneficent form of government. But a Woodrow Wilson is not born of every election, and when he is born the benevolent domination which he exercises over his party is a source, in the long run, of weakness rather than of strength. As a consequence of direct primaries, a party ceases to be a representative democracy. It obtains and retains its cohesion only as the result of a benevolent dictatorship.

Under the conditions defined in the preceding chapters official executive leadership, in the name of a temporary majority of the electorate, may be an essential and fruitful instrument of democracy; but in order to be fruitful it needs to be accompanied by some method of minority representation and by the recall. In any event it is incompatible with a really vital partisan system. If the other party leaders are men of conviction who take their joint partisan responsibility to the electorate seriously, they will not submit to a method of leadership which is necessarily dictatorial. If they are not men of conviction and are united chiefly for the attainment of local or personal ends, they will submit; but they will submit to the official dictation of the President just as they formerly submitted to the unofficial dictation of the boss. They are accustomed to take orders; and when orders are lacking, they flounder hopelessly around. The old system cannot be galvanized into any real life by virtue of executive leadership. The necessity of such leadership is itself an evidence of the decrepitude of the two-party system.

. . .

VII

THE ELECTION OF 1912

22

Progressive Platform of 1912*

Progressive Party

When Theodore Roosevelt lost the 1912 Republican presidential nomination to William Howard Taft, he pulled his delegates from the convention and formed his own party, which nominated him for the presidency and California's Hiram Johnson for the vice presidency. The following is the platform adopted by the new party at its convention in Chicago, where Roosevelt thundered that "We stand at Armageddon, and we battle for the Lord."

DECLARATION OF PRINCIPLES OF THE PROGRESSIVE PARTY

The conscience of the people, in a time of grave national problems, has called into being a new party, born of the nation's sense of justice. We of the Progressive party here dedicate ourselves to the fulfillment of the duty laid upon us by our fathers to maintain the government of the people, by the people and for the people whose foundations they laid.

We hold with Thomas Jefferson and Abraham Lincoln that the people are the masters of their Constitution, to fulfill its purposes and to safeguard it from those who, by perversion of its intent, would convert it into an instrument of injustice. In accordance with the needs of each generation the people must use their sovereign powers to establish and maintain equal opportunity and industrial justice, to secure which this Government was founded and without which no republic can endure.

* Editors' Note: George Henry Payne, *The Birth of the New Party: Or Progressive Democracy* (New York: J. L. Nichols & Company, 1912), 303–20.

This country belongs to the people who inhabit it. Its resources, its business, its institutions and its laws should be utilized, maintained or altered in whatever manner will best promote the general interest.

It is time to set the public welfare in the first place.

THE OLD PARTIES

Political parties exist to secure responsible government and to execute the will of the people.

From these great tasks both of the old parties have turned aside. Instead of instruments to promote the general welfare, they have become the tools of corrupt interests which use them impartially to serve their selfish purposes. Behind the ostensible government sits enthroned an invisible government owing no allegiance and acknowledging no responsibility to the people.

To destroy this invisible government, to dissolve the unholy alliance between corrupt business and corrupt politics is the first task of the statesmanship of the day.

The deliberate betrayal of its trust by the Republican party, the fatal incapacity of the Democratic party to deal with the new issues of the new time, have compelled the people to forge a new instrument of government through which to give effect to their will in laws and institutions.

Unhampered by tradition, uncorrupted by power, undismayed by the magnitude of the task, the new party offers itself as the instrument of the people to sweep away old abuses, to build a new and nobler commonwealth.

A COVENANT WITH THE PEOPLE

This declaration is our covenant with the people, and we hereby bind the party and its candidates in State and Nation to the pledges made herein.

THE RULE OF THE PEOPLE

The National Progressive party, committed to the principles of government by a self-controlled democracy expressing its will through representatives of the people, pledges itself to secure such alterations in the fundamental law of the several States and of the United States as shall insure the representative character of the government.

In particular, the party declares for direct primaries for the nomination of State and National officers, for nation-wide preferential primaries for candidates for the presidency; for the direct election of United States Senators by the people; and we urge on the States the policy of the short ballot, with responsibility to the people secured by the initiative, referendum and recall.

AMENDMENT OF THE CONSTITUTION

The Progressive party, believing that a free people should have the power from time to time to amend their fundamental law so as to adapt it progressively to the changing needs of the people, pledges itself to provide a more easy and expeditious method of amending the Federal Constitution.

NATION AND STATE

Up to the limit of the Constitution, and later by amendment of the Constitution, if found necessary, we advocate bringing under effective national jurisdiction those problems which have expanded beyond reach of the individual States.

It is as grotesque as it is intolerable that the several States should by unequal laws in matter of common concern become competing commercial agencies, barter the lives of their children, the health of their women and the safety and well being of their working people for the benefit of their financial interests.

The extreme insistence on States' rights by the Democratic party in the Baltimore platform demonstrates anew its inability to understand the world into which it has survived or to administer the affairs of a union of States which have in all essential respects become one people.

EQUAL SUFFRAGE

The Progressive party, believing that no people can justly claim to be a true democracy which denies political rights on account of sex, pledges itself to the task of securing equal suffrage to men and women alike.

CORRUPT PRACTICES

We pledge our party to legislation that will compel strict limitation of all campaign contributions and expenditures, and detailed publicity of both before as well as after primaries and elections.

PUBLICITY AND PUBLIC SERVICE

We pledge our party to legislation compelling the registration of lobbyists; publicity of committee hearings except on foreign affairs, and recording of all votes in committee; and forbidding federal appointees from holding office in State or National political organizations, or taking part as officers or delegates in political conventions for the nomination of elective State or National officials.

THE COURTS

The Progressive party demands such restriction of the power of the courts as shall leave to the people the ultimate authority to determine fundamental questions of social welfare and public policy. To secure this end, it pledges itself to provide:

1. That when an Act, passed under the police power of the State, is held unconstitutional under the State Constitution, by the courts, the people, after an ample interval for deliberation, shall have an opportunity to vote on the question whether they desire the Act to become law, notwithstanding such decision.

2. That, every decision of the highest appellate court of a State declaring an Act of the Legislature unconstitutional on the ground of its violation of the Federal Constitution shall be subject to the same review by the Supreme Court of the United States as is now accorded to decisions sustaining such legislation.

ADMINISTRATION OF JUSTICE

The Progressive party, in order to secure to the people a better administration of justice and by that means to bring about a more general respect for the law and the courts, pledges itself to work unceasingly for the reform of legal procedure and judicial methods.

We believe that the issuance of injunctions in cases arising out of labor disputes should be prohibited when such injunctions would not apply when no labor disputes existed.

We also believe that a person cited for contempt in labor disputes, except when such contempt was committed in the actual presence of the court or so near thereto as to interfere with the proper administration of justice, should have a right to trial by jury.

SOCIAL AND INDUSTRIAL JUSTICE

The supreme duty of the Nation is the conservation of human resources through an enlightened measure of social and industrial justice. We pledge ourselves to work unceasingly in State and Nation for:

Effective legislation looking to the prevention of industrial accidents, occupational diseases, overwork, involuntary unemployment, and other injurious effects incident to modern industry;

The fixing of minimum safety and health standards for the various occupations, and the exercise of the public authority of State and Nation, including the Federal Control over interstate commerce, and the taxing power, to maintain such standards;

The prohibition of child labor;

Minimum wage standards for working women, to provide a "living wage" in all industrial occupations;

The general prohibition of night work for women and the establishment of an eight hour day for women and young persons;

One day's rest in seven for all wage workers;

The eight hour day in continuous twenty-four-hour industries;

The abolition of the convict contract labor system; substituting a system of prison production for governmental consumption only; and the application of prisoners' earnings to the support of their dependent families;

Publicity as to wages, hours and conditions of labor; full reports upon industrial accidents and diseases, and the opening to public inspection of all tallies, weights, measures and check systems on labor products;

Standards of compensation for death by industrial accident and injury and trade disease which will transfer the burden of lost earnings from the families of working people to the industry, and thus to the community;

The protection of home life against the hazards of sickness, irregular employment and old age through the adoption of a system of social insurance adapted to American use;

The development of the creative labor power of America by lifting the last load of illiteracy from American youth and establishing continuation schools for industrial education under public control and encouraging agricultural education and demonstration in rural schools;

The establishment of industrial research laboratories to put the methods and discoveries of science at the service of American producers;

We favor the organization of the workers, men and women, as a means of protecting their interests and of promoting their progress.

DEPARTMENT OF LABOR

We pledge our party to establish a department of labor with a seat in the cabinet, and with wide jurisdiction over matters affecting the conditions of labor and living.

COUNTRY LIFE

The development and prosperity of country life are as important to the people who live in the cities as they are to the farmers. Increase of prosperity on the farm will favorably affect the cost of living, and promote the interests of all who dwell in the country, and all who depend upon its products for clothing, shelter and food.

We pledge our party to foster the development of agricultural credit and cooperation, the teaching of agriculture in schools, agricultural college extension, the use of mechanical power on the farm, and to re-establish the Country Life Commission, thus directly promoting the welfare of the farmers, and bringing the benefits of better farming, better business and better living within their reach.

HIGH COST OF LIVING

The high cost of living is due partly to world-wide and partly to local causes; partly to natural and partly to artificial causes. The measures proposed in this platform on various subjects such as the tariff, the trusts and conservation, will of themselves remove the artificial causes.

There will remain other elements such as the tendency to leave the country for the city, waste, extravagance, bad system of taxation, poor methods of raising crops and bad business methods in marketing crops.

To remedy these conditions requires the fullest information and based on this information, effective government supervision and control to remove all the artificial causes. We pledge ourselves to such full and immediate inquiry and to immediate action to deal with every need such inquiry discloses.

HEALTH

We favor the union of all the existing agencies of the Federal Government dealing with the public health into a single national health service without discrimination against or for anyone set of therapeutic methods, school of medicine, or school of healing with such additional powers as may be necessary to enable it to perform efficiently such duties in the protection of the public from preventable diseases as may be properly undertaken by the Federal authorities, including the executing of existing laws regarding pure food, quarantine and cognate subjects, the promotion of vital statistics and the extension of the registration area of such statistics, and co-operation with the health activities of the various States and cities of the Nation.

BUSINESS

We believe that true popular government, justice and prosperity go hand in hand, and, so believing, it is our purpose to secure that large measure of general prosperity which is the fruit of legitimate and honest business, fostered by equal justice and by sound progressive laws.

We demand that the test of true prosperity shall be the benefits conferred thereby on all the citizens, not confined to individuals or classes, and that the test of corporate efficiency shall be the ability better to serve the public; that those who profit by control of business affairs shall justify that profit and that control by sharing with the public the fruits thereof.

We therefore demand a strong National regulation of inter-State corporations. The corporation is an essential part of modern business. The concentration of modern business, in some degree, is both inevitable and necessary for national and international business efficiency. But the existing concentration of vast wealth under a corporate system, unguarded and uncontrolled by the Nation, has placed in the hands of a few men enormous, secret, irresponsible power over the daily life of the citizen—a power insufferable in a free Government and certain of abuse.

This power has been abused, in monopoly of National resources, in stock watering, in unfair competition and unfair privileges, and finally in sinister influences on the public agencies of State and Nation. We do not fear commercial power, but we insist that it shall be exercised openly, under publicity, supervision and regulation of the most efficient sort, which will preserve its good while eradicating and preventing its ill.

To that end we urge the establishment of a strong Federal administrative commission of high standing, which shall maintain permanent active supervision over industrial corporations engaged in inter-State commerce, or such of them as are of public importance, doing for them what the Government now does for the National banks, and what is now done for the railroads by the Inter-State Commerce Commission.

Such a commission must enforce the complete publicity of those corporation transactions which are of public interest; must attack unfair competition, false capitalization and special privilege, and by continuous trained watchfulness guard and keep open equally all the highways of American commerce.

Thus the business man will have certain knowledge of the law, and will be able to conduct his business easily in conformity therewith; the investor will find security for his capital; dividends will be rendered more certain, and the savings of the people will be drawn naturally and safely into the channels of trade.

Under such a system of constructive regulation, legitimate business, freed from confusion, uncertainty and fruitless litigation, will develop normally in response to the energy and enterprise of the American business man.

We favor strengthening the Sherman Law by prohibiting agreement to divide territory or limit output; refusing to sell to customers who buy from business rivals; to sell below cost in certain areas while maintaining higher prices in other places; using the power of transportation to aid or injure special business concerns; and other unfair trade practices.

PATENTS

We pledge ourselves to the enactment of a patent law which will make it impossible for patents to be suppressed or used against the public welfare in the interests of injurious monopolies.

INTER-STATE COMMERCE COMMISSION

We pledge our party to secure to the Inter-State Commerce Commission the power to value the physical property of railroads. In order that the power of the commission to protect the people may not be impaired or destroyed, we demand the abolition of the Commerce Court.

CURRENCY

We believe there exists imperative need for prompt legislation for the improvement of our National currency system. We believe the present method of issuing notes through private agencies is harmful and unscientific.

The issue of currency is fundamentally a Government function and the system should have as basis principles soundness and elasticity. The control should be lodged with the Government and should be protected from domination or manipulation by Wall Street or any special interests.

We are opposed to the so-called Aldrich currency bill, because its provisions would place our currency and credit system in private hands, not subject to effective public control.

COMMERCIAL DEVELOPMENT

The time has come when the Federal Government should cooperate with manufacturers and producers in extending our foreign commerce. To this end we demand adequate appropriations by Congress, and the appointment of diplomatic and consular officers solely with a view to their special fitness and worth, and not in consideration of political expediency.

It is imperative to the welfare of our people that we enlarge and extend our foreign commerce.

In every way possible our Federal Government should co-operate in this important matter. Germany's policy of co-operation between government and business has, in comparatively few years, made that nation a leading competitor for the commerce of the world.

CONSERVATION

The natural resources of the Nation must be promptly developed and generously used to supply the people's needs, but we cannot safely allow them to be wasted, exploited, monopolized or controlled against the general good. We heartily favor the policy of conservation, and we pledge our party to protect the National forests without hindering their legitimate use for the benefit of all the people.

Agricultural lands in the National forests are, and should remain, open to the genuine settler. Conservation will not retard legitimate development. The honest settler must receive his patent promptly, without hindrance, rules or delays.

We believe that the remaining forests, coal and oil lands, water powers and other natural resources still in State or National control (except agricultural lands) are more likely to be wisely conserved and utilized for the general welfare if held in the public hands.

In order that consumers and producers, managers and workmen, now and hereafter, need not pay toll to private monopolies of power and raw material, we demand that such resources shall be retained by the State or Nation, and

opened to immediate use under laws which will encourage development and
make to the people a moderate return for benefits conferred.

In particular we pledge our party to require reasonable compensation to the
public for water power rights hereafter granted by the public.

We pledge legislation to lease the public grazing lands under equitable provisions now pending which will increase the production of food for the people and thoroughly safeguard the rights of the actual homemaker. Natural resources, whose conservation is necessary for the National welfare, should be
owned or controlled by the Nation.

GOOD ROADS

We recognize the vital importance of good roads and we pledge our party to
foster their extension in every proper way, and we favor the early construction of National highways. We also favor the extension of the rural free delivery service.

ALASKA

The coal and other natural resources of Alaska should be opened to development at once. They are owned by the people of the United States, and are safe
from monopoly, waste or destruction only while so owned.

We demand that they shall neither be sold nor given away, except under the
Homestead Law, but while held in Government ownership shall be opened to
use promptly upon liberal terms requiring immediate development.

Thus the benefit of cheap fuel will accrue to the Government of the United
States and to the people of Alaska and the Pacific Coast; the settlement of extensive agricultural lands will be hastened; the extermination of the salmon
will be prevented and the just and wise development of Alaskan resources
will take the place of private extortion or monopoly.

We demand also that extortion or monopoly in transportation shall be prevented by the prompt acquisition, construction or improvement by the Government of such railroads, harbor and other facilities for transportation as the
welfare of the people may demand.

We promise the people of the Territory of Alaska the same measure of legal self-government that was given to other American territories, and that
Federal officials appointed there shall be qualified by previous *bone-fide* residence in the Territory.

WATERWAYS

The rivers of the United States are the natural arteries of this continent. We demand that they shall be opened to traffic as indispensable parts of a great Nation-wide system of transportation, in which the Panama Canal will be the central link, thus enabling the whole interior of the United States to share with the Atlantic and Pacific seaboards in the benefit derived from the canal.

It is a National obligation to develop our rivers, and especially the Mississippi and its tributaries, without delay, under a comprehensive general plan covering each river system from its source to its mouth, designed to secure its highest usefulness for navigation, irrigation, domestic supply, water power and the prevention of floods.

We pledge our party to the immediate preparation of such a plan, which should be made and carried out in close and friendly co-operation between the Nation, the States and the cities affected.

Under such a plan, the destructive floods of the Mississippi and other streams, which represent a vast and needless loss to the Nation, would be controlled by forest conservation and water storage at the headwaters, and by levees below; land sufficient to support millions of people would be reclaimed from the deserts and the swamps, water power enough to transform the industrial standings of whole States would be developed, adequate water terminals would be provided, transportation by river would revive, and the railroads would be compelled to co-operate as freely with the boat lines as with each other.

The equipment, organization and experience acquired in constructing the Panama Canal soon will be available for the Lakes-to-the-Gulf deep waterway and other portions of this great work, and should be utilized by the Nation in cooperation with the various States, at the lowest net cost to the people.

PANAMA CANAL

The Panama Canal, built and paid for by the American people, must be used primarily for their benefit.

We demand that the canal shall be so operated as to break the transportation monopoly now held and misused by the transcontinental railroads by maintaining sea competition with them; that ships directly or indirectly owned or controlled by American railroad corporations shall not be permitted to use the canal, and that American ships engaged in coastwise trade shall pay no tolls.

The Progressive party will favor legislation having for its aim the development of friendship and commerce between the United States and Latin-American nations.

TARIFF

We believe in a protective tariff which shall equalize conditions of competition between the United States and foreign countries, both for the farmer and the manufacturer, and which shall maintain for labor an adequate standard of living.

Primarily the benefit of any tariff should be disclosed in the pay envelope of the laborer. We declare that no industry deserves protection which is unfair to labor or which is operating in violation of Federal law. We believe that the presumption is always in favor of the consuming public.

We demand tariff revision because the present tariff is unjust to the people of the United States. Fair dealing toward the people requires an immediate downward revision of those schedules wherein duties are shown to be unjust or excessive.

We pledge ourselves to the establishment of a non-partisan scientific tariff commission, reporting both to the President and to either branch of Congress, which shall report, first, as to the costs of production, efficiency of labor, capitalization, industrial organization and efficiency and the general competitive position in this country and abroad of industries seeking protection from Congress; second, as to the revenue producing power of the tariff and its relation to the resources of Government; and, third, as to the effect of the tariff on prices, operations of middlemen, and on the purchasing power of the consumer.

We believe that this commission should have plenary power to elicit information, and for this purpose to prescribe a uniform system of accounting for the great protected industries. The work of the commission should not prevent the immediate adoption of acts reducing these schedules generally recognized as excessive.

We condemn the Payne-Aldrich bill as unjust to the people. The Republican organization is in the hands of those who have broken, and cannot again be trusted to keep, the promise of necessary downward revision.

The Democratic party is committed to the destruction of the protective system through a tariff for revenue only—a policy which would inevitably produce widespread industrial and commercial disaster.

We demand the immediate repeal of the Canadian Reciprocity Act.

INHERITANCE AND INCOME TAX

We believe in a graduated inheritance tax as a National means of equalizing the obligations of holders of property to Government, and we hereby pledge our party to enact such a Federal law as will tax large inheritances, returning to the States an equitable percentage of all amounts collected.

We favor the ratification of the pending amendment to the Constitution giving the Government power to levy an income tax.

PEACE AND NATIONAL DEFENSE

The Progressive party deplores the survival in our civilization of the barbaric system of warfare among nations with its enormous waste of resources even in time of peace, and the consequent impoverishment of the life of the toiling masses. We pledge the party to use its best endeavors to substitute judicial and other peaceful means of settling international differences.

We favor an international agreement for the limitation of naval forces. Pending such an agreement, and as the best means of preserving peace, we pledge ourselves to maintain for the present the policy of building two battleships a year.

TREATY RIGHTS

We pledge our party to protect the rights of American citizenship at home and abroad. No treaty should receive the sanction of our Government which discriminates between American citizens because of birthplace, race, or religion, or that does not recognize the absolute right of expatriation.

THE IMMIGRANT

Through the establishment of industrial standards we propose to secure to the able-bodied immigrant and to his native fellow workers a larger share of American opportunity.

We denounce the fatal policy of indifference and neglect which has left our enormous immigrant population to become the prey of chance and cupidity.

We favor Governmental action to encourage the distribution of immigrants away from the congested cities, to rigidly supervise all private agencies dealing with them and to promote their assimilation, education and advancement.

PENSIONS

We pledge ourselves to a wise and just policy of pensioning American soldiers and sailors and their widows and children by the Federal Government. And we approve the policy of the southern States in granting pensions to the ex-Confederate soldiers and sailors and their widows and children.

PARCEL POST

We pledge our party to the immediate creation of a parcel post, with rates proportionate to distance and service.

CIVIL SERVICE

We condemn the violations of the Civil Service Law under the present administration, including the coercion and assessment of subordinate employees, and the President's refusal to punish such violation after a finding of guilty by his own commission; his distribution of patronage among subservient congressmen, while withholding it from those who refuse support of administration measures; his withdrawal of nominations from the Senate until political support for himself was secured, and his open use of the offices to reward those who voted for his renomination.

To eradicate these abuses, we demand not only the enforcement of the civil service act in letter and spirit, but also legislation which will bring under the competitive system postmasters, collectors, marshals, and all other non-political officers, as well as the enactment of an equitable retirement law, and we also insist upon continuous service during good behavior and efficiency.

GOVERNMENT BUSINESS ORGANIZATION

We pledge our party to readjustment of the business methods of the National Government and a proper co-ordination of the Federal bureaus, which will increase the economy and efficiency of the Government service, prevent duplications, and secure better results to the taxpayers for every dollar expended.

GOVERNMENT SUPERVISION OVER INVESTMENTS

The people of the United States are swindled out of many millions of dollars every year, through worthless investments. The plain people, the wage earner and the men and women with small savings, have no way of knowing the merit of concerns sending out highly colored prospectuses offering stock for sale, prospectuses that make big returns seem certain and fortunes easily within grasp.

We hold it to be the duty of the Government to protect its people from this kind of piracy. We, therefore, demand wise, carefully thought out legislation that will give us such Governmental supervision over this matter as will furnish to the people of the United States this much-needed protection, and we pledge ourselves thereto.

CONCLUSION

On these principles and on the recognized desirability of uniting the Progressive forces of the Nation into an organization which shall unequivocally represent the Progressive spirit and policy we appeal for the support of all American citizens, without regard to previous political affiliations.

23

Introduction to *Progressive Democracy**

Herbert Croly

> Herbert Croly arguably makes the keenest and clearest observations on the contemporary state of progressive movement from within the movement itself. In the following account of the situation on the ground in the aftermath of the 1912 election, Croly highlights the differences between Theodore Roosevelt and Woodrow Wilson, while perceptively conceding that these differences had less to do with principle and more to do with political calculation. Croly also concedes, correctly, that President Wilson was governing in a way that should make new-nationalist progressives quite content.

. . .

More than any other single leader, Theodore Roosevelt contributed decisively to the combination of political with social reform and to the building up of a body of national public opinion behind the combination. Under his leadership as President, reform began to assume the characteristics, if not the name, of progressivism. He was peculiarly qualified to bring about the transition. His own early political career had been associated with the movements towards civil service and municipal reform, but he had never been an ordinary Mugwump. Instead of representing a limited class in the eastern cities, he had mixed with all sorts of Americans in many different parts of the country. Neither did he allow his power of effective political association with others to die of nonpartisanship. His human sympathies were lively and varied

* Editors' Note: Herbert Croly, *Progressive Democracy* (New York: The Macmillan Company, 1914), 11–25. Excerpt.

enough to prevent him from becoming a "doctrinaire," or from staking, as did the Mugwumps, his own personal future and the supposed welfare of the country on a rigid political and economic creed. Thus he remained flexible and open-minded. He was able, as was no other political leader, to collect under his own leadership a large proportion of the old reformers and a large measure of the new and more liberal progressivism. He was the hero of the first moral revulsion against the abuses of the established order—a revulsion which for the time being united a substantial majority of the good citizens of the country.

This first union of effective progressive sentiment could not last. Under Mr. Roosevelt's leadership there had been tied together many discordant factions. The bond of union was partly derived from the leader's own personal popularity. It was partly partisan, because he continued to control the machinery of the Republican party. It was partly moral, because of the indignation which had been aroused by the exposures. Finally, it was beginning to be partly ideal and formative, in that many progressives began to discern the need of the substitution of a new and better order for the old. After the term of Mr. Roosevelt's official leadership ceased, the latent discord among these elements soon rose to the surface. The hollowness of the conversion of official Republicanism to progressivism almost immediately developed and resulted in an outbreak of insurgency on the part of the genuine progressives in that party. At the same time the tide of moral indignation began to subside, and progressives began to search much more frankly and unscrupulously for some positive political and economic principle and method which would constitute a sufficient basis for agitation and a sufficient bond of union. In the pursuance of this search they necessarily became more than ever curious. They began to inquire whether the domination of partisan machines was a normal result of the American system of government or an unwholesome eruption on its comely countenance. They went on to ask whether any relation could be traced between an autocratic economic organization or an individualistic legal system and the reign of political bosses. And in considering these questions they were pushed more and more towards the supposition that the United States never had been a genuine political democracy, and that if it were to become one, effective measures must be taken to make of it an economic and social democracy.

Just in proportion, however, as progressivism began to be radically inquisitive and to seek the bond of a positive political and social principle, it began to alienate many of its earlier supporters and to gain a more enthusiastic following of a different kind. The earlier reforming agitations had been conceived essentially as attempts to remove excrescences from the traditional system and to restore it to a suppositious condition of pristine purity. They could be defended as a kind of higher conservatism, which proposed to get rid of all the diseased tissue by means of a surgical operation, and then to leave the political and economic body to its own powers of recuperation. They needed to take no risk as to the safety of the patient and to incur no responsibility as to his subsequent behavior. The reformers, who were tied to such a conception of the meaning of the movement, did not relish the transition to progressivism. Certain of them, consisting chiefly of former Republicans and Independents, refused to become progressives, and began to look upon those who did as dangerous and frivolous political empirics. Progressivism, as it developed, began to differ from reform both in its friends and in its enemies.

The result of these new lines of attraction and repulsion has been the bestowal of different values both on progressivism and on conservatism. They both have tended to become more self-conscious than formerly, more definitely formulated and more antagonistic. The progressives found themselves obliged to carry their inquisition to its logical conclusion—to challenge the old system, root and branch, and to derive their own medium and power of united action from a new conception of the purpose and methods of democracy. The conservatives, on their side, could claim without hypocrisy or exaggeration that essential parts of the traditional system were being threatened, and they could ask prudent men to rally to its defence. A sharp issue was created between radical progressivism and its opponents, which could not be evaded or compromised.

It should, however, be added that the issue so created has not been universally accepted as the dividing line between all men of progressive and all men of conservative tendencies. The majority of thoroughgoing progressives are Republican insurgents, whose progressivism has been sharply defined as a result of warfare with their former partisan associates. No similar change has as yet taken place within the Democratic party, which still presents the spectacle of avowed progressives and avowed conservatives lying without apparent discomfiture in the same political bed. The controversies between the two factions of the former Republican party are to a large extent ignored by the Democrats, who have been seeking to convince public opinion that progressivism consists chiefly in the advocacy of certain specific economic reforms, which were not sufficiently emphasized by either of the former Republican factions.

The divergent economic interpretations which have been attached to progressivism as a result of this situation can, perhaps, best be made explicit by considering the differences, as developed during the presidential campaign of 1912, between the progressives who supported Mr. Wilson and those who supported Mr. Roosevelt. Roosevelt progressivism can fairly be charged with many ambiguities, but in one essential respect its meaning is unmistakable.

Its advocates are committed to a drastic reorganization of the American political and economic system, to the substitution of a frank social policy for the individualism of the past, and to the realization of this policy, if necessary, by the use of efficient governmental instruments. The progressivism of President Wilson, on the other hand, is ambiguous in precisely this essential respect. The slightest question need not be raised as to his sincerity, but his deliberate purpose seems to have been to keep progressivism vague—with a vagueness that is elusive and secretive rather than merely flexible. His tendency is to emphasize those aspects of progressivism which can be interpreted as the emancipation of an essentially excellent system from corrupting and perverting parasites. His version of progressivism, notwithstanding its immediately forward impulse, is scrupulously careful not to be too progressive, and, like the superseded reform movements, poses as a higher conservatism.

This aspect of Wilson progressivism receives its least equivocal expression in the doctrine of the "New Freedom." The purpose of the "New Freedom" is much clearer than its meaning. It is to serve as a kind of an intellectual antidote to such heresies as "New Nationalism" and the "New Democracy." It seems to be based upon the principle, enunciated by Mr. Wilson during the campaign, that the history of human liberty is the history of the restriction of governmental functions. The most important policies in which it is embodied are tariff reform and the ruthless eradication of any monopolistic control over business transactions. By reducing the tariff, not only is commerce liberated and the competitive system freed from its shackles, but necessarily unjust privileges are abolished. By eradicating any trace of monopoly, or any possibility of organized control over business, and by comprehensively identifying restraint of trade with restraint of competition, the wholesome action of automatic economic forces is further encouraged. Such is the "New Freedom" on its economic side, and its difference from the old freedom is plainly one of method rather than of purpose. Not a word that President Wilson uttered during or since the campaign indicated any tendency on his part to substitute for an automatic competitive economic regime one in which a conscious social purpose, equipped with an adequate technical method, was to play a decisive part. The "New Freedom" looks in general like a revival of Jeffersonian individualism. It proposes to contribute to human amelioration chiefly by the negative policy of doing away with discrimination, by expressly disparaging expert contribution to the business of government, by opposing the extension of national responsibility, and by intrusting the future of democracy to the results of cooperation between an individualistic legal system and a fundamentally competitive economic system.

I am aware that the foregoing interpretation of Wilson progressivism may not be entirely just. Any attempt to define the "New Freedom" incurs the danger of attaching too precise a meaning to a doctrine which has been left so essentially and apparently so deliberately vague. Be it recognized that Mr. Wilson's version of progressivism, whatever its underlying tendency and meaning, is a high and serious doctrine, which is the outcome of real elevation of purpose and feeling, and which up to date has had on the whole a beneficial effect on public opinion. Be it recognized also that in Mr. Wilson's situation a certain amount of ambiguity has a manifest practical value. He is a Democrat as well as a progressive. Harmony within his party has been essential to the successful passage of legislation to which he and his party were committed. The Democrats were undoubtedly the only organized political agency to which could be intrusted the work of passing a sufficiently drastic revision of the tariff; and drastic revision of the tariff may well be considered of so much importance to the welfare of the country that a leader would be justified in purchasing its accomplishment by a very considerable tribute to party unity. He would have good reason, consequently, for emphasizing any possible analogies between progressivism and the historic tradition of his own party. But there is no necessary finality about an emphasis. He is, I think, by way of being a realist in politics rather than a doctrinaire. He can understand the authority of human opinions and social needs which do not fit into antecedent theories. If at some future time the practical importance of interpreting progressivism along the lines of traditional Democracy should be diminished, and the need of a different method of handling economic and social problems should become more imposing, the progressive principle might receive at his hands a very different emphasis.

But while sound reasons may exist for the elusive and secretive nature of Mr. Wilson's progressivism, derived both from his own temperament and from his practical necessities, it is surely a fair matter for criticism. Just because progressivism is a high and serious affair, just because it seeks and needs to win converts as well as accomplish results, just because it can advance towards its goal only by entering into the souls of men and taking possession, it requires candor and integrity of spirit as well as flexibility. Wilson progressivism is, on the one hand, either too vague and equivocal to inspire sufficient energy of conviction, or else it is progressivism with its eyes fastened more on the past than on the future. It obscures the fundamental issue. What we need above all to know is the effect of progressivism upon the old order and the spiritual opportunities afforded by it for the establishment of a new order. "We are witnessing," says President Wilson in the "New Freedom," "we are witnessing a renaissance of public spirit, a reawakening of sober public opinion, a revival of the power of the people, the beginning of an age of thoughtful reconstruction, that makes our thought hark back to the great age in which democracy was set up in America." Remark how every phrase of this version of a doctrine which is called progressive confronts the past and turns its back upon the future. Progressivism is not a new birth of public spirit; it is a rebirth. It is not an awakening of public opinion to something novel; it is a reawakening. It is not aiming at an unprecedented vitalizing of democracy, but at its revival along traditional lines. A "thoughtful reconstruction" is promised; but the "thought" which prompts the revision "harks back to the great age" of primitive American democracy. The projected reconstruction is only a restoration. Small wonder that a progressivism of this kind finds a large part of its support among conservatives.

Yet if there is one aspect of progressivism about which American public opinion needs to be fully and clearly informed it is the relation between progressivism and conservatism. Are they supplementary ideas, as President Wilson seems to imply in the foregoing quotation, in such wise that the most thoroughgoing progressive reconstruction will merely restore us to a condition analogous to that of the primitive American democracy? Or does a real antagonism exist between the old order and the new order which some progressives are trying to substitute for it? By promoting progressive sentiment, is Mr. Wilson bestowing increasing authority and popularity upon a state of mind which in its ultimate results will prove inimical to institutions and ideas cherished by a large part of his followers? Will the increase of progressivism inevitably involve responsibilities and incur dangers to which prudent people should not be committed without full warning? In short, are conservatives, like Senator Root, justified in being alarmed at the innovations which contemporary radicalism is proposing? Or will it be possible to accomplish all the reforms demanded by the progressive principle without doing harm to any essential ingredient of the traditional American political and economic order?

In this connection I do not want to raise any question as to the relation between conservatism and progressivism in their essential aspects. An opportunist realistic conservatism may well exist, which is supplementary rather than inimical to progressivism. But such is not the character of contemporary American conservatism. The particular expression of the conservative spirit to which progressivism finds itself opposed is essentially, and, as it seems, necessarily doctrinaire and dogmatic. It is based upon an unqualified affirmation of the necessity of the traditional constitutional system to the political salvation of the American democracy. That system is not being appraised by its friends primarily as a serviceable political and legal instrument, wrought under the stress of historical vicissitudes, for the satisfaction of comparatively permanent but possibly changing social needs. It has been and is being acclaimed rather as a consummate system of law and government, framed under the guidance of a final political philosophy, to satisfy the essential conditions of individual liberty and wholesome political association. "The fact is,"

says one of its defenders on its behalf, "that in the history of mankind some
things after long toil and tribulation are settled once for all. They neither in-
vite nor permit amendment or improvement." Another of its apologists declares in relation to the quoted approval of an essential part of the system,
"These are sentiments not for a particular epoch, but for all time. To assume
that society can ever be constructed on any other principle is like assuming
that we may get beyond the influence of the law of gravitation." Or, again, according to Chief Justice Miller, the Constitution declares "those natural and
fundamental rights of individuals for the security and common enjoyment of
which governments are established." Thus the peculiar justification of our traditional constitutional government does not consist in its past and present serviceability or in its nice adaptation to our special political needs and customs,
but rather in its quality of embodying the permanent principles of righteous
and reasonable political action.

The foregoing quotations have been derived either from contemporary or
almost contemporary defenders of the traditional system; but as every one familiar with American political literature knows, they could be duplicated by
similar quotations from publicists, dating from every period of American history and belonging to every important American partisan organization. Ever
since the Constitution was established, a systematic and insidious attempt has
been made to possess American public opinion with a feeling of its peculiarly
sacred character. All commentators do not declare in so many words that it
embodies ultimate political truth; but no matter whether they verbally disparage the superstitious worship of the Constitution or participate in it, the practical effect of their interpretation remains much the same. They consider the
preservation of the existing constitutional system in its fundamental characteristics as essential to the political safety of the American democracy as
Joseph de Maistre considered the preservation of legitimacy essential to the
safety of European nations.

Such being the merits of the traditional system in the eyes of its friends,
they not unnaturally feel licensed to scold its adversaries. The paramount
duty of every patriotic citizen must be the defence of this priceless political
heritage. In the performance of such a sacred duty words should be used as
weapons rather than counters. Progressives who propose to eradicate or seriously to alter a system which does not admit of essential improvement
must be exposed rather than merely refuted. They are accused of being neu-
rotic perverts or unscrupulous demagog[ue]s. Those who manifestly cannot
be grouped in either of these classes are required to make up for a sound
nervous system and an apparent public spirit by grave deficiencies of knowledge and intelligence. They are charged with hopeless superficiality and utter ignorance of the recorded history of government and human society.

They become a conspicuous illustration of the vital truth that the failure or unpopularity of such an admirable system can result only from the inability of American citizens to live up to the high intellectual and moral responsibilities imposed upon them by its successful operation.

Conservatives always take a grave risk when they flourish such portentous claims on behalf of a group of time-honored political institutions. A position becomes vulnerable in proportion as it is exposed, and once the critical and inquisitive spirit is aroused, no position could be more exposed than that assumed at present by American conservatism. As I shall point out in a later discussion, it was obliged in candor to occupy this aggressive and advanced strategic situation; and progressives may well rejoice in such a sharp definition of the issue and such an opportunity for an open fight. They have more to fear from a furtive than from a frank enemy.

But before they engage in any attack a careful study needs to be made of the coveted citadel. The position which American conservatism has elected to defend, exposed as it is, may still be defensible. It assuredly does arouse on the part of its defenders an admirable loyalty of conviction. Many abuses have flourished under, the protection of the traditional constitutional system; but it has none the less a long and honorable career, and it has contributed enormously to American political safety and prosperity. It has given stability, order and security to a political experiment, undertaken in a new country under peculiarly hazardous and trying conditions. Whether or not it actually makes for permanent political health and individual and social welfare, it has apparently been doing so, and its friends ardently believe that it is as useful as ever. Some such conviction bestowed a semblance of respectability and even of dignity upon the opposition within the Republican party to the nomination of Mr. Roosevelt in the spring of 1912—an opposition which in the absence of genuine conviction would scarcely have dared to defy the plainly declared will of a majority of Republicans. Conservatism of this kind, much as it likes to abuse its progressive opponents, cannot be vanquished by the imputation of selfish motives or by the free use of derogatory epithets. Progressivism will not be able to overthrow it without the support of a very good cause, very large battalions, great tenacity of purpose and very thorough preparation and organization.

Many sincere conservatives are profoundly suspicious of progressivism, because they fail to discover in the new doctrine any trustworthy substitute for the existing system—a system which with all its deficiencies has probably enabled a larger proportion of its beneficiaries to live bravely than any other political and economic system. The providing of such a substitute is the peculiar, the indispensable need of progressivism. It would be mere nihilism for progressives to attack the exposed citadel of conservatism, unless they were equipped permanently to occupy at least an equally advanced and exposed position. If progressivism is to be constructive rather than merely restorative, it must be prepared to replace the old order with a new social bond, which will be no less secure than its predecessor, but which will serve still more effectually as an impulse, an inspiration and a leaven. The new system must provide, that is, not merely a new method, important as a new method may be, but a new faith, upon the rock of which may be built a better structure of individual and social life.

. . .

VIII

PROGRESSIVISM, WAR, AND PEACE

24

War Message to Congress*

April 2, 1917

Woodrow Wilson

Within months of the beginning of World War I, Woodrow Wilson encouraged Americans to remain "impartial in thought as well as action." He found it increasingly difficult, however, to maintain his professed neutrality while simultaneously favoring Britain on the issue of neutral rights, insisting, for example, that Americans could travel on ships of belligerent nations. When Germany's U-boat campaign resulted in the sinking of the *Lusitania* in 1915 and the loss of 128 American lives, Wilson extracted a promise from Germany to abide by the rules of cruiser warfare. Britain, however, was not held to "strict accountability" when it came to violation of neutral shipping. Indeed, Wilson's Secretary of State William Jennings Bryan resigned over what he viewed as inconsistencies in Wilson's policy regarding neutral rights that would lead the United States to enter the war. Germany's resumption of submarine warfare in 1917 and the continued loss of American lives finally led Wilson to ask for a declaration of war.

Gentlemen of the Congress,—I have called the Congress into extraordinary session because there are serious, very serious, choices of policy to be made, and made immediately, which it was neither right nor constitutionally permissible that I should assume the responsibility of making.

On the 3d of February last I officially laid before you the extraordinary announcement of the Imperial German Government that on and after the first day of February it was its purpose to put aside all restraints of law or of humanity

---

* Editors' Note: Titled by Woodrow Wilson "We Must Accept War," in Woodrow Wilson, *In Our First Year of War: Messages and Addresses to the Congress and the People, March 5, 1917, to January 8, 1918* (New York: Harper & Brothers Publishers, 1918), 9–25. Wilson's subheadings have been omitted.

and use its submarines to sink every vessel that sought to approach either the ports of Great Britain and Ireland or the western coasts of Europe or any of the ports controlled by the enemies of Germany within the Mediterranean. That had seemed to be the object of the German submarine warfare earlier in the war, but since April of last year the Imperial Government had somewhat re- strained the commanders of its undersea craft in conformity with its promise then given to us that passenger boats should not be sunk and that due warning would be given to all other vessels which its submarines might seek to destroy, when no resistance was offered or escape attempted, and care taken that their crews were given at least a fair chance to save their lives in their open boats.

The precautions taken were meager and haphazard enough, as was proved in distressing instance after instance in the progress of the cruel and unmanly business, but a certain degree of restraint was observed.

The new policy has swept every restriction aside. Vessels of every kind, whatever their flag, their character, their cargo, their destination, their errand, have been ruthlessly sent to the bottom without warning and without thought of help or mercy for those on board, the vessels of friendly neutrals along with those of belligerents. Even hospital ships and ships carrying relief to the sorely bereaved and stricken people of Belgium, though the latter were pro- vided with safe conduct through the proscribed areas by the German Govern- ment itself and were distinguished by unmistakable marks of identity, have been sunk with the same reckless lack of compassion or of principle.

I was for a little while unable to believe that such things would in fact be done by any government that had hitherto subscribed to the humane practices of civilized nations. International law had its origin in the attempt to set up some law which would be respected and observed upon the seas, where no nation had right of dominion and where lay the free highways of the world. By painful stage after stage has that law been built up, with meager enough results, indeed, after all was accomplished that could be accomplished, but al- ways with a clear view, at least, of what the heart and conscience of mankind demanded.

This minimum of right the German Government has swept aside under the plea of retaliation and necessity and because it had no weapons which it could use at sea except these which it is impossible to employ as it is employing them without throwing to the winds all scruples of humanity or of respect for the understandings that were supposed to underlie the intercourse of the world.

I am not now thinking of the loss of property involved, immense and seri- ous as that is, but only of the wanton and wholesale destruction of the lives of non-combatants, men, women, and children, engaged in pursuits which have always, even in the darkest periods of modern history, been deemed innocent and legitimate. Property can be paid for; the lives of peaceful and innocent people cannot be.

The present German submarine warfare against commerce is a warfare against mankind. It is a war against all nations. American ships have been sunk, American lives taken, in ways which it has stirred us very deeply to learn of, but the ships and people of other neutral and friendly nations have been sunk and overwhelmed in the waters in the same way. There has been no discrimination. The challenge is to all mankind. Each nation must decide for itself how it will meet it. The choice we make for ourselves must be made with a moderation of counsel and a temperateness of judgment befitting our character and our motives as a nation. We must put excited feeling away.

Our motive will not be revenge or the victorious assertion of the physical might of the nation, but only the vindication of right, of human right, of which we are only a single champion.

When I addressed the Congress on the twenty-sixth of February last I thought that it would suffice to assert our neutral rights with arms, our right to use the seas against unlawful interference, our right to keep our people safe against unlawful violence. But armed neutrality, it now appears, is impracticable. Because submarines are in effect outlaws when used as the German submarines have been used against merchant shipping, it is impossible to defend ships against their attacks as the law of nations has assumed that merchantmen would defend themselves against privateers or cruisers, visible craft giving chase upon the open sea.

It is common prudence in such circumstances, grim necessity, indeed, to endeavor to destroy them before they have shown their own intention. They must be dealt with upon sight, if dealt with at all.

The German Government denies the right of neutrals to use arms at all within the areas of the sea which it has proscribed, even in the defense of rights which no modern publicist has ever before questioned their right to defend. The intimation is conveyed that the armed guards which we have placed on our merchant ships will be treated as beyond the pale of law and subject to be dealt with as pirates would be.

Armed neutrality is ineffectual enough at best; in such circumstances and in the face of such pretensions it is worse than ineffectual: it is likely only to produce what it was meant to prevent; it is practically certain to draw us into the war without either the rights or the effectiveness of belligerents.

There is one choice we cannot make, we are incapable of making: we will not choose the path of submission and suffer the most sacred rights of our nation and our people to be ignored or violated. The wrongs against which we now array ourselves are no common wrongs; they cut to the very roots of human life.

With a profound sense of the solemn and even tragical character of the step I am taking and of the grave responsibilities which it involves, but in unhesitating obedience to what I deem my constitutional duty, I advise that the Congress declare the recent course of the Imperial German Government to be in fact nothing less than war against the government and people of the United States; that it formally accept the status of belligerent which has thus been thrust upon it; and that it take immediate steps not only to put the country in a more thorough state of defense but also to exert all its power and employ all its resources to bring the Government of the German Empire to terms and end the war.

What this will involve is clear. It will involve the utmost practicable cooperation in counsel and action with the governments now at war with Germany, and, as incident to that, the extension to those governments of the most liberal financial credits, in order that our resources may so far as possible be added to theirs.

It will involve the organization and mobilization of all the material resources of the country to supply the materials of war and serve the incidental needs of the nation in the most abundant and yet the most economical and efficient way possible.

It will involve the immediate full equipment of the navy in all respects but particularly in supplying it with the best means of dealing with the enemy's submarines.

It will involve the immediate addition to the armed forces of the United States already provided for by law in case of war at least five hundred thousand men, who should, in my opinion, be chosen upon the principle of universal liability to service, and also the authorization of subsequent additional increments of equal force so soon as they may be needed and can be handled in training.

It will involve also, of course, the granting of adequate credits to the Government, sustained, I hope, so far as they can equitably be sustained by the present generation, by well conceived taxation. I say sustained so far as may be equitable by taxation because it seems to me that it would be most unwise to base the credits which will now be necessary entirely on money borrowed.

It is our duty, I most respectfully urge, to protect our people so far as we may against the very serious hardships and evils which would be likely to arise out of the inflation which would be produced by vast loans.

In carrying out the measures by which these things are to be accomplished we should keep constantly in mind the wisdom of interfering as little as possible in our own preparation and in the equipment of our own military forces with the duty,—for it will be a very practical duty,—of supplying the nations already at war with Germany with the materials which they can obtain only from us or by our assistance. They are in the field and we should help them in every way to be effective there.

I shall take the liberty of suggesting, through the several executive departments of the Government, for the consideration of your committees, measures for the accomplishment of the several objects I have mentioned. I hope that it will be your pleasure to deal with them as having been framed after very careful thought by the branch of the Government upon which the responsibility of conducting the war and safeguarding the nation will most directly fall.

While we do these things, these deeply momentous things, let us be very clear, and make very clear to all the world what our motives and our objects are. My own thought has not been driven from its habitual and normal course by the unhappy events of the last two months, and I do not believe that the thought of the nation has been altered or clouded by them.

I have exactly the same things in mind now that I had in mind when I addressed the Senate on the 22nd of January last; the same that I had in mind when I addressed the Congress on the 3d of February and on the 26th of February.

Our object now, as then, is to vindicate the principles of peace and justice in the life of the world as against selfish and autocratic power and to set up amongst the really free and self-governed peoples of the world such a concert of purpose and of action as will henceforth ensure the observance of those principles.

Neutrality is no longer feasible or desirable where the peace of the world is involved and the freedom of its peoples, and the menace to that peace and freedom lies in the existence of autocratic governments backed by organized force which is controlled wholly by their will, not by the will of their people. We have seen the last of neutrality in such circumstances.

We are at the beginning of an age in which it will be insisted that the same standards of conduct and of responsibility for wrong done shall be observed among nations and their governments that are observed among the individual citizens of civilized states.

We have no quarrel with the German people. We have no feeling towards them but one of sympathy and friendship. It was not upon their impulse that their government acted in entering this war. It was not with their previous knowledge or approval.

It was a war determined upon as wars used to be determined upon in the old, unhappy days when peoples were nowhere consulted by their rulers and wars were provoked and waged in the interest of dynasties or of little groups of ambitious men who were accustomed to use their fellow-men as pawns and tools.

Self-governed nations do not fill their neighbor states with spies or set the course of intrigue to bring about some critical posture of affairs which will give them an opportunity to strike and make conquest. Such designs can be successfully worked out only under cover and where no one has the right to ask questions.

Cunningly contrived plans of deception or aggression, carried, it may be, from generation to generation, can be worked out and kept from the light only within the privacy of courts or behind the carefully guarded confidences of a narrow and privileged class. They are happily impossible where public opinion commands and insists upon full information concerning all the nation's affairs.

A steadfast concert for peace can never be maintained except by a partnership of democratic nations. No autocratic government could be trusted to keep faith within it or observe its covenants. It must be a league of honor, a partnership of opinion. Intrigue would eat its vitals away; the plottings of inner circles who could plan what they would and render account to no one would be a corruption seated at its very heart. Only free peoples can hold their purpose and their honor steady to a common end and prefer the interests of mankind to any narrow interest of their own.

Does not every American feel that assurance has been added to our hope for the future peace of the world by the wonderful and heartening things that have been happening within the last few weeks in Russia?

Russia was known by those who knew it best to have been always in fact democratic at heart, in all the vital habits of her thought, in all the intimate relationships of her people that spoke their natural instinct, their habitual attitude towards life.

The autocracy that crowned the summit of her political structure, long as it had stood and terrible as was the reality of its power, was not in fact Russian in origin, character, or purpose; and now it has been shaken off and the great, generous Russian people have been added in all their naive majesty and might to the forces that are fighting for freedom in the world, for justice, and for peace. Here is a fit partner for a league of honor.

One of the things that has served to convince us that the Prussian autocracy was not and could never be our friend is that from the very outset of the present war it has filled our unsuspecting communities and even our offices of government with spies and set criminal intrigues everywhere afoot against our national unity of counsel, our peace within and without, our industries and our commerce.

Indeed it is now evident that its spies were here even before the war began; and it is unhappily not a matter of conjecture but a fact proved in our courts of justice that the intrigues which have more than once come perilously near to disturbing the peace and dislocating the industries of the country have been carried on at the instigation, with the support, and even under the personal direction of official agents of the Imperial Government accredited to the Government of the United States.

Even in checking these things and trying to extirpate them we have sought to put the most generous interpretation possible upon them because we knew that their source lay, not in any hostile feeling or purpose of the German people towards us (who were, no doubt as ignorant of them as we ourselves were), but only in the selfish designs of a Government that did what it pleased and told its people nothing. But they have played their part in serving to convince us at last that that Government entertains no real friendship for us and means to act against our peace and security at its convenience. That it means to stir up enemies against us at our very doors the intercepted note to the German Minister at Mexico City is eloquent evidence.

We are accepting this challenge of hostile purpose because we know that in such a government, following such methods, we can never have a friend; and that in the presence of its organized power, always lying in wait to accomplish we know not what purpose, there can be no assured security for the democratic governments of the world.

We are now about to accept gauge of battle with this natural foe to liberty and shall, if necessary, spend the whole force of the nation to check and nullify its pretensions and its power. We are glad, now that we see the facts with no veil of false pretense about them, to fight thus for the ultimate peace of the world and for the liberation of its peoples, the German peoples included: for the rights of nations great and small and the privilege of men everywhere to choose their way of life and of obedience. The world must be made safe for democracy. Its peace must be planted upon the tested foundations of political liberty.

We have no selfish ends to serve. We desire no conquest, no dominion. We seek no indemnities for ourselves, no material compensation for the sacrifices we shall freely make. We are but one of the champions of the rights of mankind. We shall be satisfied when those rights have been made as secure as the faith and the freedom of nations can make them.

Just because we fight without rancor and without selfish object, seeking nothing for ourselves but what we shall wish to share with all free peoples, we shall, I feel confident, conduct our operations as belligerents without passion and ourselves observe with proud punctilio the principles of right and of fair play we profess to be fighting for.

I have said nothing of the governments allied with the Imperial Government of Germany because they have not made war upon us or challenged us to defend our right and our honor.

The Austro-Hungarian Government has, indeed, avowed its unqualified endorsement and acceptance of the reckless and lawless submarine warfare adopted now without disguise by the Imperial German Government, and it has therefore not been possible for this Government to receive Count Tarnowski, the Ambassador recently accredited to this Government by the Imperial and Royal Government of Austria-Hungary; but that Government has not actually engaged in warfare against citizens of the United States on the seas, and I take the liberty, for the present at least, of postponing a discussion of our relations with the authorities at Vienna.

We enter this war only where we are clearly forced into it because there are no other means of defending our rights.

It will be all the easier for us to conduct ourselves as belligerents in a high spirit of right and fairness because we act without animus, not in enmity towards a people or with the desire to bring any injury or disadvantage upon them, but only in armed opposition to an irresponsible government which has thrown aside all considerations of humanity and of right and is running amuck.

We are, let me say again, the sincere friends of the German people, and shall desire nothing so much as the early re-establishment of intimate relations of mutual advantage between us,—however hard it may be for them, for the time being, to believe that this is spoken from our hearts. We have borne with their present government through all these bitter months because of that friendship,—exercising a patience and forbearance which would otherwise have been impossible.

We shall, happily, still have an opportunity to prove that friendship in our daily attitude and actions towards the millions of men and women of German birth and native sympathy who live amongst us and share our life, and we shall be proud to prove it towards all who are in fact loyal to their neighbors and to the Government in the hour of test. They are, most of them, as true and loyal Americans as if they had never known any other fealty or allegiance. They will be prompt to stand with us in rebuking and restraining the few who may be of a different mind and purpose. If there should be disloyalty, it will be dealt with with a firm hand of stern repression; but, if it lifts its head at all, it will lift it only here and there and without countenance except from a lawless and malignant few.

It is a distressing and oppressive duty, Gentlemen of the Congress, which I have performed in thus addressing you. There are, it may be, many months of fiery trial and sacrifice ahead of us. It is a fearful thing to lead this great peaceful people into war, into the most terrible and disastrous of all wars, civilization itself seeming to be in the balance. But the right is more precious than peace, and we shall fight for the things which we have always carried nearest our hearts,—for democracy, for the right of those who submit to authority to have a voice in their own governments, for the rights and liberties of small nations, for a universal dominion of right by such a concert of free peoples as shall bring peace and safety to all nations and make the world itself at last free.

To such a task we can dedicate our lives and our fortunes, everything that we are and everything that we have, with the pride of those who know that the day has come when America is privileged to spend her blood and her might for the principles that gave her birth and happiness and the peace which she has treasured. God helping her, she can do no other.

25

Opposition to Wilson's War Message*

Robert M. La Follette

Two days after Woodrow Wilson's request for a declaration of war against Germany, Robert M. La Follette addressed the Senate and accused Wilson of failing to follow a policy of neutrality in regard to the war. Instead, La Follette contends, Wilson thwarted popular will by ignoring Congress's refusal to pass a bill arming merchant ships—a decision that ultimately led the United States to enter World War I.

$\mathbf{M}$r. President, I had supposed until recently that it was the duty of Senators and Representatives in Congress to vote and act according to their convictions on all public matters that came before them for consideration and decision.

I. STANDING BACK OF THE PRESIDENT.

Quite another doctrine has recently been promulgated by certain newspapers, which unfortunately seems to have found considerable support elsewhere, and that is the doctrine of "standing back of the President," without inquiring whether the President is right or wrong.

For myself I have never subscribed to that doctrine and never shall. I shall support the President in the measures he proposes when I believe them to be right. I shall oppose measures proposed by the President when I believe them

* Editors' Note: Robert M. La Follete, "Opposition to Wilson's War Message," 65th Cong., 1st sess., *Congressional Record* (April 4, 1917), 223–26. Excerpt.

to be wrong. The fact that the matter which the President submits for consideration is of the greatest importance is only an additional reason why we should be sure that we are right and not to be swerved from that conviction or intimidated in its expression by any influence of power whatsoever. If it is important for us to speak and vote our convictions in matters of internal policy, though we may unfortunately be in disagreement with the President, it is infinitely more important for us to speak and vote our convictions when the question is one of peace or war, certain to involve the lives and fortunes of many of our people and, it may be, the destiny of all of them and of the civilized world as well. If, unhappily, on such momentous questions the most patient research and conscientious consideration we could give to them leave us in disagreement with the President, I know of no course to take except to oppose, regretfully but not the less firmly, the demands of the Executive.

II. ARMED NEUTRALITY.

On the 2d of this month the President addressed a communication to the Senate and House in which he advised that the Congress declare war against Germany and that this Government "assert all its powers and employ all its resources to bring the Government of the German Empire to terms and end the war."

On February 26, 1917, the President addressed the Senate and the House upon the conditions existing between this Government and the German Empire, and at that time said, "I am not now proposing or contemplating war or any steps that need lead to it." . . . "I request that you will authorize me to supply our merchant ships with defensive arms, should that become necessary, and with the means of using them" against what he characterized as the unlawful attacks of German submarines.

A bill was introduced, and it was attempted to rush it through the closing hours of the last session of Congress, to give the President the powers requested, namely, to arm our merchant ships, and to place upon them guns and gunners from our Navy, to be used against German submarines, and to employ such other instrumentalities and methods as might in his judgment and discretion seem necessary and adequate to protect such vessels. That measure did not pass.

It is common knowledge that the President, acting without authority from Congress, did arm our merchant ships with guns and gunners from our Navy, and sent them into the prohibited "war zone." At the time the President addressed us on the 2d of April there was absolutely no change in the conditions between this Government and Germany. The effect of arming merchant ships had not been tested as a defensive measure. Late press reports indicate, however, that the *Aztec*, a United States armed merchantman, has been sunk in the prohibited zone, whether with mines or a torpedo, I believe, has not been established, so the responsibility for this sinking can not, so far as I know at this time, be placed.

When the request was made by the President on February 26 for authority to arm merchant ships, the granting of such authority was opposed by certain Members of the House and by certain Senators, of which I was one. I made at that time a careful investigation of the subject, and became convinced that arming our merchant ships was wholly futile and its only purpose and effect would be to lure our merchantmen to danger, and probably result in the destruction of the vessels and in the loss of the lives of those on board. The representatives of the President on this floor then having that bill in charge saw fit, by methods I do not care to characterize, to prevent my speaking upon the measure and giving to the Senate and to the country such information as I had upon the subject.

Under the circumstances, I did the only thing that seemed practical to me, and that was to give such publicity as I was able through the press to the fact that the proposition to arm merchant ships would be wholly futile, and could only result in loss of the lives and property of our own people, without accomplishing the results intended. I regret to say that the President, according to statements in the public press purporting to emanate from him, and which have never been denied, saw fit to characterize as "willful" the conduct of the Senators who, in obedience to their consciences and their oaths of office, opposed the armed-ship bill, and to charge that in so doing they were not representing the people by whose suffrages they are here. I know of no graver charge that could be made against the official conduct of any Member of this body than that his official action was the result of a "willful"—that is, an unreasoned and perverse—purpose.

Mr. President, many of my colleagues on both sides of this floor have from day to day offered for publication in the *Record* messages and letters received from their constituents. I have received some 15,000 letters and telegrams. They have come from 44 States in the Union. They have been assorted according to whether they speak in criticism or commendation of my course in opposing war.

Assorting the 15,000 letters and telegrams by States in that way, 9 out of 10 are an unqualified indorsement of my course in opposing war with Germany on the issue presented. I offer only a few selected hastily just before I came upon the floor which especially relate to public sentiment on the question of war.

. . .

Do not these messages indicate on the part of the people a deep-seated conviction that the United States should not enter the European war? The armed-ship bill meant war. Senators who opposed its being forced through Congress in the closing hours of the session were rebuked by the President. It is highly important, therefore, to note at this time that the President in his address on the 2d of this month takes the same view of arming merchant ships that was entertained by at least some of the Senators, including myself, when the armed-ship bill was before us for consideration.

. . .

So, too, Mr. President, we find that the framers of that great instrument wrote into it that one-fifth of the Members of either one of the two bodies of Congress might hold in check the autocratic use of power by the majority on any question whatsoever. They armed a minority of one-fifth of the body with the power to filibuster; the power to demand a roll call—not a roll call, as some of the State constitutions provide, only upon matters which carry appropriations, but a roll call on every single question upon which it pleases one-fifth of the body to demand a roll call.

SUPREME POWER IS IN THE PEOPLE

What was the purpose of it? Not to make a record, for parliamentary legislative history shows that they had that right prior to that time, and always had it and could exercise it. No, no; it was the foresight of the makers of the Constitution of this great Government of ours desiring to perpetuate not the semblance of democracy but real democracy, and they said, "There may be times when a majority, swept either by passion or misinformation, may do a wrongful thing to this Republic, and we will arm the minority in such emergencies against the undue exercise of majority power by placing in the hands of one-fifth the right to demand a roll call on every question." Exercised in the late hours of the session of a Congress it would easily be possible for them to demand roll calls in such a way as to make an extra session necessary. But, oh, Mr. President, we have always and ever in this Republic of ours back of Congresses and statutes and back of Presidents the supreme power, the sovereign power of the people, and they can correct our errors and mistakes and our wrongdoing. They can take us out of our places, and if we abuse any power which the Constitution puts in the hands of a minority, it lies with them to call us to account; and the more important, the more profoundly and intensely important the question upon which such as power is abused by a minority, the more swift and sweeping will be the punishment by the people for the wrongful exercise of it.

We need not disturb ourselves because of what a minority may do. There is always lodged, and always will be, thank the God above us, power in the people supreme. Sometimes it sleeps, sometimes it seems the sleep of death; but, sir, the sovereign power of the people never dies. It may be suppressed for a time, it may be misled, be fooled, silenced. I think, Mr. President, that it is being denied expression now. I think there will come a day when it will have expression.

26

Fourteen Points*

January 8, 1918

Woodrow Wilson

With the addition of millions of American "doughboys" to the allied war effort, Germany's ability to continue the war began to fade. Woodrow Wilson went before Congress with his plan for peace—fourteen points that demonstrated both his liberal internationalist aspirations and his idealistic hope for a "peace without victory." His ideas, however, did not prevail at Versailles, where the realities of a brutal war resulted in a punitive peace.

Gentlemen of the Congress,—Once more, as repeatedly before, the spokesmen of the Central Empires have indicated their desire to discuss the objects of the war and the possible bases of a general peace. Parleys have been in progress at Brest-Litovsk between representatives of the Central Powers, to which the attention of all the belligerents has been invited for the purpose of ascertaining whether it may be possible to extend these parleys into a general conference with regard to terms of peace and settlement.

The Russian representatives presented not only a perfectly definite statement of the principles upon which they would be willing to conclude peace, but also an equally definite program of the concrete application of those principles. The representatives of the Central Powers, on their part, presented an outline of settlement which, if much less definite, seemed susceptible of liberal interpretation until their specific program of practical terms was added. That program

---

* Editors' Note: Titled by Woodrow Wilson "The Terms of Peace," in Woodrow Wilson, *In Our First Year of War: Messages and Addresses to the Congress and the People, March 5, 1917, to January 8, 1918* (New York: Harper & Brothers Publishers, 1918), 150–61. Wilson's subheadings have been omitted.

proposed no concessions at all either to the sovereignty of Russia or to the preferences of the populations with whose fortunes it dealt, but meant, in a word, that the Central Empires were to keep every foot of territory their armed forces had occupied,—every province, every city, every point of vantage,—as a permanent addition to their territories and their power. It is a reasonable conjecture that the general principles of settlement which they at first suggested originated with the more liberal statesmen of Germany and Austria, the men who have begun to feel the force of their own peoples' thought and purpose, while the concrete terms of actual settlement came from the military leaders who have no thought but to keep what they have got. The negotiations have been broken off. The Russian representatives were sincere and in earnest. They cannot entertain such proposals of conquest and domination.

The whole incident is full of significance. It is also full of perplexity. With whom are the Russian representatives dealing? For whom are the representatives of the Central Empires speaking? Are they speaking for the majorities of their respective parliaments or for the minority parties, that military and imperialistic minority which has so far dominated their whole policy and controlled the affairs of Turkey and of the Balkan states which have felt obliged to become their associates in this war? The Russian representatives have insisted, very justly, very wisely, and in the true spirit of modern democracy, that the conferences they have been holding with the Teutonic and Turkish statesmen should be held within open, not closed doors, and all the world has been audience, as was desired.

To whom have we been listening, then? To those who speak the spirit and intention of the Resolutions of the German Reichstag of the ninth of July last, the spirit and intention of the liberal leaders and parties of Germany, or to those who resist and defy that spirit and intention and insist upon conquest and subjugation? Or are we listening, in fact, to both, unreconciled and in open and hopeless contradiction? These are very serious and pregnant questions. Upon the answer to them depends the peace of the world.

But, whatever the results of the parleys at Brest-Litovsk, whatever the confusions of counsel and of purpose in the utterances of the spokesmen of the Central Empires, they have again attempted to acquaint the world with their objects in the war and have again challenged their adversaries to say what their objects are and what sort of settlement they would deem just and satisfactory. There is no good reason why that challenge should not be responded to, and responded to with the utmost candor. We did not wait for it. Not once, but again and again, we have laid our whole thought and purpose before the world, not in general terms only, but each time with sufficient definition to make it clear what sort of definitive terms of settlement must necessarily spring out of them.

Within the last week Mr. Lloyd George has spoken with admirable candor and in admirable spirit for the people and Government of Great Britain. There is no confusion of counsel among the adversaries of the Central Powers, no uncertainty of principle, no vagueness of detail. The only secrecy of counsel, the only lack of fearless frankness, the only failure to make definite statement of the objects of the war, lies with Germany and her Allies. The issues of life and death hang upon these definitions. No statesman who has the least conception of his responsibility ought for a moment to permit himself to continue this tragical and appalling outpouring of blood and treasure unless he is sure beyond a peradventure that the objects of the vital sacrifice are part and parcel of the very life of Society and that the people for whom he speaks think them right and imperative as he does.

There is, moreover, a voice calling for these definitions of principle and of purpose which is, it seems to me, more thrilling and more compelling than any of the many moving voices with which the troubled air of the world is filled. It is the voice of the Russian people. They are prostrate and all but helpless, it would seem, before the grim power of Germany, which has hitherto known no relenting and no pity. Their power, apparently, is shattered. And yet their soul is not subservient. They will not yield either in principle or in action. Their conception of what is right, of what is humane and honorable for them to accept, has been stated with a frankness, a largeness of view, a generosity of spirit, and a universal human sympathy which must challenge the admiration of every friend of mankind; and they have refused to compound their ideals or desert others that they themselves may be safe.

They call to us to say what it is that we desire,—in what, if in anything, our purpose and our spirit differ from theirs; and I believe that the people of the United States would wish me to respond, with utter simplicity and frankness. Whether their present leaders believe it or not, it is our heartfelt desire and hope that some way may be opened whereby we may be privileged to assist the people of Russia to attain their utmost hope of liberty and ordered peace.

It will be our wish and purpose that the processes of peace, when they are begun, shall be absolutely open and that they shall involve and permit henceforth no secret understandings of any kind. The day of conquest and aggrandizement is gone by; so is also the day of secret covenants entered into in the interest of particular governments and likely at some unlooked-for moment to upset the peace of the world. It is this happy fact, now clear to the view of every public man whose thoughts do not still linger in an age that is dead and gone, which makes it possible for every nation whose purposes are consistent with justice and the peace of the world to avow now or at any other time the objects it has in view.

We entered this war because violations of right had occurred which touched us to the quick and made the life of our own people impossible unless they were corrected and the world secured once for all against their recurrence. What we demand in this war, therefore, is nothing peculiar to ourselves. It is that the world be made fit and safe to live in; and particularly that it be made safe for every peace-loving nation which, like our own, wishes to live its own life, determine its own institutions, be assured of justice and fair dealing by the other peoples of the world as against force and selfish aggression. All the peoples of the world are in effect partners in this interest, and for our own part we see very clearly that unless justice be done to others it will not be done to us.

The program of the world's peace, therefore, is our program; and that program, the only possible program, as we see it, is this:

I. Open covenants of peace, openly arrived at, after which there shall be no private international understandings of any kind but diplomacy shall proceed always frankly and in the public view.

II. Absolute freedom of navigation upon the seas, outside territorial waters, alike in peace and in war, except as the seas may be closed in whole or in part by international action for the enforcement of international covenants.

III. The removal, so far as possible, of all economic barriers and the establishment of an equality of trade conditions among all the nations consenting to the peace and associating themselves for its maintenance.

IV. Adequate guarantees given and taken that national armaments will be reduced to the lowest point consistent with domestic safety.

V. A free, open-minded, and absolutely impartial adjustment of all colonial claims, based upon a strict observance of the principle that in determining all such questions of sovereignty the interests of the populations concerned must have equal weight with the equitable claims of the government whose title is to be determined.

VI. The evacuation of all Russian territory and such a settlement of all questions affecting Russia as will secure the best and freest cooperation of the other nations of the world in obtaining for her an unhampered and unembarrassed opportunity for the independent determination of her own political development and national policy and assure her of a sincere welcome into the society of free nations under institutions of her own choosing; and, more than a welcome, assistance also of every kind that she may need and may herself desire. The treatment accorded Russia by her sister nations in the months to come will be the acid test of their good will, of their comprehension of her needs as distinguished from their own interests, and of their intelligent and unselfish sympathy.

VII. Belgium, the whole world will agree, must be evacuated and restored, without any attempt to limit the sovereignty which she enjoys in common with all other free nations. No other single act will serve as this will serve to restore confidence among the nations in the laws which they have themselves set and determined for the government of their relations with one another. Without this healing act the whole structure and validity of international law is forever impaired.

VIII. All French territory should be freed and the invaded portions restored, and the wrong done to France by Prussia in 1871 in the matter of Alsace-Lorraine, which has unsettled the peace of the world for nearly fifty years, should be righted, in order that peace may once more be made secure in the interests of all.

IX. A readjustment of the frontiers of Italy should be effected along clearly recognizable lines of nationality.

X. The peoples of Austria-Hungary, whose place among the nations we wish to see safeguarded and assured, should be accorded the freest opportunity of autonomous development.

XI. Rumania, Serbia, and Montenegro should be evacuated; occupied territories restored; Serbia accorded free and secure access to the sea; and the relations of the several Balkan states to one another determined by friendly counsel along historically established lines of allegiance and nationality; and international guarantees of the political and economic independence and territorial integrity of the several Balkan states should be entered into.

XII. The Turkish portions of the present Ottoman Empire should be assured a secure sovereignty, but the other nationalities which are now under Turkish rule should be assured an undoubted security of life and an absolutely unmolested opportunity of autonomous development, and the Dardanelles should be permanently opened as a free passage to the ships and commerce of all nations under international guarantees.

XIII. An independent Polish state should be erected which should include the territories inhabited by indisputably Polish populations, which should be assured a free and secure access to the sea, and whose political and economic independence and territorial integrity should be guaranteed by international covenant.

XIV. A general association of nations must be formed under specific covenants for the purpose of affording mutual guarantees of political independence and territorial integrity to great and small states alike.

In regard to these essential rectifications of wrong and assertions of right we feel ourselves to be intimate partners of all the governments and peoples associated together against the Imperialists. We cannot be separated in interest or divided in purpose. We stand together until the end.

For such arrangements and covenants we are willing to fight and to continue to fight until they are achieved; but only because we wish the right to prevail and desire a just and stable peace such as can be secured only by removing the chief provocations to war, which this program does remove. We have no jealousy of German greatness, and there is nothing in this program that impairs it. We grudge her no achievement or distinction of learning or of pacific enterprise, such as have made her record very bright and very enviable. We do not wish to injure her or to block in any way her legitimate influence or power. We do not wish to fight her either with arms or with hostile arrangements of trade if she is willing to associate herself with us and the other peace-loving nations of the world in covenants of justice and law and fair dealing. We wish her only to accept a place of equality among the peoples of the world,—the new world in which we now live,—instead of a place of mastery.

Neither do we presume to suggest to her any alteration or modification of her institutions. But it is necessary, we must frankly say, and necessary as a preliminary to any intelligent dealings with her on our part, that we should know whom her spokesmen speak for when they speak to us, whether for the Reichstag majority or for the military party and the men whose creed is imperial domination.

We have spoken now, surely, in terms too concrete to admit of any further doubt or question. An evident principle runs through the whole program I have outlined. It is the principle of justice to all peoples and nationalities, and their right to live on equal terms of liberty and safety with one another, whether they be strong or weak. Unless this principle be made its foundation no part of the structure of international justice can stand. The people of the United States could act upon no other principle; and to the vindication of this principle they are ready to devote their lives, their honor, and everything that they possess. The moral climax of this the culminating and final war for human liberty has come, and they are ready to put their own strength, their own highest purpose, their own integrity and devotion to the test.

Index

About the Editors

Ronald J. Pestritto holds the Charles and Lucia Shipley Chair in the American Constitution at Hillsdale College, where he serves as associate professor of political science. He is also a senior fellow of the Claremont Institute for the Study of Statesmanship and Political Philosophy. He has held fellowships from the Bradley, Earhart, Olin, and Salvatori Foundations, and has served as visiting scholar at the Social Philosophy and Policy Center at Bowling Green State University. Among his books are *Woodrow Wilson and the Roots of Modern Liberalism* (2005) and *Woodrow Wilson: Essential Political Writings* (2005).

William J. Atto is assistant professor of American history at the University of Dallas. He also holds an appointment to the Graduate Faculty of Ashland University, where he teaches in the Master of History and American Government program. He has held a summer fellowship in military history from the United States Military Academy at West Point, and has published articles and reviews in a number of journals including *The Catholic Social Science Review*, *The Historian*, *Military History of the West*, *The Texas Journal of Genealogy and History*, and *Catholic Southwest*.